Kathrin Leuze
Smooth Path or Long and Winding Road?

Kathrin Leuze

Smooth Path or Long and Winding Road?

How Institutions Shape the Transition
from Higher Education to Work

Budrich UniPress Ltd.
Opladen & Farmington Hills, MI 2010

A CIP catalogue record for this book is available from
Die Deutsche Bibliothek (The German Library)

ISBN   978-3-940755-42-1

Budrich UniPress Ltd.
Stauffenbergstr. 7. D-51379 Leverkusen Opladen, Germany

28347 Ridgebrook. Farmington Hills, MI 48334. USA
www.budrich-unipress.eu

Jacket illustration by disegno, Wuppertal, Germany – www.disenjo.de
Printed in Europe on acid-free paper by paper & tinta, Warszaw

Contents

Acknowledgements 9

Preface 11

1.   Introduction 13

2.   Graduate Employment in the Era of Mass Higher Education
      and European Harmonisation 21
2.1   The Legacy of Mass Higher Education 21
2.2   The Changing Nature of Labour Markets 23
2.3   Graduate Employment in Western Europe 26

3.   The Institutional Embeddedness of Graduate Employment –
      An Analytical Framework 31
3.1   The Institutional Embeddedness of Life Course Transitions 31
3.1.1 The Matching Problem as Life Course Transition Process 33
3.1.2 The Institutional Embeddedness of Life Courses 35
3.1.3 Institutional Effects and the Transition from Higher Education
      to Work 38
3.2   The Institutional Determinants of Graduate Employment 39
3.2.1 The Importance of Institutions for Explaining Vocational
      Training to Work Transitions 40
3.2.2 The Institutional Determinants of the Transition from Higher
      Education to Work 43
3.2.3 Political Economies, Institutional Complementarities and the
      Transition Process 64
3.2.4 Assessing Continuity and Change in Different Political
      Economies 67
3.3   Embedding the Transition from Higher Education to Work into
      Varieties of Capitalism 70

**4. Analysing Graduate Employment Trajectories –
The Methodological Approach** 73

4.1   Motives and Means of Cross-National Comparisons 73

4.2   The Country Cases: Germany and Britain 77

4.3   Quantitative Data Analysis of Individual Transitions from Higher
       Education to Work 79

4.3.1 The Data Sources: German Socio-Economic Panel and two
       British Cohort Studies 79
4.3.2 The Method: Event History Analysis 85

4.4   Operationalisations of Concepts and Variables 88

**5. Higher Education and Labour Market Institutions
in Germany and Britain** 99

5.1   Stratification in Higher Education: Vertical and Horizontal
       Institutional Differentiation 100

5.1.1 The Road to Mass Higher Education 100
5.1.2 Institutional Differentiation and the Stratification
       of Higher Education 107
5.1.3 Pathways into Higher Education 120
5.1.4 Stratification of German and British Higher Education:
       Diverse Trends 123

5.2   Occupational Specificity: Generalist and Specialist
       Curricular Orientations 125

5.2.1 Historical Frames: Professional vs. Liberal Higher Education 126
5.2.2 General Objectives of Higher Education Institutions 129
5.2.3 Occupation-specific Training of Different Types of Degrees
       and Fields of Study 133
5.2.4 Professional and Liberal Orientations in German and British
       Higher Education 139

5.3   Graduate Labour Market Segmentation: Between Professional
       and Public Spheres 140

5.3.1 Higher Education and the Social Closure of Professional
       Labour Markets 141
5.3.2 Public Services between Status Protection and New Public
       Management 146

5.3.3 Trends in Public Sector Employment 152
5.3.4 The Social Closure of Graduate Labour Markets in Germany
       and Britain 154

5.4   Labour Market Regulation and the Protection of
       (Un-)Employment 155

5.4.1 Employment Protection Legislation and the Stability of
       Employment Relations 156
5.4.2 Unemployment Protection and the Level of Skill Protection 160
5.4.3 Strictness and Flexibility of German and British Labour Markets ..165

**6.   Graduate Employment between Elitist Ideals and the
         Realities of Mass Higher Education** 167

6.1   Early Employment Patterns after Graduation 168

6.2   Institutional Differentiation and the Stratification of Labour
       Market Returns 172

6.2.1 Labour Market Returns of Initial Employment Positions 175
6.2.2 Mechanisms of Stratification and the Transition to Employment ...181

6.3   Occupational Specificity and the Match between Field of Study
       and Occupation 189

6.3.1 Transition to a Job in an Occupation Matching the Field of Study 192
6.3.2 Occupational Mobility after First Placement 200

6.4   The Importance of Occupational and Internal Labour Markets
       for Graduate Employment 205

6.4.1 Labour Market Segments and Entry Ports after Graduation 208
6.4.2 The Educational Determinants of Employment in Entry
       Port Occupations 213
6.4.3 Mobility Within and Between Professional and Public Labour
       Market Segments 218

6.5   Labour Market Regulation and the Stability of Employment
       Positions 224

6.5.1 Stability of Initial Employment Positions after Graduation 226
6.5.2 Occurrence and Effects of Unemployment 229
6.5.3 Upward and Downward Labour Market Mobility 233

7.   Smooth Path or Long and Winding Road? 237

7.1   The Importance of National Institutions for the
        Transition Process 237

7.2   Building Institutional Complementarities between Higher
        Education and Work 242

7.3   National Paths in Transition? 247

References 251

Appendix 269

Appendix A: Description of German and British Data Sets 269

Appendix B: The Erikson-Goldthorpe Class Scheme 270

Appendix C: The New Casmin Educational Classification 270

Appendix D: Vocational Training in Germany and Britain 271

Appendix E: Gender-specific Transition Patterns 273

List of Tables 274

List of Figures 274

List of Abbreviations 276

Acknowledgements

This book is based on my PhD thesis, which I wrote between October 2003 and March 2007 at the Graduate School of Social Sciences (GSSS), University of Bremen. Writing a thesis is never possible without the help and encouragement of others. I, too, had many people around me who supported me throughout the process, from writing the first proposal until finalising the manuscript. First of all, I would like to thank my three supervisors, Ansgar Weymann, Reinhold Sackmann and Jutta Allmendinger, who from the beginning encouraged me in my research, provided me with practical ideas on how to proceed further, gave me constructive feedback on papers and chapters I gave them to read, and always found the right words to keep me going. In addition, I owe a lot of thanks to the GSSS, which provided me with all the necessary facilities and, most importantly, with financial support. In particular, I am grateful to Werner Dressel and Anne Schlüter, whose organisational talents often helped me to navigate through the University of Bremen's administrative "jungle" and made my life much easier. The fellows of my cohort at the GSSS also played a very important role throughout the whole PhD process, since they went with me through the same ups and downs which are bound to come when writing a thesis. I am especially thankful to Susanne Strauss, Daniela Kroos and Bettina Kohlrausch for the fruitful discussions we had, and for the constructive remarks they made on my data analysis and on many things I have written. In addition, I profited strongly from the support of other researchers not institutionally connected to my PhD. I would like to thank in particular Vernon Gayle and Paul Lambert of the University of Stirling, Alessandra Rusconi of the Social Science Research Center Berlin (WZB), Karin Gottschall and Matthias Wingens of the University of Bremen, and the researchers of the SOEP group from the German Institute of Economic Research (DIW), who all gave me useful advice regarding my theoretical and methodological approach. I am also grateful to Tilman Brand, Aletta Diefenbach, Diana Lange and Friederike Theilen-Kosch, who helped me with literature searches, proof-reading, formatting and layout of graphs. Finally, getting through this PhD would not have been possible without all the people that are close to me. I would never have made it through my time in Bremen without the help of my friends, Jasmina, Melanie, Andi, Steffen and Tine, as well as those friends mentioned above. Also the loving support of my parents and my sister were very important to keep me going. Thanks a lot to all of you.

Berlin, January 2010   Kathrin Leuze

Preface

Comparative research on higher education often lacks context and dynamics. OECD benchmark studies report the proportion of students of a given age cohort, their average competence scores, the distribution across disciplines, the unemployment rate by educational level and age. No efforts are made to trace the career trajectories of students asking e.g. how long it takes to find a job, how much it fits the qualifications obtained, how long people hold a job. Such studies leave us puzzled and ignorant on processes and dynamics of entering the labour market and the first years in employment. Consequently, we have no grasp on the extent to which national institutions and professions matter. We look at individual outcomes but ignore their institutional embeddedness.

The study of Kathrin Leuze "A smooth path or long and winding road? Comparing the institutional embeddedness of graduate careers in Germany and Britain" fills this gap. The design is both longitudinal, using life history data from Germany and Britain, and institutional, focussing on labour market institutions in particular. Hence, differences in career trajectories between British and German students are not only described but are explained using concepts of stratification of the educational system, the role of the professions, labour market segmentation and labour market regulation. The study shows that institutions do matter. It also shows that converging educational systems - the aim and focus of the Bologna process – hit on widely differing labour markets that shape the transition from school to work and educational outcomes at large. Special attention is also given to the role of the professions, a usually neglected terrain.

The results are rich and path setting. University graduates in Germany have comparatively smooth paths. Compared to British students, they move faster from education into the labour market, they stay longer in their jobs, their qualifications fit better to the positions obtained. After some years in employment, however, smooth paths and long and winding roads converge, and the career trajectories of German and British graduates look very much the same.

Kathrin Leuze presents a rich and highly compelling book, very well written, and excellent in both theory and methodology. The study is an essential read for researchers and policy makers alike pointing at the pitfalls of limited and unembedded reforms. Hence, Bologna is only one small step towards a truly European transition regime between school and work.

Berlin. March 2010   Jutta Allmendinger

1. Introduction

Today, universities are often blamed for not delivering the skills required by the labour market. There appears to be wide-spread consensus among politicians, education practitioners and scientific experts that higher education systems in Europe lack efficiency. Too theory-laden, too little oriented towards application and mostly out-dated: these are the main points of criticism directed against university graduates and their degree courses . This criticism has been provoked by the systems' seeming inability to deliver an ever greater variety of educational products to an expanding number of students. The changing skills requirements of higher education graduates are determined to a great extent by changing demands of the labour market, which include a continuous increase in tertiary and service sector employment, progressive technological development and change, as well as the rising importance of knowledge-based products and services. As a consequence, scholars, media and employers criticise universities for supplying skills that are insufficient for the requirements of the labour market. With it aims „to create a European space for higher education in order to enhance the employability and mobility of citizens and to increase the international competitiveness of European higher education" (CRE 2000), the Bologna Declaration on the European Space for Higher Education seems to offer a solution to these national problems.

This public debate, however, seems to be only a partial reflection of empirical reality. Studies on graduate employment demonstrate that the crisis of European higher education systems is not accompanied by a crisis in the labour market opportunities of higher education graduates. All over Europe, higher education graduates still have a good chance of finding work immediately after graduation despite the enormous increase in total numbers of students and rising unemployment among the labour force as a whole. But it has also been shown that the quality of early labour market positions obtained by higher education graduates differs strongly cross-nationally. While in some countries, university graduates quickly move into upper status positions as professionals or managers, other countries offer less favourable prospects. There, less favourable starting positions are often coupled with a high number of job shifts and periods of unemployment (Brennan et al. 1996a; Kivinen and Nurmi 2003; Lindberg 2007; Schomburg 2007; Schomburg and Teichler 2006; Teichler 2000; 2002b; 2007a).

How can we explain and interpret these findings? This book seeks to disentangle the reciprocal relationship between higher education systems, labour markets, and graduate career mobility in a comparative perspective. It argues that the institutional set-up of both, higher education systems and graduate labour markets, is the decisive factor for shaping the career prospects of higher education graduates. It is an understanding of these national institutions, i.e. of their structure and ideational principles, which explains commonalities and differences in graduate employment across Europe. Accordingly, the main research question is: How do national institutions influence individual transitions from higher education to work? Existing research on the relationship between higher education and work has not yet systematically linked institutional arrangements of higher education systems and graduate labour markets with individual employment outcomes. It is crucial to fill this gap because it is a necessary precondition for doing expedient cross-national comparison of the transition from higher education to work. Furthermore, only an analysis of the institutional embeddedness of graduate careers can provide a blueprint for evaluating the changing nature of graduate employment in the era of globalisation, European harmonisation, and the rise of a knowledge-based society. In this regard, further theoretical conceptualisation of the institutional embeddedness of the transition process in combination with longitudinal analysis of individual career trajectories from higher education to work is needed and provided by this book.

It thus fills a gap in the existing literature on comparative higher education research. It develops a novel theoretical approach for embedding graduate careers into a country's wider political economy and identifies four institutional spheres that are important for the transition from higher education and work: the structure of higher education systems, the content of study, the structure of graduate labour markets, and labour market regulation. Empirically, this book conducts two in-depth case-studies of countries most different in their institutional set-up, Britain and Germany. The institutional analysis carried out for these two countries draws upon secondary literature and relevant policy documents published over a twenty year period between the early 1980s and the early 2000s. This institutional analysis is accompanied by a quantitative longitudinal study of graduate career development during the first five years after graduation in Germany and Britain to show how institutional configurations translate into career outcomes.

The book makes *three* unique contributions to comparative research on the transition from higher education to work in Europe: First, it uses an innovative analytical framework for analysing the institutional embeddedness of career mobility processes; second, it combines an institutional analysis of higher education systems and graduate labour markets with a longitudinal analysis of the transition from higher education to work; and third, it covers a period of more than 20 years, which makes this book unique in its empirical scope. Regarding the analytical framework, it applies established theoretical concepts for vocational education and training (VET) to work transitions to the sphere of higher education. In the field of VET, many studies have investigated the impact of various forms of education and labour market institutions on individual career development. It has become commonplace to distinguish between two basic types of institutional contexts related to the wider political economy. One the one hand, there is a more occupationalised one operating in countries like Germany, Austria or Denmark, where young people are predominantly trained within a standardised apprenticeship system and from thereon experience rather smooth trajectories into the labour market. On the other hand, a more organisation-based system is said to exist in Anglo-Saxon countries such as Britain or the US, where the transition process appears to be less structured by the education system, resulting in more protracted transition phases with stop-gap-job patterns and higher risks of unemployment (Allmendinger 1989a; Kogan and Müller 2003; Marsden 1999; Maurice et al. 1986; Müller and Gangl 2003; Shavit and Müller 1998). It is an important goal of this book to demonstrate that, for the transition from higher education to work, the effects of different political economies are as pronounced as for vocational education and training.

Second, this book combines a thorough institutional analysis of *both*, higher education and labour market institutions with a longitudinal statistical study of individual career mobility. Particularly since the 1990s there has been a rising interest in evaluating labour market outcomes of higher education graduates in a comparative perspective (see for example Altbach and McGill Peterson 1999; Brennan et al. 1996a; Teichler 1996; 1999). Two strands of research can be distinguished. One focuses on micro level developments and analyses labour market careers of higher education graduates by comparing employment outcomes in different countries (Jahr et al. 2003; Kivinen and Nurmi 2003; Lindberg 2007; Schomburg 2007; Schomburg and Teichler 2006; Teichler 2000; 2002b; 2007a). These studies are important for demonstrating similarities as well as differences of graduate employment across countries. However, they lack a consistent institutional analysis which helps to integrate and interpret their micro-level findings. The comparative analysis of higher education policy and policy change is the focus of the second strand of research. Since the 1970s, scholars have been concerned with higher education and its function for the labour market and society as a whole (see for example Archer 1972; Ben-David 1977). In the 1990s, comparative research on higher education systems as well as on policy reforms became a "hot topic" (see for example Altbach and McGill Peterson 1999; Bleiklie and Byrkejeflot 2002; Clark 1995; Enders 2004; Huisman et al. 2001; Martens et al. 2007; Scott, P. 1995; Teichler 2007b). While these studies give a profound account of the institutional development of higher education systems and how it varies across countries, a systematic connection with individual data on career mobility has not yet been made. This book integrates both strands of research and adds a third, the study of labour markets, which has so far been neglected in comparative research on graduate employment. This book introduces well-established concepts of comparative labour markets research, such as labour market segmentation and labour market regulation, into the specific realm of graduate labour markets. The central goal of this book, therefore, is to take into account higher education *and* labour market institutions as explanatory points of reference.

Besides applying a novel analytical approach and analysing higher education and labour market institutions in combination with individual career mobility, this book is unique in its empirical scope of both institutional and career analysis, covering a period of more than 20 years. It is necessary to study a longer period of observation than has been done in previous research in order to show how institutional configurations develop and translate into labour market outcomes. This book is written against the background of the changes in higher education currently evolving across Europe. In the course of the Bologna Process, degree structures are being reformed and quality assurance and accreditation systems introduced in order to make the European higher education area the most competitive in the world. Yet, these reforms build on national systems that vary strongly in terms of higher education philosophy, structure, and graduate labour markets. It is too early to draw final conclusions about whether the Bologna Process will indeed serve the harmonisation and convergence of higher education systems and, accordingly, graduate career prospects. But in order to understand the changes it introduces not only to higher education systems, but also to the very nature of graduate careers itself, we have to go one step back and ask how national institutions influenced graduate career developments in different countries *prior* to Bologna.

Especially since the beginning of the 1980s, the institutional variation among higher education systems and graduate labour markets became very pronounced across Western Europe. Regarding the organisation of higher education systems, countries began to develop their own political solutions to meet the challenges of mass higher education (Teichler 2007b). Some countries such as such as Britain undertook major reforms and even reversed the dual structure of universities and technical colleges by forming a unitary system. Others, such as Germany, proved to be very resistant to any attempt of re-organisation and only allowed for marginal modifications of higher education structures (Eurydice 2000). At the same time, labour markets became more diverse during these decades, in particular regarding the (de-)regulation of sectors and occupations that have traditionally been important labour market destinations for higher education graduates. For example, public service sector employment was subject to scrutiny in the wake of a "New Public Management" (Hood, Christohper 1995). Britain went furthest in its attempt to strip away previous privileges, which shielded public servants from the disciplines of the market and its attendant job insecurity, while German public service still provides a high degree of job security (Hesse 2003; Hood, Christopher 2003). But professional services, too, historically marked by a high degree of social closure from external markets, have been confronted with deregulation, intensified competition, cost containment and more service-conscious clients (Lane et al. 2000). This book demonstrates that the diversification of higher education structures and the re-organisation and deregulation of graduate labour markets during the 1980s and 1990s are important factors for explaining cross-national differences of career mobility patterns among higher education graduates.

In pursuit of these three tasks, the book is structured in the following way.

Following this introduction, chapter 2 sets out the historical and institutional developments of higher education systems and labour markets which have led to the current situation of graduate employment in Western Europe. These macro-level developments are contrasted with actual labour market outcomes of higher education graduates in different countries in order to show where further research is needed and how this book is going to accomplish this task.

Chapter 3 develops the theoretical framework for analysing the transition from higher education to work in a comparative perspective. Based on the theoretical concepts of VET research and the Varieties of Capitalism approach (Hall and Soskice 2001), it is argued that country-specific career patterns depend to a large extent on the *institutional complementarities* between higher education systems and graduate labour markets. The main hypothesis of this book states that country-specific linkages between higher education and the world of work create distinct transition regimes for individuals. These regimes follow a specific path-dependent logic that is intimately related to the wider political economy, and has been relatively stable over time. Four institutional spheres and their likely effect on graduate employment are explored in more detail: the structure of higher education systems (stratification), the content of study (occupational specificity), the structure of graduate labour market (segmentation), and finally, labour market flexibility (regulation). By applying the theoretical concepts related to these institutional spheres to higher education-to-work-transitions, it becomes possible to formulate precise hypotheses regarding the extent to which institutions influence graduate career mobility.

Chapter 4 gives an account of the methodological approach and the methods used. The empirical analysis comprises an in-depth analysis of Germany and Britain by conducting, in a first step, an institutional analysis of higher education systems and graduate labour markets based on legal and policy documents as well as on secondary literature on policy development in the respective institutional spheres. In a second step, a longitudinal analysis of graduate labour market careers during the first five years after graduation is conducted to examine whether and how institutional variations translate into career outcomes. This is done by estimating event-history models based on the German Socio-economic Panel (SOEP) and two British cohort studies, namely the National Child Development Study (NCDS) and the 1970 British Cohort Study (BCS70).

Chapter 5 examines the historical development as well as the institutional set-up of higher education systems and graduate labour markets during the 1980s and 1990s in order to look for national configurations within Germany and Britain. To analyse the stratification of higher education, it gives an account of the legal basis and structural set-up of British and German higher education, and explicates the educational pathways that are necessary preconditions for entry into higher education. In order to account for varying degrees of occupation-specific training provided by higher education systems, it sketches in broad terms the different philosophies and principles that underpin higher education in both countries and examines the training of professionals, engineers and managers in more detail. The analysis of the structure of graduate labour markets focuses on the institutional organisation of labour market segments that have traditionally been associated with graduate employment, the professions and the public service. A final institutional aspect to be analysed for graduate careers is the degree of labour market regulation, as it relates to employment and unemployment protection.

Chapter 6 investigates labour market careers of higher education graduates during the first five years after graduation. Each sub-section will shortly review empirical results that have been found for (vocational) education in general and for higher education in particular in order to embed the findings of this study into the broader framework of country-specific transition patterns. In particular, this chapter shows how the stratification of different higher education systems influences the status of initial employment positions and the role that higher education expansion plays in this regard. Furthermore, various forms of occupation-specific training and their importance for the match between higher education credentials and early labour market outcomes as well as for occupational mobility are studied. To assess the impact of different labour market structures, the transition to and mobility between professional and public labour market segments are examined. This is closely related to the analysis of more or less flexible labour market regulation and its impact on the stability of career paths.

In the concluding Chapter 7, the empirical findings are summarised and re-analysed with special reference to the wider institutional framework and the Varieties of Capitalism approach. From the analysis conducted in the previous chapters, it follows that national institutions indeed matter; they have a strong influence on the development of graduate careers. In Germany, the transition from higher education to work follows a smooth path, while in Britain it is more comparable to a long and winding road. Based on these findings, the concluding chapter will construct a common point of reference by developing a theoretical explanation for the overall transition patterns in both countries. It argues that country-specific institutional complementarities between higher education systems and graduate labour markets make it possible to provide varying degrees of *skill* and *status* protection. Due to the higher degree of skill and status protection prevalent in CMEs, the connection between higher education and the graduate labour market tends to be more "decommodified" and sheltered from market competition as compared to LMEs. This guarantees a smooth transition process, while a lower degree of skill and status protection is associated with more turbulent labour market entry patterns. The development of specific institutional complementarities between higher education systems and labour markets of different political economies leads to a more general theoretical conceptionalisation of the transition process in Western Europe.

Built on its theoretical impetus and empirical evidence, this book sheds light on the factors that shape the working careers of graduates. It also contributes to the further conceptualisation of the linkage between higher education and work. In particular, it demonstrates that the skills provided by higher education and required by the labour market are not universal; rather, their demand and supply follows a national institutional logic. The skills of higher education graduates required by the labour market are shaped by specific institutional structures and historical trajectories that cannot be easily transferred from one country to the next. In the end, cross-national differences in the relationship between higher education and labour markets will therefore have to be closely monitored against the background of the Bologna Process, which aims to harmonise the structures of higher education systems across Europe. Such a perspective neglects, however, the existence of path dependencies of higher education systems and graduate labour markets. What this indicates is that national higher education reform projects initiated by the Bologna Process are likely to follow a tortuous route to convergence. This book aims to gain a better understanding of some of the obstacles that stand in its way.

2. Graduate Employment in the Era of Mass Higher Education and European Harmonisation

2.1 The Legacy of Mass Higher Education

Historically, the remarkable changes in higher education began as early as in the first half of the 20th century when Western European universities changed from elite education to mass education (Teichler 1988). Despite existing differences between national higher education systems, countries all over Western Europe followed a similar path of development for several decades after World War II. Initially, higher education expansion was driven from below. Ongoing processes of democratisation, which enabled an ever larger number of citizens to participate in society, lead to an increasing demand in education participation among all social groups (Klemm 2000; Müller 1998). Soon more and more pupils acquired upper secondary credentials, the prerequisite for entry into higher education, and the demand for attending universities rose considerably. Given the relatively low number of university institutions in all European countries at that time, education policies had to respond to the rising numbers of students by expanding higher education institutions accordingly.

The expansion of higher education accelerated in most Western European countries during the 1950s and 1960s and was marked by the optimistic belief that an increase in the number of students was the necessary and unavoidable precondition for economic, technological and social progress. One major driving force was enabling students from lower socioeconomic backgrounds to achieve higher levels of education in order to reduce social inequalities (Krais 1996; Müller 1998). Another key aspect was the increasing complexity of modern societies and economies, which required a more highly trained workforce. Overall, the shift from elite to mass higher education meant that new forms of institutional organisation and management needed to be found that could effectively and efficiently cater to more students, more diverse students, and new demands of the labour market.

It was soon discovered, however, that traditional university systems, originally designed to educate the elites of society, could not fulfil their societal function anymore. As a response, major university reforms were introduced all over Western Europe during the 1960s and 1970s, which basically led to a stronger differentiation among institutions mainly through the introduction of technical colleges (Teichler 2002a). In some countries such as Germany, the higher education system responded to the new challenges by establishing *Fachhochschulen* to respond to the labour market's "manpower requirements" by providing education with a high degree of applied knowledge transfer and occupational training. Other nations such as Britain rather pursued the goal of increasing educational equality, *polytechnics* were introduced to allow more students from lower socioeconomic backgrounds to acquire higher education.

By the beginning of the 1980s, however, the expansion euphoria had levelled off in a lot of countries since none of the proclaimed goals had actually been achieved. What was more, new problems resulting from mass higher education began to emerge. Despite all reform efforts, a student's socioeconomic background continues to be a strongly influential factor determining educational achievement and labour market opportunities in many countries (Blossfeld and Shavit 1993; Krais 1996; Müller 1998). In addition, funding of higher education institutions is more and more seen as one of the major problems resulting from higher education expansion (Jongbloed 2004), leading to crowded lecture halls, rising student-teacher ratios, poorly equipped facilities, and, consequently, to a deterioration of overall study conditions. During this phase of disillusionment, countries began to search for more flexible solutions to the problems caused by mass higher education, and higher education policies in different countries started to diverge. Western European countries began to develop their own political solutions, and country-specific differences in the organisation of higher education became more pronounced (Teichler 1988). In cross-national comparison, differences were particularly strong regarding the speed and the extent of reforms. Some countries, such as Germany, proved to be very resistant to any attempt of reorganisation and only allowed for marginal modifications of university structures and institutional procedures. Others, such as Britain, undertook major changes and even reversed the dual structure of universities and technical colleges by forming a unitary system (Eurydice 2000).

It was not until the end of the 20th century that European countries again sought to find common answers to their problems. In 1999, 29 European governments signed a declaration in Bologna, which proposed the creation of a European area of higher education by 2010. The Bologna Declaration represents the attempt to formulate a common European answer to common European problems in higher education. This common higher education is designed to facilitate student mobility, enhance the transparency and the recognition of qualification and quality and establish a European dimension in higher education (CRE 2000; Keller 2003). The process originated from the recognition that, in spite of their valuable differences, European higher education systems were facing common internal and external challenges related to the growth and diversification of higher education, such as the financing of university systems, the promotion of students' and researchers' international mobility, the provision of equal access to education, the governing capacity of the state, and the changing importance of the curricular contents for the job market (Sporn 1999).

The dynamics of this process continues to evolve, and the consequences for graduate careers are only starting to emerge. Optimists believe that higher education systems across Europe are eventually going to converge, which as a consequence will make career prospects more similar across countries and thereby increase the employability of higher education graduates. The effects of previous path-dependent developments on gradate careers shall not be underestimated, however. However, the present study makes use of these path dependencies and concentrates specifically on the two decades prior to Bologna in order to see how national higher education institutions and the legacy of mass higher education shape the transition from higher education to work in different countries.

2.2 The Changing Nature of Labour Markets

Higher education expansion is only one of the major challenges that graduate employment is facing today. Other problems stem from changes in the labour market itself. Due to increasing rates of unemployment over past decades even among those sections of the population with higher education degrees, the social consequences of educational expansion with regard to the labour market have gained more and more attention. First of all, there were widespread concerns that large numbers of graduates might have completed their higher education in vain, either because they would end up in unemployment or would obtain low-status positions, where their competencies were not needed (Büchel et al. 2003; Müller 1998; Teichler 2002b). Even though the upgrading of participation in education was paralleled by an upgrading of labour market structures, the latter proceeded at a slower pace. Therefore, the fear of an overqualified "academic proletariat" has been prevailing since the mid-1970s and has shifted the focus of politicians, practitioners and experts to the question of labour market success of higher education graduates (Teichler 1999).

Occasionally, this concern about an oversupply of graduates had been expressed earlier, but it gained momentum after the "oil-shock" in 1973, when unemployment began to grow substantially in market-oriented economies (Teichler 1999: 29). Since then, not only the risk of overqualifica-tion but also the threat of unemployment itself began to create problems for the employment chances of higher education graduates. Between 1980 and the mid-1990s, most countries in Western Europe had experienced their highest rates of unemployment since the Second World War. The persistence of high unemployment rates were equally frightening; these were no transitory peaks produced by stagnating demand, but the result of longer term and less reversible developments, especially the enormous rise in world commodity prices and a dramatic decline in the demand for low-skilled workers caused by technological change (Wood 2001). While for a long time, this crisis of the labour market only concerned employees with no or lower-level educational credentials, unemployment has increased in various Western European countries especially since the early 1990s among higher education graduates as well (Teichler 1999: 34).

Western European countries underwent major efforts to react to this steady increase in unemployment by starting to reform their labour markets. Many changes of labour market legislation went in the direction of more flexible structures, such as a decentralised bargaining, lower employment protection and the abolition of minimum standards. These reforms were based on the assumption that the lack of labour market flexibility could be considered a major reason for the pertaining unemployment problem across Europe, since labour markets could not respond adequately to increased technological change and the globalisation of products and financial markets (Heckman 2002). Existing cross-national differences in the flexibility of labour market legislation became even more pronounced during this period. Britain is sold as "success story" in this regard, since it was able to reduce unemployment drastically and deregulate the labour market strongly (Pissarides 2003). Other countries, such as Germany, still lag behind in their attempts to introduce higher flexibility into the labour market, which is said to be one of the causes of high unemployment (Heckman 2002). In general, the consequences of increased labour market flexibility are supposed to be most pronounced at the beginning of one's career, leading to a declining proportion of direct and stable transitions into the labour market. Thus, increased labour market flexibility and deregulation may have strong implications for the transition from higher education to work, not only regarding unemployment experiences, but also related to the stability of early labour market positions.

Increased flexibility within the labour market, however, did not only imply that non-standard working relations such as part-time work, fixed-term contracts and precarious employment became more pronounced, while the creation of continuous full-time standard employment relationships declined. Even those sectors of the labour market that have traditionally enjoyed a high degree of protection from market competition increasingly became the target of deregulatory policies. Public service sector employment in particular was subject to scrutiny in the wake of a "New Public Management" (Hood, Christohper 1995), leading to a successful reduction of what were considered unwarranted "privileges" of the public service through cut-backs, retrenchment and contracting-out, privatisation and deregulation initiatives in many European countries. Britain went furthest in its attempt to strip public servants of their privileges, which shielded them from the disciplines of the market and its attendant job insecurity. But professional services, historically marked by a high degree of social closure from external markets, have also been confronted with deregulation, intensified competition, cost containment and more service-conscious clients (Lane et al. 2000). Both public and professional sectors are important destinations for higher education graduates. Varying degrees of deregulatory policies promoted by different European governments should have specific consequences for graduate career prospects.

The deregulation of labour markets was accompanied by drastic changes in the overall labour market structure throughout Western Europe. One of the most important of these changes concerns the tertiarisation of employment sectors. Since the 1970s, there has been a massive, steady shift in the employment structures of all advanced industrialised economies, away from manufacturing and towards service provision (Pierson 2001; Rubery and Grimshaw 2003). This shift was especially pronounced in the European Union prior to its enlargement, where between 1998 and 2003 the share of employment in the service sector increased by 11.3 per cent (European Commission 2004). Since service sector employment is often associated with the low-wage sector as well as with precarious employment positions, this post-industrial transition confronts governments with a "trilemma of the service economy" (Pierson 2001: 86), in which the goals of employment growth, wage equality, and budgetary constraint come into increasing conflict. One effect of the trend towards tertiarisation might be worsening career prospects for the labour force as a whole, but also for higher education graduates. On the other hand, service sector occupations are also found at the upper level of the job hierarchy, such as professions and semi-professions, which have also been growing steadily, creating new opportunities for university leavers.

Overall, the developments of Western European labour markets over the past decades should have important consequences for graduate employment. The extent to which labour markets have become more deregulated and service-sector oriented should be an important factor for explaining cross-national similarities and differences of mobility patterns across Europe. At the same time, the structure of labour markets might create specific interaction effects with the restructuring of higher education systems as a consequence of mass higher education. The present study therefore takes into account both institutions of the higher education systems and the labour market in order to shed light on the national specifics of graduate employment.

2.3 Graduate Employment in Western Europe

The trends of higher education expansion and labour market change are common to all European countries, although there is evidence that they occur at different levels of pace and intensity. Overall, these changes are assumed to have consequences for the career perspectives of higher education graduates. However, it is not clear yet how the apparent crisis of higher education systems resulting from mass higher education in combination with changing labour market dynamics influences graduate employment opportunities in different countries. Of course, there are many empirical studies that have addressed the transition from higher education to work in one way or the other. The 1990s in particular saw a rising interest in evaluating labour market outcomes of higher education graduates in a cross-national perspective (Teichler 1999). Nevertheless, no comprehensive study exists that has thoroughly investigated the impact of country-specific institutional environments related to higher education systems and labour markets on individual career prospects.

Two of the most comprehensive comparative studies of graduate employment so far were conducted by the CHEERS project (Careers after Higher Education: a European Research Study, at http://www.uni-kassel.de/wz1/tseregs.htm) and its successor, the REFLEX project (The Flexible Professional in the Knowledge Society New Demands on Higher Education in Europe, at http://www.fdewb.unimaas.nl/roa/reflex/). CHEERS surveys early labour market careers of 1995 graduates in ten Western European countries, one transition country and one economically advanced country outside Europe. REFLEX is directed at graduates of the academic year 1999-2000 and more strongly focuses on the competencies required by higher education graduates and the role higher education institutions play in providing these competences. It is conducted in 14 European countries and one economically advanced country outside Europe. In both surveys, the respondents answered questions regarding their study paths, transition from higher education to employment, early career outcomes, their job satisfaction, and their retrospective view on higher education. Results from the CHEERS survey reveals that most higher education graduates end up, after a brief period of transition, in early career positions and work tasks which can be viewed as more or less matching their knowledge and their educational level (Kivinen and Nurmi 2003; Schomburg and Teichler 2006; Teichler 2002b; 2007a). However, results also indicate that transition patterns are more differentiated with respect to the type of job obtained after graduation, the perceived utilisation of knowledge, the self-rated adequacy of employment positions, and job satisfaction. By and large, according to this study, graduate employment in Western Europe displays both similarities and differences across countries. The following table illustrates these findings by giving some examples of objective and subjective employment measures of higher education graduates during the first four years after graduation (Teichler 2002a):

Table 1: Objective and subjective measures of graduate employment in Western Europe

	AUT	ES	FIN	FR	GER	IT	NL	NOR	SWE	UK
Duration of job search after graduation (month)	6.0	11.6	5.1	7.1	5.5	8.9	4.7	3.3	4.9	4.4
Still on job search after 12 months (%)	2	10	4	20	3	4	3	1	2	4
Employed four years after graduation (%)	87	73	93	69	87	79	93	87	83	87
as professionals, managers, etc.	95	73	93	66	87	61	68	46	--	74
as clerks, service personnel, workers etc.	2	24	3	10	5	9	7	1	--	11
Wrong field of study / HE not necessary (%)	17	15	9	26	15	14	12	3	7	27
Dissatisfaction with current job / work	10	13	9	14	12	18	7	4	11	18

Source: CHEERS Graduate Survey, Teichler 2002a

Even though these results provide interesting insights into early career outcomes of higher education graduates in different countries, the problem with the findings of large scale graduate surveys is often the lack of an encompassing explanation of the empirical patterns observed. Are they a result of economic circumstances, individual capabilities, or rather cultural specificities? A lot of comparative empirical studies share the common view of analysing employment "success" of higher education graduates; however, they fail to consider that the definition of successful labour market integration might differ between countries. The specific social mechanisms underlying the transition process from higher education to work in different countries remain rather under-investigated. This book aims at filling the gap by providing an institutional perspective on graduate employment.

When assessing the shortcomings of previous research, it is notable that large scale assessments and many of the case studies do not combine their analysis of graduate careers with an analysis of institutions. As a result, they often remain on rather descriptive levels of analysis, showing similarities and differences of graduate employment, but failing to explain the observed patterns. In the field of vocational training, in contrast, a lot of studies have already investigated the impact of various forms of education and labour market institutions on individual career development. It has become commonplace to distinguish between two basic types of institutional contexts of the transition process. On the one hand, there is a more occupationalised one operating in countries like Germany, Austria or Denmark, where young people are predominantly trained within a standardised apprenticeship system and from thereon experience rather smooth trajectories into the labour market. On the other hand, there is a more organisation-based system as it is said to exist in Anglo-Saxon countries like Britain or the US, where the transition process appears to be less structured by the educational system, while discretionary employer recruitment and promotion strategies play a crucial role for shaping early labour market careers (see Allmendinger 1989b; Kerckhoff 2001; Kogan and Müller 2003; Marsden 1999; Maurice et al. 1986; Müller and Gangl 2003; Müller and Shavit 1998). It stands to reason to assume that for the transition from higher education to work, the effects of different institutional environments should be as pronounced as for vocational training. From an institutional perspective, national strategies of organising higher education systems and the graduate labour market should be the decisive determinants of divergent graduate employment patterns.

But even if an empirical examination of institutions is conducted in combination with the analysis of labour market careers, most of the studies refer to institutional differences of higher education systems, while they neglect institutional influences of labour markets. For example, a lot of studies deal with the consequences of educational expansion. Many of them examine the labour market outcomes of students with different educational credentials by comparing the effects of higher education to those of general secondary education and vocational training on individual career development. Those studies show that the transition from education to the world of work is still more favourable for university leavers than for holders of other credentials despite rising numbers of students (Brauns, Müller et al. 1997; Brennan, Kogan et al. 1996; Scherer 2001; Shavit and Müller 1998; Teichler 2000; 2002b). Graduates are still likely to start their professional life in the upper sector of the job hierarchy (Allmendinger and Aisenbrey 2002; Hillmert 2001; Krais 1996), are facing unemployment less often and for shorter periods (Hillmert 2001; Müller 1998; Teichler 1999), and tend to have higher incomes than the rest of the labour force (Butz 2000; Teichler 1999).

Other empirical studies focus on labour market opportnunities of higher education graduates exclusively to investigate the consequences of higher education expansion. In his literature review on "Higher education and Graduate Employment in Europe", Teichler (1999) sketches the common trends of previous decades. Since the 1970s, the transition to employment became a more protracted process, which required participants to seek information about their own employment opportunities, to develop more elaborate search activities, and often led them to accept a period of "non-matching" employment. Furthermore, unemployment of recent graduates increased in many countries, which led graduates to continue study beyond graduation to protect themselves against unemployment and to increase their levels of qualification. Additionally, the growth trend of the service sector naturally provided more employment for graduates, but fixed-term contracts also became more frequent. A lot of attention was also paid to the vertical change of graduate employment resulting from higher education expansion. Most scholars agree that the proportion of demanding jobs continued to increase within most sectors during the 1970s and 1980s, but not to such an extent that it would ensure "adequate" employment for all graduates. As to the correspondence between field of study and subsequent employment, research suggests that over the years, students' selection of fields of study changed in Europe to some extent in the direction of more applied subjects, which is interpreted as a sign of growing 'vocationalism'. Another important finding is that the equalisation of women's education opportunities increased over the last few decades. The share of women graduating from higher education nowadays more or less equals and sometimes even exceeds the share of male graduates.

More in-depth cross-country comparisons, some of them conducted with fewer country-cases, have shown that graduate employment differs substantially across Europe due to country-specific higher education structures. Assessing the implications of higher education expansion for graduate labour market outcomes, Müller et al. (2002) show that higher education systems of different countries vary considerably in the extent to which they guarantee access to favourable class and labour market positions by various higher education institutions. Examining gender segregation by fields of study, Kim and Kim (Kim and Kim 2003) find smaller gender differences in class outcomes in some countries, but this rather egalitarian result disappears if the type of jobs, for example part-time vs. full-time jobs, is controlled for. Other studies show that in some countries, possession of higher education credentials is more important for obtaining a job than in others, or that the content taught at universities is less applicable in the labour market (Brennan et al. 1996b).

Even though all these studies are valuable contributions to the study of the transition from higher education to work, by neglecting labour market structures, they fail to address an important aspect for explaining cross-national similarities and differences. To account for variation of graduate employment across countries, a study of the changing structure of labour markets is a necessary precondition in order to avoid a constrained assessment of empirical findings. An important goal of this book, therefore, is to take into account the institutional set-up of both higher education systems and labour markets as explanatory points of reference.

Another critical failure of previous research on higher education to work transitions is related to methodology, namely the application of inadequate statistical methods. A lot of the cited studies on graduate employment use cross-sectional data analysed at one particular point in time. They can be criticised for being too static and not taking into account the duration of transition processes and the time-dependent variations of initial labour market outcomes. On the basis of cross-sectional data it is not possible to depict the complexity of mobility patterns associated with the transition from higher education to work. If quantitative methods are used, the focus therefore should be on pathways, on life course trajectories rather than on labour market outcomes at a single point in time, to overcome a static and sometimes misleading approach for studying labour market entries. Consequently, another major purpose of this study is to analyse the dynamics of the transition from higher education to work by applying more appropriate statistical techniques. In summary, previous research on graduate employment often fails to develop a coherent explanatory framework, to take explicitly into account the structure graduate labour markets, and to adopt of a longitudinal life course perspective on labour market careers.

3. The Institutional Embeddedness of Graduate Employment – An Analytical Framework

Finding a job after graduation is an important step in every graduate's life. This chapter will set up the theoretical framework that explains how early career processes are shaped by national institutions. The overall hypothesis is that transition patterns from higher education to work differ systematically due to country-specific institutional linkages between higher education systems and labour markets. At first sight, labour market entry seems to be merely influenced by a student's educational attainment, for example the type of degree obtained, the subject studied, or the type of institution attended. These characteristics seem to be essential prerequisites for any form of labour market outcomes, such as type of occupation, unemployment experiences, length of job search, or number of job shifts taking place after graduation. However, it will be argued that these individual transition processes are the result of a country's institutional framework. National higher education systems and graduate labour markets are linked in such a way that they produce specific patterns of labour market entry and career mobility. In order to develop a comprehensive theoretical framework for studying the transition from higher education to work, it is necessary to consider concepts of education and labour market theory on the micro and the macro level.

The following chapter provides an overview of the most prominent theories in these research fields. The aim of this outline is neither to provide a comprehensive summary of all existing theories nor to weigh or test them against each other, but rather to explore whether their most distinctive features are suitable for comparing labour market careers of higher education graduates in different countries. But before moving to the specific realm of education and labour market theories, it is crucial to reflect upon general assumptions of how individual life courses are shaped by national institutions.

3.1 The Institutional Embeddedness of Life Course Transitions

At the micro level, the general theoretical problem of successfully assigning job seekers to jobs and thus of analysing the transition from higher education to work is often referred to as a matching problem. Economic job-matching theory (Jovanovic 1979; Sattinger 1993) stresses that a good labour market match is two-sided since it not only results from an employee's adequate education and experience but also depends on job characteristics and employer preferences. For a successful assignment to come about, employer and job applicant have to make a positive rational decision[1]: the employer to hire, the applicant to accept the job conditions. But since both have to make their decisions under conditions of imperfect information, job mismatches, i.e. a low degree of fit between required and acquired skills are likely to occur. Career mobility takes place because employers and employees are interested in finding an optimal match and accordingly try to re-adjust the assignment until this has been achieved. Consequently, from the perspective of job-matching theory, initial employment positions after higher education and early career mobility are the outcome of such a two-sided matching process.

This micro-economic approach will be taken as a starting point for the analytical framework of the transition from higher education to work. However, it lacks two central aspects: the principle of time and the importance of institutions, which are both vital for understanding how early career mobility patterns come about. Institutions in particular are also important for explaining cross-national differences, since decision making processes not only depend on specific job requirements, preferences and recourses of the actors involved, but also on the institutional environment which affects the range and sequence of alternatives of the choice-agenda (North 1990). Country-specific variations of the institutional settings will accordingly give rise to different matching processes and create particular mobility patterns. The life course approach offers suitable concepts in this regard and will therefore be adopted to specify and enrich the theoretical model of the matching process.[2]

---

1   In this work Boudon's (2003) premises of rational choice theory – individualism, understanding and rationality – are adopted to outline the understanding of human behaviour. 1) Any social phenomenon is the effect of individual decisions, actions and attitudes (individualism). 2) An action can be understood (understanding). 3) Any action is caused by reasons in the mind of individuals (rationality). It is assumed that actors act purposively following a set of preferences and priorities that they seek to realise in a satisfying way. This is done under bounded rationality, meaning that they act on uncertain expectations, restricted information and partial knowledge (Boudon 2003). This concept of rationality goes far beyond the mere instrumental notion of rationality, proposed by *Rational Choice Theory* (Coleman 1994). It rather takes into account that any social action generally depends on beliefs. Therefore both preferences and priorities as well as individual actions and choices have to be explained in terms of their meaning for the actors. They are rational not because of rational means-ends calculations, but because the actors perceive the effect of their reasoning to be rational.

2   In other words, this study analyses the institutional embeddedness of life courses, conceptualising the matching problem as a life course transition. Other perspectives on the higher education to work link, which will not be taken into consideration, might include an economic point of view on market returns to human capital (Becker, G. S. 1964; Becker, G.

3.1.1 The Matching Problem as Life Course Transition Process

In contrast to the timeless realm of abstract social theories such as neo-economic approaches or functionalism, life course approaches stress the importance of social institutions and time for the development of human lives. Life course research analyses the social pathways of human lives in their historical time and place, from childhood to old age, by considering how these pathways are influenced at the micro level by the course of individual action and ageing, and at the macro level by the importance of historical and geographic contexts. In pursuit of models of the life course that reflect historical and biographical time, a number of useful concepts have been developed (see Elder et al. 2003: 8-15). Each provides a way of thinking about the way lives are socially organised by showing that the time structure of individual lives is by no means only the outcome of individual choice and decision making processes but rather shaped by societal forces. A life course *trajectory* can be described as a "pathway defined by the ageing process or movement across the age structure" (Elder 1985: 31). In modern societies trajectories are the social pathways of education and work, family and residences that are followed by individuals and groups through society. These pathways are shaped by historical forces and are often structured by social institutions. Trajectories are themselves made up of *transitions*, which are changes in state or role. Examples of transitions include leaving parental home, becoming a parent, or – as it is the case in this study – entering the labour market after having finished education. The linkage between a single transition and a complex trajectory is a *sequence*, defined as any life course movement that includes at least two transitions between states (Sackmann and Wingens 2003: 96). The time between transitions is known as *duration*. Long durations enhance behavioural stability through acquired obligations and vested interests (Elder 1994).

Regarding the transition from education to work and the associated matching problem, life course research has already identified several particularities associated with this particular stage in life. First of all, labour market entry after finishing education is rather a process than one single change of state or one single match (Allmendinger 1989a; b; Kerckhoff 2001). As a consequence, the transition from higher education to work is better characterised as a transition period with several transitions occurring simultaneously or sequentially. Such sequences of transitions after full-time education might include obtaining a part-time job, being unemployed for

---

S. and Chiswick 1966; Mincer 1970; Schultz 1961), a functionalist analysis of mass higher education in modern societies (Archer 1972; Clark 1995), the spread of best practice higher education models for the labour market in a world society (Meyer 1977; Meyer et al. 1992; Ramirez and Meyer 1980), or a conflict theoretical point of view on labour market inequalities produced by the higher education system (Collins 1979).

some time, returning to education, obtaining a full-time job, and then being on parental leave. Transitions in early life may also have lifelong implications for shaping later events, experiences and transitions. Initial labour market experiences after leaving full-time education have a particularly long-lasting impact on career development. Furthermore, the timing of transitions is important for developmental consequences. The same events or experiences may affect individuals in different ways, depending on when they occur in the life course.

All these concepts – transitions, trajectories, sequences – are closely related to the process of ageing, which has become another primary theoretical vehicle in life course research. Ageing not only indicates that a person is becoming older, but also that specific states, roles and experiences are normatively associated with a particular age in society (Kohli 1985). Since age is highly collinear with labour force experience, it is difficult to separate the effects of age, job experience and other state durations. There is, however, the possibility of examining the effect of age norms for career development. It might be that those who enter the labour market or are promoted at relatively young ages are perceived as those who are especially able and likely to achieve more. Moreover, it is expected in general that the rate of job shifting slows down with age or labour force experience due to a declining discrepancy between current and potential positions, or due to the development of skills particular to a given job or employer (Rosenfeld 1992). Particularly in different national contexts, the age norms of finishing higher education and entering the labour market might strongly differ and have to be taken into account.

The duration of the matching process is therefore of utmost importance for analysing early labour market careers of higher education graduates. It is essential to pay attention to the length of early labour market spells, to take into account the timing of transition events during the life course, and to focus on sequences of transitions occurring during a longer transition period after finishing education instead of analysing only a single point in time. In addition to these duration aspects of the transition process, the quality of early labour market outcomes is certainly important as well. A very basic criterion in this regard is that transitions after graduation can occur between different life phases, such as the transition from higher education to work, from work to unemployment, or from work to parental leave. But transitions can also take the form of changes between different labour market states, such as being employed full-time, then part-time, and then out of the labour force. Furthermore, transitions between different kinds of jobs with particular employment characteristics, such as those transitions between various types of occupations or between high and low status positions, are essential for characterising the quality of the matching process. In this regard, mobility studies have pointed to the importance of job shifts for career development.

34

While a job is a particular kind of work with a particular employer, a career can be defined as a sequence of jobs, usually with some notion of progress or at least coherence (Rosenfeld 1992: 40). Job shifts can be considered as the building blocks of individuals' careers and thus as important transitions during career development.

With the help of the information about the duration and the quality of the matching process taking place after graduation, it becomes possible to investigate sequences of transitions in the beginning of graduate careers that, taken together, constitute specific transition patterns from higher education to work. This conceptualisation of the matching process will be used as *explanandum* for the cross-national analysis of graduate career trajectories. However, the concepts discussed so far still remain at the individual level and pay attention to the conduct of individual lives based on rational decision making, while they neglect their institutional embeddedness. In this regard, life course research also stresses also that certain macro level phenomena, namely institutions and historical circumstance, are decisive for structuring the nature of individual life courses.

3.1.2 The Institutional Embeddedness of Life Courses

Ryder (1965) has shown that historical changes often have different implications for people of different age, because these age differences become manifest in different experiences and recourses when confronted with new situations and consequently lead to different adoption processes to new conditions. In general, a *cohort* is a group of people who have shared the same critical experience during the same interval of time, for example in the most common sense the year of birth, but also the year of labour market entry or of retirement (Alwin and McCammon 2003; Heinz 1996; Ryder 1965). Thus, cohorts link age and historical time by showing how people of different age bring different resources to situations and consequently adapt differently to social conditions. When historical change differentiates the lives of successive cohorts, it generates a *cohort effect*. For the transition from education to work, it has been shown that as a consequence of educational expansion, younger cohorts face different employment prospects than older ones (Falk et al. 2000; Hillmert 2001). In addition, history can take the form of a *period effect* when the impact of social change is relatively uniform across several cohorts. Both period and cohort effects constitute evidence of historical influences, which always have to be taken into account when explaining cross-national similarities and differences of transition patterns.

These multiple meanings of history brought time and temporality of the macro level to life course thinking. However, it is not only the principle of time that explains the social embeddedness of lives, but also the principle of place or societal institutions. The institutionalisation of life courses refers to the process by which normative, legal or organisational rules define the social and temporal organisation of human lives. This institutionalisation either refers to stages or states in life, which can be formally or informally structured like education, employment or partnership, or to life course events and transitions like leaving school, entry into and exits from labour contracts, or ages of pension entitlements (Kohli 1985; Weymann 1989; 2003b).

Life course research remains very vague in its definition of institutions and often refers to institutions of the welfare state as major determinants for the organisation of modern life courses (Mayer and Müller 1989). Explicit theoretical accounts of institutions, however, are missing. Therefore, this study adopts the comprehensive definition of institutions given by Scott (2001) who sees institutions as social structures that have attained a high degree of resilience and are composed of regulative, normative and cultural-cognitive elements that provide stability and meaning to social life. Regulative elements refer to a society's formal and informal rules such as legislation or traditions. Normative elements define roles and expectations for its members. And cultural-cognitive elements structure the knowledge of how appropriate behaviour in a society looks like (Scott, R. W. 2001). According to Scott (2001), institutions operate at multiple levels of jurisdiction, from the world system to localised interpersonal relationships, and by definition connote stability while also being subject to change (Scott, R. W. 2001: 47f). In this conception, institutions are multifaceted, durable social structures, made up of material resources, social activities, and symbolic elements. They have developed historically in a time and place-specific manner and are thus path dependent. Despite being relatively stable over time, they are also subject to change, both because of the impact of the broader institutional environment in which they are embedded and because of the impact of the aggregation of lives that follow these pathways. This draws attention to a dynamic analysis of institutional development taking into account the historical processes of institutional evolution, stability and change.[3]

This societal macro level of institutions enables and constrains individual life course conduct by setting a regulative, normative and cognitive framework for individual preferences, capacities and expectations. Institutions can affect individual behaviour by giving information about the legitimacy of social practices (Scott, R. W. 2001), by providing actors with greater or lesser degrees of certainty about the appropriateness of behaviour

---

3   A definition of institutional path dependency and explicit mechanisms generating institutional stability and change remain underdeveloped in life course research. The dynamics of institutional development will therefore be examined more thoroughly within the *Varieties of Capitalism* approach (Hall and Soskice 2001), which offers more theoretical considerations in this regard (see p. 54ff of this study).

of other actors (March and Olson 1989), by affecting the range and sequence of alternatives of the choice-agenda (North 1990), or by supplying actors with moral or cognitive templates for interpreting actions (Meyer and Rowan 1977; Zucker 1977). Actors are thus choosing between different possibilities by referring to an institutional environment that gives meaning and thus perceived (bounded) rationality to their actions.

The major focus of this study will be on regulatory institutions, the formal and informal rules guiding job search and job placement activities after graduation. Regulatory institutions that are especially relevant for shaping individual life course transitions in modern times are national life course policies, such as education, labour market, unemployment, family, or retirement policies. There have been different cross-national attempts to link theories of welfare regimes and political economies to the life course approach, and thereby develop a comparative model of nations from a life course perspective (Leisering and Leibfried 1999; Mayer and Müller 1989; Weymann 2003a). According to these studies, country-specific life course policies lead to different life course regimes, and, consequently, to different patterns of transition within life course stages. The term *life course regime* indicates that the life course in one country has some overall logic that reflects the institutional structure (Leisering and Leibfried 1999: 14).

Country-specific political regulations provide institutional support for the conduct of life by giving structure and helping to stabilise expectations, transitions, and trajectories. For the transition from higher education to work, both education and labour market policies play an important role in life course politics, for example by providing age entry and exit norms of the higher education system, by defining the available range of educational credentials, by establishing rules for the distribution of labour market outcomes and rewards, or by providing assistance in the case of unemployment. Family policies, too, are important institutions for shaping labour market careers since they influence the way work and family can be combined, an essential aspect especially for the life courses of women. In addition to regulatory institutions, normative and cognitive institutions are also taken into account when explaining transition patterns from higher education to work. Normative institutions, for example, influence the expectations regarding the skills and knowledge a higher education graduate is confronted with when applying for a job. Cognitive institutional elements influence the range of jobs students consider appropriate for their type of higher education and accordingly influence their labour market behaviour.

Institutions are not free-floating, however, they must manifest themselves in one way or another to be applicable to individual lives. Some authors consider organisations as such manifestations of societal institutions (Meyer and Rowan 1977; Scott, R. W. 2001), which mediate between institutions and life courses. However, contrary to the point of view of sociological neo-institutionalism, which considers organisations to be institutions themselves and thus prevents an analytical separation of the two concepts, organisations in this study are regarded as distinct from institutions in terms of their main principle, the way they operate, the factors that influence their establishment and dissolution, etc. North (1990) explicitly differentiates institutions from organisations: While institutions are defined as rules and the related enforcement characteristics of these rules within a given social system, organisations are groups of individuals bound together by a common purpose (North 1990: 5). Organisations just as individuals follow the rules given by institutions. In the field of higher education, the regulative institutions of higher education policies define the structural set-up of university organisations, their financial structure, or their personnel recruitment practices. Furthermore, societal expectations define what kind of values and normative functions universities have to fulfil in society. Consequently, for explaining cross-national similarities and differences in the transition from higher education to work, relevant organisations such as different types of universities organisations, or various forms of employment organisations have to be taken into account.

3.1.3 Institutional Effects and the Transition from Higher Education to Work

From applying the concepts of life course research to the labour market entry of higher education graduates in different countries it follows that the overall aim of this study is to analyse the duration and the quality of the matching process and to explain how these two are influenced by the institutional set-up of higher education systems and labour markets. Rather than focussing on a single point in time, it is important to follow graduates from the end of higher education throughout their early labour market careers to analyse the sequences of life course states, labour market states, and/or job shifts they are experiencing. The timing of transition processes has to be taken into account as well, since transitions have different implications for later career development, depending on when they happened during the life course.

For explaining the similarities and differences observed with regard to the labour market entry of higher education graduates in different countries, national higher education and labour market institutions serve as important blueprints against which individual transition processes may be studied cross-nationally. This does not mean that these institutions determine individual career development completely, but that they enhance people's ability to act by providing general preconditions for individual behaviour required for achieving individual projects in a country-specific way. In this regard, an analysis of the historical evolution of the institutional structure is

38

pivotal in establishing which national rules, norms and cognitive scripts are related to the labour market entry of higher education graduates. They influence what both students and employers perceive as "adequate" graduate employment, constitute the perceived arena of choice and transition options, and define the value of university certificates as well as higher education in general. These overall effects of the national institutional environment can be called *institutional effects* since they form a national frame of reference.

Apart from these more general institutional effects stemming from the institutional set-up of higher education systems and graduate labour markets, historical events can also have an impact on the transition from higher education to work. As a cohort effect they result in similar work trajectories of students that share a common historical experience, such as being born at the same time, or, what seems even more important, having graduated at the same time. If history takes the form of a period effect, such as German reunification, it influences a country's population as a whole. Only by analysing the various time dependent and independent impacts of institutions on life courses one is able to gain deeper insights in the formation of national transition regimes. But which institutional features of higher education systems and labour markets are important constituents of a national transition regime? In order to establish a more distinct picture of the social mechanisms underlying the transition from higher education to work, concepts of existing education and labour market theories will be introduced in the following sections and applied to explain patterns of graduate career mobility.

3.2 The Institutional Determinants of Graduate Employment

Institutions of higher education and labour markets shape matching processes as they affect both worker and employer action in the labour market. One can define higher education as any kind of post-secondary education which is either largely theoretically based and intended to provide sufficient qualifications for gaining entry into advanced research programmes (for example history, philosophy, mathematics, etc.) or professions with high skill requirements (for example medicine, dentistry, pharmacy, etc.), or which is rather practically oriented, designed for participants to acquire the practical skills and know-how needed for employment in a particular occupation (for example architecture, engineering, management studies, etc.) (UNESCO 1997). Higher education institutions define the design of education programmes, the range of achievable credentials, the structural set-up, governance, and financing of higher education organisations, or the societal norms and cognitive scripts associated with this kind of education. Labour markets can be characterised abstractly as "arenas in which workers exchange their labor power in return for wages, status, and other job rewards" (Kalleberg and Sorensen 1979: 351). Labour market institutions include the means by which employees are matched to and distributed among jobs and the rules that govern employment, mobility, skill and training requirements, as well as the distribution of wages and other rewards obtained contingent upon the embeddedness in a specific societal system.

The comparison of higher education systems and labour markets among nation states, where institutional arrangements, social conditions, the forms of economic organisation and the role and attitudes of social actors all vary, provides a very rich field for developing theoretical mechanisms that explain transition patterns in different countries. The purpose of the following theoretical explications, however, is not, simply to describe different institutional arrangements but rather to understand how these are linked to generate a particular societal logic or path of development, and to impart different meanings and significance for individual life course development. However, since research conducted on the relationship between higher education and work has so far failed to relate to institutional arrangements for life course developments in a systematic manner, theoretical concepts of other research traditions have to be borrowed. In the field of vocational education and training (VET) there have been different attempts to link institutional theories to the life course approach and thereby develop models of VET to work transitions, which might be applied to graduate employment as well. In the following, the concepts developed in this particular area of research will be applied to the field of higher education.

3.2.1 The Importance of Institutions for Explaining Vocational Training to Work Transitions

In the field of vocational education and training, the notion of a dichotomy of institutional arrangements shaping VET to work transitions in advanced societies has been popular in comparative transition research for more than a decade. Fuelled by numerous studies from educational sociology, life course analysis and labour market mobility research, it has become commonplace to distinguish between two basic types of institutional contexts creating specific transition patterns (see Allmendinger 1989b; Kerckhoff 2001; Marsden 1999; Maurice et al. 1986; Müller and Shavit 1998): a more occupationalised one at work in countries like Germany, where young people are predominantly trained within a highly standardised and occupation-specific apprenticeship system and from thereon experience rather smooth trajectories into the labour market, and a less standardised, more organisation-based system that supposedly exists in Anglo-Saxon countries, where general and comprehensive education without institutionalised vocational training leads to early entry into the labour market, but the transition period is more turbulent and marked by a sequence of stop-gap jobs. These country-specific transition patterns are deemed to result directly from the differences in institutional environments, which are found under a variety of headings. Some authors frame the dichotomy as the difference between *occupational* and *organisational* spaces (Maurice et al. 1986), others refer to *systems of occupational* vs. *systems of internal labour markets* (Marsden 1990), still others distinguish between *highly* or *weakly standardised* and *stratified* education systems (Allmendinger 1989b) or, similarly, between *highly occupation-specific* and *general* skill arrangements of school-to-work transitions (Hannan et al. 1999; Kerckhoff 2001; Müller and Shavit 1998).

Empirical studies making use of these typologies point to the fact that the coupling between vocational education and trainings systems and labour markets is the major reason why transition patterns differ cross-nationally (Gangl 2001; 2002a; 2004; see, for example, Kogan and Müller 2003; Kohlrausch 2009; Müller and Gangl 2003; Shavit and Müller 1998). In this perspective, educational resources are not in general beneficial for individual labour market outcomes.[4] Rather, the structure of education systems, by providing either fairly general training or more specific vocational training, has an effect on the structure of labour market entry processes via the different linkages established between education and employment systems. Thus, the notion of two distinct institutional environments and associated patterns of labour market integration of young people is common to all these approaches. A tight coupling between VET and work guarantees smooth trajectories for leavers, and educational credentials are the primary criterion for career mobility. In loosely coupled systems, on the other hand, the transition process appears to be less structured by the education system, while individual bargaining processes and promotion strategies as well as training on the job are important determinants for structuring early labour market careers.

---

4   This assumption is very popular in economic theories of labour market matching. Human capital theorists (Kalleberg and Sorensen 1979), for example, interpret employment outcomes as a matching of demand and supply on a perfect market. They explain observed earning differentials among the labour force with differences in human capital acquired through education, work-based training, and work experience. The basic claim is that the more human capital an individual obtains, the higher are his or her physical and mental abilities, and consequently the higher is his or her productivity in the labour market, which is rewarded by higher incomes. The main criticism of this theoretical approach is its assumption of a perfectly competitive market. It assumes that all actors, workers and employers, have perfect information, maximise utilities in particular earnings, and are unable to individually influence the prices given by the market (Amable 2000: 656). However, the fact that human capital theory cannot shed light on cross-national differences is even more important for this work, since it refers to general mechanisms of labour market matching on the micro level and refrains from institutional explanations.

The most comprehensive account in this regard is provided by Maurice et al. (1986) with their seminal study on the recruitment practices in French and German firms. Their results suggest two concepts for understanding national differences in the linkage between VET and employment systems: *qualificational* and *organisational* mobility space. Transition regimes, in this perspective, are structured by the reciprocal constitution of actors and spaces, i.e. the way in which qualifications are produced in the education system and their subsequent use by employers, leading to complex system-specific relationships between qualifications and jobs. In qualificational spaces vocational qualifications are used by employers to organise jobs and to allocate personnel. In organisational spaces, education is less closely related to occupational training, and vocational skills are mainly obtained by training on the job. According to Maurice et al. (1986), qualificational spaces have a much higher "capacity to structure" (Kerckhoff 2001: 6) the distribution of young people into employment, and students more often fit smoothly into stable labour market locations and experience relatively orderly careers. In contrast, young people in organisational spaces more often experience a period of "turbulence" during which they may move in and out of the labour force and change jobs with some frequency.

Regarding the transition from higher education to work, national institutions should also have a capacity to structure individual career patterns. In order to get a first grasp of the concepts that might account for country-specific institutional linkages between higher education and work and resulting transition patterns it seems reasonable to make use of the theoretical concepts that have already been identified for studying VET to work transitions, namely stratification and occupational specificity as institutions of the higher education system, and labour market segmentation as well as labour market regulation as institutions of the labour market. Standardisation, another concept developed in this research tradition, will also be discussed theoretically, but not be applied in the empirical part of the study due to data limitations. The applications of these concepts to graduate career mobility will be a first step in analysing how individual life courses are shaped by higher education and graduate labour market institutions.

Figure 1: Theoretical model for studying the transition from higher education to work

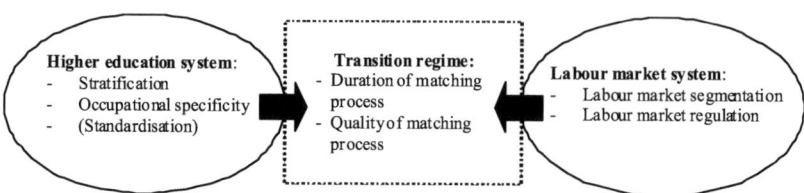

Figure 1 gives an overview of the theoretical model to be applied in the empirical part of the book. By studying the impact of institutional configurations on the duration and quality of the matching process, one can get insights into how country-specific trajectories evolve and come into practice. However, since higher education differs substantially from vocational education, the adaptation of these theoretical concepts has to take into consideration the specificities that this type of education brings about. In the following sections, each concept will be discussed separately and analysed in terms of how it might be applicable to explain transition patterns from higher education to work in different countries.

3.2.2 The Institutional Determinants of the Transition from Higher Education to Work

Even though the concepts of stratification, occupational specificity, standardisation, labour market segmentation and labour market regulation have been developed by different scholars and applied in different research contexts, they all demonstrate how national institutions structure individual labour market outcomes and career mobility. Yet so far, none of these concepts has been applied exclusively to the transition from higher education to work. Taken together, however, they should have the capability of elucidating how and why graduate careers differ cross-nationally.

Cross-National Differences in the Institutional Set-up of Higher Education Systems

With respect to the stage of entering the labour market, researchers have long been convinced that the structure of education and training systems has important effects on the transition process between education and work (see Allmendinger 1989b; Blossfeld and Shavit 1993; Hannan et al. 1999; Heinz 1999; Kerckhoff 2001; Müller and Shavit 1998). In contrast to micro theories which strongly focus on the amount of human capital and related productivity as decisive factors for successful labour market entry, the concepts of stratification, occupational specificity, and standardisation show how education institutions have the capacity to structure transition processes. The interface between the higher education system and the labour market will be examined along these three dimensions.

Stratification and Institutional Differentiation

An initial concept for analysing higher education to work transitions is the concept of *stratification*. This concept was originally developed to explain the relationship between the structural set-up of an education system and the structure of the labour market. The stratification of national education systems comprises two dimensions: the degree of differentiation within given education levels (tracking), coupled with the proportion of a birth cohort that attains the maximum number of school years provided by the education system (Allmendinger 1989b; Kerckhoff 2001; Müller and Shavit 1998). The degree of stratification is high where there is a relatively low percentage of a birth cohort graduating from higher education combined with a relatively high number of tracks at a particular education level.

The main hypothesis related to this institutional aspect holds that the stratified structure of an education system is a key factor in determining how qualifiers are matched to a stratified occupational structure. Institutional stratification therefore mainly influences individuals' job prospects with respect to future employers' expectations because, in highly stratified systems, employers can rely upon the "meritocratic" pre-selection through a stratified education system. More precisely, the stratification of an education system affects the way different education credentials correspond to the differentiated social structure of the labour market. A high degree of educational stratification is assumed to be complementary to a high degree of occupational stratification, making the match between higher education credentials and initial employment positions more likely and therefore reducing the time it takes to find a matching employment position.

What is theoretically interesting about the concept of stratification is the question of which micro mechanisms have an influence upon the stratification of the labour force. Even though it is rarely stated in clear terms, researchers applying this concept either refer to stratification by productivity differences or by socio-structural differences. The first follow the logic of human capital theory (Becker, G. S. 1962; Mincer 1970; Schultz 1961) and the signalling approach (Spence 1973)[5], arguing that in highly stratified systems, educational credentials clearly signal differences in productivity of applicants and their subsequent usefulness for specific labour market positions. If a larger variety of educational tracks exists, employers can rely on an effective pre-sorting of individuals by the education system, which allows for a matching process based on certified human capital. From this point of view, observed stratification in form of status or earning

---

5   Spence's signalling approach (1973) tries to incorporate employer decisions under uncertainty into the matching problem. On the basis of previous experience in the market, employers have conditional probability assessments over productive capacity related to specific education signals. Job matching occurs in the context of a feedback loop, in which employer expectations lead to offered wages which are related to various levels of education, which in turn leads to investment in education by individuals. After hiring, the discovery of the actual relationships between education and productivity results in revised expectations and beliefs, and the cycle starts again. In stratified systems, these learning processes are less important since educational credentials give enough information about job applicants' productive capacities.

differentials among the labour force can be explained with differences in human capital acquired in different tracks of the education system. In the absence of such a pre-sorting system, labour market matching has to rely relatively more on previous work experience or other socio-structural factors such as gender or ethnicity serving as signals of productivity. However, a critical evaluation of this line of reasoning might conclude that education credentials are less a means of identifying human capital, but rather are a means of reproducing persisting power structures and inequalities (Collins 1979). Even though it has been shown that the influence of parental socio-economic status decreases with each transition taken in the education system, a class-specific positive selection nevertheless prevails even at the highest level of education (Blossfeld and Shavit 1993). In highly stratified systems the positive selection of upper class children should be particularly pronounced and accordingly, an important mechanism for the stratification of the labour force. Therefore, parental class background is an essential aspect of analysing stratified labour market outcomes.

In order to make predictions about the impact of stratification on graduate labour market careers, the first dimension – tracking within a particular level of education – has to be adapted to higher education by explicating the dimensions along which a pre-sorting of students can occur. In this regard, it seems useful to consider the institutional differentiation of higher education. National systems of higher education became more diversified in the process of education expansion. Especially during the 1980s and 1990s, they varied substantially according to the extent of diversity and the major dimensions of diversification, such as different types of higher education institutions (for example universities vs. technical colleges), different field of study programmes (for example humanities vs. engineering), different types of degree levels (for example Bachelor vs. Master), and variations in reputation and prestige within formally equal institutions and programmes (Teichler 2002a; 2007b). All of these dimensions are indicators of an institutional differentiation within a higher education system along which tracking can occur[6]. It is important to note, however, that the quality of tracking might differ between these dimensions.

---

6   The importance of institutional differentiation for graduate employment has been stressed
     by various scholars (1995). Clark (1998) for example underlines the increasing necessity
     for professional training by universities. He proposes a differentiated structure of university
     degrees, which institutionally separates a generalist education for "under graduates"
     oriented at satisfying the broad demands of the labour market from a master's education
     preparing for leadership positions in business, and PhD programmes preparing students for
     a career in academia. This implies that institutional differentiation will lead to specific
     labour market careers of higher education graduates stemming from different levels of
     productivity as well as labour market demands. Specific mechanisms governing this labour
     market entry and explanations of cross-national variation, however, have not yet been
     conceptualised in this line of research.

Various types of institutions or degrees can project both a horizontal and a vertical differentiation within the higher education system, depending on whether they are hierarchically structured (such as BA and MA) or not. Different fields of study normally pertain to the same hierarchical level and therefore only differentiate the system horizontally. Institutional reputation, in contrast, by definition creates a hierarchy among institutions and is thus exclusively related to vertical differentiation. Both forms of differentiation might stratify the labour force; however, only a high degree of vertical differentiation is assumed to stratify labour market outcomes hierarchically and as such is associated with a high degree of stratification. As a consequence, occupational rewards of initial employment positions in vertically differentiated systems should be more unequal in status.

H1.1: The higher the vertical differentiation of a higher education system, the stronger differ the (status) returns to different higher education tracks.

The other dimension of stratification – the proportion of a birth cohort that attains the maximum number of school years provided by the education system – does not have to be adapted for higher education graduates, since it directly refers to the number of students obtaining a higher education degree. Based on this dimension, stratification can be taken as a good indicator of higher education expansion. It is important to note, however, that this dimension does not refer to the structure of higher education, but rather to the set-up of secondary education and its sorting function for entry into higher education. This sorting in secondary schooling acts as an important filtering mechanism for the process of higher education expansion since it restricts the number of students with entry certificates. The basic premise of this mechanism is that in secondary education systems with a low level of stratification, less sorting takes place through secondary schooling, which, as a consequence leads to a higher proportion of higher education graduates. In highly stratified systems, on the other hand, the main sorting of pupils into different tracks occurs already in secondary education, which subsequently yields lower graduation rates in higher education. In some systems, therefore, it is easier to obtain the highest available degree than in others based on the structure of secondary education. Accordingly, the degree of a country's higher education expansion is not only the result of individual choice (more students willing or demanding to attend higher education) and higher education structures (more available higher education institutions), but also depends on the selectivity of secondary education.

Building on this mechanism, Müller and Shavit (1998) argue that increases in the proportion of higher education graduates tend to decrease returns to the educational level below, but also overall status outcomes of higher education graduates (Müller and Shavit 1998). Their theoretical explanation is based on Thurow's labour queue model (Thurow 1975), which assumes that most skills necessary for job performance are obtained on the job. Educational qualifications are not valued by employers for the skills the represent *per se*, but for the indirect information (signals) they provide, for example, about a candidate's intelligence (trainability), work habits, or disciplines. Due to the importance of these indicators, employers establish a hierarchical queue among applicants based on their educational credentials, which places higher education graduates ahead of other qualification holders. If such a job-queue is at work, there is a built-in incentive for young people to acquire more education qualifications in order to stay ahead of the queue. But as ever larger proportions of a given age cohort obtain the highest credentials, the labour market value of these credentials declines (Müller 1998; Müller and Shavit 1998). Thus, secondary education systems with a low level of stratification tend to produce an excessive supply of higher education graduates, thereby lowering the value of these credentials in the labour market. By contrast, in systems with highly stratified secondary education, the value of higher education credentials is preserved because only a lower percentage of a birth cohort is able to attain a higher education degree. This indicates that in (secondary) education systems with a low level of stratification, the labour market returns of higher education graduates in general should be lower than in stratified systems, where a smaller proportion of higher education graduates are still able to outperform the rest of the labour force. At the same time, the time needed to find a job matching the level of education should be much shorter in stratified than in unstratified systems.

H1.2:   The higher the stratification of secondary education and the lower the proportion of a birth cohort that obtains a higher education degree, the higher the overall labour market returns of initial employment positions after graduation.

H1.3:   The higher the stratification of secondary education and the lower the proportion of a birth cohort that obtains a higher education degree, the less time it takes graduates to obtain favourable labour market positions.

In summary, an analysis of higher education stratification operating in different political economies will show how the flow of students is channelled to initial employment -positions. At the level of higher education, a high degree of stratification leads to strong status differences between students with different higher education credentials and strongly stratifies labour market returns accordingly. Vertically differentiated higher education systems in particular are supposed to allocate individuals to positions of matching status within the differentiated occupational structure and to decrease the duration of the job search to achieve a good match. Higher education systems that are highly stratified by type of institutions, degrees, institutional reputation, or fields of study should be associated with track-specific timing and matching effects. The stratification of secondary education and the degree of higher education expansion more generally affects the comparative advantage of higher education graduates as compared to qualifiers from other educational levels. If secondary education is highly stratified and the proportion of higher education graduates remains low, graduates will generally stay ahead of the queue and obtain higher-status positions as compared to secondary education systems with a low level of stratification, where credential inflation lowers the overall labour market returns of higher education graduates.

Since the concept of stratification refers to the structural set-up of education systems, it is a good example of how regulatory institutions are likely to influence the transition from higher education to work. The concept of occupational specificity is less concerned with institutional structures, but focuses more strongly on the content taught at higher education institutions. Therefore, it serves as an example of how norms and historical ideas have an impact on career development.er education tracks.

Occupational Specificity and the Nature of Training

According to the concept of occupational specificity, higher education systems may vary in the extent to which they offer curricula that are designed to prepare students for particular occupations and award credentials that are occupationally specific. Occupations can be defined as groups of individuals who perform similar activities, have similar skills and competencies, as well as similar amounts of social power deriving from their occupational position within the social division of labour (Kalleberg and Sorensen 1979: 361). For both employers and employees, occupations serve as a meaningful internal structure of the labour market, facilitating the acknowledgement of status transfer as well as the process of matching qualifications to skill requirements. However, the way qualifications correspond to certain occupations and accordingly the match between contents learned in the education system and job requirements differ cross-nationally.

Comparative studies on VET systems have shown that only in systems with a high degree of occupational specificity, a close match between vocational training and occupation is achieved immediately after leaving education, while in systems with a stronger focus on general skills the training for specific occupations does not take place within the education system, but has to be attained after entering the labour market (Gangl 2000a;

2001; Kerckhoff 2001; Müller and Shavit 1998).[7] The theoretical argument holds that educational resources are not beneficial for individual career outcomes *per se*, but rather that the structure of education systems as providing either general training or more specific occupational training has an effect on individual labour market entry via the different linkages established between educational and employment systems. The micro mechanism associated with occupation specific training is related to employers' *relative* reliance on formal qualifications vs. labour market experience as a reliable measure of individual skills during recruitment and allocation processes. To the extent that educational credentials do little to convey job applicants' potential capabilities for a particular occupation, employers will be more likely to assess individual skills either from their past work records or from training on the job. In turn, if training systems provide qualifications that are meaningful indicators of skills for a particular occupation, employers should be more likely to use this inexpensive signal of individual capabilities and hire job applicants on the basis of their credentials.

Interestingly, the concept of occupational specificity helps to overcome one of the major criticisms of neo-economic models of the matching process, namely that employers possess perfect information about the applicants' skills (Kalleberg and Sorensen 1979). The assumption that a high degree of occupation-specific training can influence employers' expectations about what has been learned in the education system implies, first of all, that education is indeed able to transfer specific knowledge and skills to students, and second, that employers possess perfect knowledge about the relationship between productivity and specific educational certificates. Accordingly, in occupation-specific systems, more information about productivity is available to both employers and job applicants and matching of applicants to jobs can be based merely on credentials. In systems conferring more general skills, on the other hand, employers cannot trust that a specific level of

---

7   Becker's version of human capital theory explicitly draws attention to the problem of general vs. specific skill acquisition (Becker, G. S. 1964). While general human capital is useful in many firms, (firm-)specific human capital is only beneficial to the firm that has provided it through training on the job. In contrast to firm-specific training, general skills either are acquired through the formal education system or are provided by firms, if they offer general training in form of industry-specific apprenticeships, which provide skills that are useful for the whole industry. The main problem of general skills is the possible poaching of skilled workers by other firms. As a consequence, firms are reluctant to invest in general skills, since they are not willing to pay for skills can be used anywhere else. Instead, individuals have to pay for the acquisition of general skills themselves, by receiving no wages at all (as it is the case for general school education) or by earning wages below what could have been received elsewhere (as it is the case for apprenticeships). Firms are willing to pay for specific training since they benefit from higher productivity. At the same time no reasonable employee would invest in training that cannot be used anywhere else, especially when the rate of labour turnover is high.

productivity is related to certain credentials. Instead, when hiring people they have to screen individuals more thoroughly, have to train them on the job, which makes labour market mismatches more likely.

The major problem of applying the concept of occupational specificity to higher education is related to empirical measurement. In the sphere of vocational training, the degree of occupational specificity depends upon the number of standardised apprenticeships designed for a specific occupation and the orientation of curricula towards the teaching of specific vocational knowledge (Kerckhoff 2001; Müller and Shavit 1998). Measurement of the occupational specificity of higher education is not as straightforward, since no such entity as an apprenticeship exists. When compared directly to vocational training, higher education is often perceived as conferring only general skills and therefore national variations of occupational specificity are considered low (Estévez-Abe et al. 2001). However, it is also very likely that on the level of higher education countries place different emphasis on particular types of skills. The analysis of the importance of occupation-specific training associated with the different dimensions of institutional differentiation should yield information in this regard. The content taught by different types of higher education institutions, degree courses, and fields of study as regards their orientation towards specific knowledge, but also the incorporation of practical training may serve as appropriate measures of occupational specificity at the higher education level. In addition, the organisation of professional training should be essential, too, since professions in particular are characterised by a highly exclusive knowledge base, systematic professional education and training, and accordingly specific fields of action relevant only for this particular occupational group (Abbott 1988; Brater and Beck 1981; Heidenreich 1999).

The effect of occupation-specific training related to any of the discussed dimensions of institutional differentiation should be a smooth transition between higher education and work, where higher education credentials are the primary criterion for job placement. Qualifications with a strong focus on occupational training should result in a close match between acquired and required skills of the first job, since both employers and graduates possess enough information about the kind of education needed. As regards the duration of the matching process, occupation-specific training should also guarantee that employment in an occupation matching the higher education credential is found more quickly after graduation. In systems which exhibit only a low degree of occupational specificity, the transition process appears to be less structured by higher education credentials, while discretionary recruitment strategies, and other individual signals should play a crucial role in shaping early labour market careers. If the specialisation is low, it should not take long before graduates get their first job, since they can choose from a large variety of different occupations. However, more general certificates should result in a larger variation of occupations obtained with the same type of higher education qualification and in longer transition periods until a matching job is found.

H2.1: The higher the occupational specificity of a higher education credential, the closer the match between educational certificate and occupation of the first job.

H2.2: The higher the occupational specificity of a higher education credential, the shorter the duration of finding an occupation matching the qualification after graduation.

Apart from finding a matching job immediately after graduation, patterns of occupational mobility after higher education should also differ between higher and lower degrees of occupational specialisation. General skills are usually transferable between different occupations, while the transferability of specific skills is more limited. This indicates that students with more general skills are more likely to experience shorter initial labour market spells due to an inappropriate match. Until a matching job is found, extensive job hopping between different types of occupations should be the consequence, often in combination with some training on the job to create a firm-specific skill profile. Students trained for a specific occupation, in contrast, should – once they are in employment – keep the same occupation for a longer time as a result of the good initial match. The high occupational specialisation should decrease the number of shifts between occupations and increase the chance of stable employment in the beginning of graduate careers.

H2.3: The higher the occupational specificity of higher education, the lower the likelihood of changing the type of occupation after job shifts.

To sum up, the degree of occupational specificity related to a higher education credential influences both the quality of the match between qualification and first occupation and the time it takes before a matching job is found after graduation. But despite the assumed commonalities between occupational specificity of VET and higher education, there might also be an important difference. In cross-national comparisons of vocational training, a country's whole system is classified as having a high or low degree of occupational specialisation, which as a consequence yields similar transition patterns for any student undergoing vocational training. Due to the different dimensions of institutional differentiation, occupation-specific training in the field of higher education might be associated with particular types of institutions, degrees, or fields of study rather than with a country's higher education system as a whole. Accordingly, different degrees of occupational specialisation might not only account for cross-national variations, but also produce strong intra-national differences. It remains to be seen empirically whether differences are more pronounced between countries or between different higher education credentials.

Excursus: Standardisation and Political Centralisation

A concept that is often used in cross-national comparisons of education systems is *standardisation*. It describes the degree to which institutional features of an education system meet the same standards nationwide (Allmendinger 1989a; Kerckhoff 2001; Müller and Shavit 1998). In the field of secondary education and vocational training, for example, researchers working with this concept analyse the extent to which degrees, curricula, or teacher training are standardised throughout a country and how this influences transition processes (Allmendinger 1989a; Bernardi et al. 2004; Hannan et al. 1999). Regarding the function of standardisation for labour market entry, it is argued that the setting of standards provides a valuable tool for evaluating what students have learned during their studies and what to anticipate for their performance in work life. Thus, the concept of standardisation influences individual job perspectives mainly with respect to future employers' expectations because in standardised systems employers can assume the presence of certain contents already learned in the education system. As a consequence, they can trust the information given by certain standardised certificates and do not have to screen and/or train individuals entering the labour force. A higher degree of standardisation is therefore assumed to lead to a smooth transition process between education and work, making it easy to find a first job soon after leaving education. Furthermore, repeated job shifts should not be necessary for obtaining stable employment. If educational processes and related qualifications are not standardised, they cannot be taken as accurate indicators of educational achievement. Students educated in unstandardised systems should have longer search phases and more job shifts in the beginning of their career.

In the field of VET to work transitions in particular, the concept of standardisation is often closely related to the occupational specificity of an education system, because only if occupation-specific credentials are standardised at the national level (e.g. as the German dual system) can they provide reliable information to employers about whether certain occupation-specific skills have been learned. In general, however, literature dealing with these concepts remains ambivalent whether standardisation can be considered an explanatory concept by itself in cross-national comparisons. While Allmendinger (1989a) and Kerckhoff (2001) consider it as a separate institutional dimension, Müller and Shavit (1998) find that the effect of standardisation disappears once stratification and occupational specificity are controlled for (Müller and Shavit 1998: 38). Allmendinger in her more recent work also relates standardisation specifically to vocational training (Allmendinger and Hinz 1998). In addition, empirical studies on the occupational specificity of vocational training systems do not separate standardisation analytically from the degree of occupational specificity (Gangl 2000b; 2001; Scherer 2001; 2005).

However, this does not mean that the concept for cross-national comparisons should be abandoned completely, but rather that we should be more explicit about the institutional dimensions that are standardised throughout a country. If the content of education credentials follows particular occupation-specific standards, then standardisation clearly is part of the more encompassing concept of occupational specificity, since only standardised occupation-specific credentials lead to a close match between education and initial employment positions. But degrees, curricula, or examinations can also be standardised at the national level without necessarily conferring occupation-specific skills. This might particularly be the case at more general levels of education, such as secondary schooling or higher education. As regards secondary education, studies have shown that both examination level and examination grades are very important for employers' decisions in highly standardised systems, while no significant effects are evident in less standardised systems (Breen et al. 1995; Rosenbaum and Kariya 1991)

In the case of higher education, research has shown that there are considerable historical and cross-national variations in the degree to which higher education systems are integrated with the political structure, yielding more or less standardised institutional elements. In highly centralised higher education systems, governments intervene universally and thereby define set nationwide standards regarding admission to higher education, the organisation of curricula, or the examination of students. In contrast, in more decentralised systems these institutional features vary more strongly between different higher education institutions (Archer 1972: 7). For the transition from higher education to work this implies that in highly standardised and centralised systems employers should find it rather easy to choose between applicants with the same degree, since they simply choose the applicant with the better results. In less standardised systems neither the certificate nor the achieved result carries enough information to allow employers to make a meaningful decision between candidates. Accordingly, the degree of standardisation of a higher education system can be considered to be a result of the centralisation or decentralisation of higher education governance within a country, if particular standards are predominantly established by national governments. Since the country-cases examined in this study do not reveal significant variation in the degree of standardisation of higher education credentials and since, furthermore, data on exam results are not available in the used data-sets, the concept of standardisation cannot be tested empirically and will therefore be left out in the following analysis. Nevertheless, standardisation should be included as a valuable concept for explaining cross-national similarities and differences in the transition from higher education to work, if other country-cases are compared and better data is available.

Cross-national Differences in the Institutional Set-up of Graduate Labour Markets

The discussion of the institutional embeddedness of transition processes has so far been centred around the organisation of higher education systems and their likely impact on graduate career development. The theoretical arguments put forward have shown how country-specific transition patterns might come into place due to vertical and horizontal institutional differentiation and the occupation-specific contents of various higher education credentials. However, a mere focus on higher education institutions would fail to consider the ways in which the world of work imposes its own requirements on the higher education system. After the initial matching problem is solved, i.e. obtaining the first job after graduation, the major problems are how career development is organised and how formal degrees and certificates correspond to the hierarchies and divisions of labour within and between firms. Specific forms of higher education and training need a structure of career mobility into which they can be integrated, and graduates need potential career rewards if they are to be persuaded to undertake the effort, if not the forgone earnings, and expense, of higher education. After graduates enter the labour market, it is therefore important to study how further career development is influenced by variations in the institutional set-up of graduate labour markets.

From an institutional perspective, graduate labour markets are not only equilibria of demand and supply of skills just as the 'market metaphor' of human capital theories implies, but a combination of institutions and processes which determine the pricing, buying, selling and allocation of labour (Kalleberg and Sorensen 1979). Two different forms of labour market dynamics might be possible for explaining transition patterns from higher education to work. Graduate labour markets might either function in relative independence from the higher education system, mainly following their its own logic, or alternatively, they may strongly build on the institutional structure of the higher education system. There are various micro theories that explain how and why early career mobility is likely to proceed. At the most basic level, one may argue that career mobility is a consequence of an increasing accumulation of human capital. As soon as additional forms of human capital are acquired, employees are likely to seek promotion and employers are willing to grant it. In addition to formal certificates, general work experience or on-the-job training may signal such an increase in human capital and accordingly lead to promotion (Becker, G. S. 1962; Mincer 1970; Schultz 1961). Job matching theory, on the other hand, would predict that labour market mobility is the result of an initial job mismatch rather than of human capital growth (Jovanovic 1979; Sattinger 1993). Since employers and employees are dissatisfied with a job allocation, in which skills do not meet job requirements, both are prone to induce job shifts in order to achieve a more satisfying match. Particularly in the case of overqualification, where the level of education acquired exceeds the level of education required for a particular job, upward mobility after initial job placement is likely to occur (Büchel et al. 2003).

Supporters of job vacancy theories loosen this tight connection between educational attainment and career mobility. They consider job vacancies an important influence on individual career development, since labour market entry and mobility depend on the availability of vacant positions. The basic idea is that a person's move to a new job creates a vacancy to be filled and therefore creates a new mobility opportunity for another person. Matching and promotion probabilities are considered to be dependent on vacancy creation, on the distribution and source of vacancies (exits, new jobs), the number and nature of competitors, and managerial decisions about how to fill vacant positions (Kalleberg and Sorensen 1979; Rosenfeld 1992; Sorensen 1977). The main contrast between job vacancy approaches and human capital theories can be found in the assumptions they make about educational influences on career mobility. While human capital theories argue that (income) mobility occurs only in accordance with increases of human capital, job vacancy approaches claim that educational resources do not change over time in an organisation and thus have no necessary relationship to the opening of vacancies and resulting mobility processes. The main function of educational resources in this perspective is to determine the best possible position a person can fill. Again, overqualification may occur since at least some people will enter an organisation in positions not matching their qualifications. However, the longer they stay with the organisation, the more they can make use of vacancies, and the smaller the gap will be between their potential and their current labour market position (Rosenfeld 1992).

The discussion of higher education institutions and their impact on transition patterns has shown that they can mainly account for the match between higher education credential and initial employment position. However, they fail to explain individual job shifts and, accordingly, patterns of job mobility. The concepts of labour market segmentation and labour market regulation are well-established theoretical approaches to explain cross-national variations of career mobility; yet, they have not been applied to the field of higher education exclusively. Both theoretical strands are able to demonstrate how job vacancies and mobility opportunities might differ between countries and thus significantly influence the career development of higher education graduates.

Labour Market Segmentation between Professional and Public Spheres

The notion of labour market segmentation, a concept commonly used in cross-national comparisons of vocational education to work transitions (Gangl 2000a; b; 2001; Marsden 1999), implies that the labour market is divided in several segments, all of which offer specific career prospects. It is assumed that a country's labour market is differentiated into distinct sectors or segments characterised by a high degree of social closure. This closure is based on specific certificates serving as a necessary precondition for entering a particular segment as well as specific allocation principles and career structures serving as a means to maintain segmental closure and to prohibit mobility between the segments (Althauser 1989; Althauser and Kalleberg 1981; Kalleberg and Sorensen 1979). A segment may be defined by occupations, industries, organisational characteristics, or the like. The main difference to the theories previously discussed is the importance given to qualifications. Even though different skill levels are important tools for analysing segmented labour markets, the important distinction is made between "good" and "bad" jobs identified by such characteristics as status, pay, opportunities for promotion, or work autonomy, rather than between high or low skilled workers.

Early work on labour market segmentation identified a dual structure consisting of primary and secondary jobs with little mobility between them. The former ones offer high status positions, high wages and good career prospects, while the latter tend to offer low wages, poorer working conditions and fewer opportunities for advancement (Doeringer and Piore 1971; see Kalleberg and Sorensen 1979 for a discussion). The most prominent differentiation found in the literature, however, is made between internal and external labour markets. External labour markets function in line with "pure" market logic, where allocation and mobility decisions are controlled directly by mechanisms of labour demand and supply (Kerr 1954). Internal labour markets, in contrast, according to Doeringer (1967) are defined as "an administrative unit within which the market functions of pricing, allocation, and often training are performed. It is governed by a set of institutional rules which delineate the boundaries of the internal market and determine its internal structure" (Doeringer 1967: 207).

In an internal labour market, employees are assumed to enter via specific entry positions and thereafter pursue their careers at least partly protected from market competition by following particular career ladders and opportunities for promotion. Recruitment from the external labour market ideally takes place only once, when external applicants are employed for a restricted number of specific "entry-jobs". Since employees are recruited not only for the position at hand, but for a specific career ladder building on the initial position, the screening process at this stage is strongly associated with the amount of training necessary for future promotion. Therefore, particular credentials and entry certificates play an important role for employers in assessing whether applicants are suited not only for the current position, but for all other jobs coming thereafter. After initial placement, career mobility is less dependent on education qualifications, while other forms of human capital defined by the internal labour market, such a work experience or training-on-the-job, are the main criterion for further promotion. In this regard, Doeringer and Piore (1971) stress the importance of internal job ladders, defined as "line of progression", where "work on one job develops the skills required for the more complex tasks on the job above it" (Doeringer and Piore 1971: 58). A special case of internal job mobility depends solely on the duration spent with the same employer instead of requiring an increase in skills. In this so-called seniority-based mobility, employees move up their organisations' job hierarchy after a certain amount of time without there needing to be a vacancy (Rosenfeld 1992).

There are a number of reasons why employers and employees are keen on establishing internal labour markets. For employers, internal markets are profitable since they reduce costs for education, training and personnel selection. Screening and training investments occur only once at the beginning of an internal career, while the process for promotion follows institutionalised rules which are easy to assess. At the same time, internal labour markets keep personnel fluctuation low and ensure that initial investments in employees, such as on-the-job training or further training, pay off in the long run. For employees, internal labour markets offer long-term employment security through stable positions and foreseeable career prospects. They can make sure that training investment in firm-specific skills are not lost through job shifts. Overall, internal labour markets guarantee a lasting planning security and protect the investments in human capital for both employers and employees (Doeringer 1967; Doeringer and Piore 1971; Kalleberg and Sorensen 1979; Rosenfeld 1992).

Empirical research on internal labour markets has not sought to classify the economy as a whole into segments, but rather takes a more disaggregated approach. Two major types of internal labour markets have been differentiated (Doeringer and Piore 1971; Kalleberg and Sorensen 1979; Lutz and Sengenberger 1980). First, internal labour markets can exist within a particular firm, where entry is controlled by the firm, and employees tend to be promoted from the entry job classifications to higher-level jobs within the firm along orderly lines. Second, internal labour markets are related to a particular occupational group, usually a craft or profession. Entry is generally controlled by members of this occupational group and mobility occurs among employers within the occupation. Both types of internal labour markets are not necessarily exclusive, since firm-internal career ladders can be established for particular occupations.

Cross-national comparisons of vocational education to work transitions have shown that countries vary strongly in the prevalence of these two types of internal labour markets (Marsden 1990; 1999). While some countries are characterised by occupational labour markets (OLM), which are segmented along nationally recognised occupations that directly correspond to qualifications obtained through vocational training, others are dominated by firm-internal labour markets (ILM), where the internal hierarchical structure of firms is the driving force behind the segmentation of the labour force. The country-specific type of labour market segmentation directly influences the labour market mobility of employees, who are mobile across firms, but within occupations in OLMs, whereas they are restricted to job ladders within the firm in ILMs. The same logic might be applied to graduate labour markets as well. However, to make these concepts work in this context, we need to specify which sectors of the graduate labour market are associated with specific occupational and firm-internal career ladders.

First of all, the graduate labour market might to a large extent be segmented along the axis of public and private sectors. In the literature, public sector employment has been identified as the prototype of firm-internal labour markets (Becker, R. 1993; Blossfeld and Becker 1988; Lutz and Sengenberger 1974). Employment in public administration is strongly associated with highly protected labour arrangements within the public enterprise (i.e. with explicitly defined "ports of entry" at the lower end of the job hierarchy, stable employment relationships and predictable promotion schemes) and an almost complete closure of higher level positions from the external labour market (Becker, R. 1993; Blossfeld and Becker 1988). If a higher education degree forms the prerequisite for entering the public sector, career and mobility patterns of higher education graduates should be very similar to those associated with ILMs. Firm-internal labour markets in general offer rather low entry positions in combination with an easy acquisition of firm-specific skills, mainly obtained through on-the-job training. This high degree of reliance on firm-specific skills induces management to minimise labour turnover to reduce recruitment, screening and promotion costs, which is achieved by promotion and (dismissal) rules based on seniority entitlements. Based on these characteristics, employment in the public sector constitutes the purest form of firm-internal mobility since it is much more strongly protected from market competition than firm-internal labour markets in the private sector.

At the same time, the system of professions can be considered another important feature of graduate labour markets, which is likely to offer career prospects associated with internal labour markets. Instead of firm-internal mobility, professional labour markets should follow the dynamics of OLMs, where segmentation between different professions is most pronounced. The exclusive nature of professions is based on their knowledge base systematically delineating a specific occupational domain. Accordingly, its structured professional training forms the prerequisite for entry into the profession, based on which the specific fields of activity become exclusively reserved for the members of a professional group. If higher education credentials provide such exclusive professional training for entry-level jobs, higher education graduates with the required entry qualifications should be well ahead of the queue of job applicants. Further career development thereafter strongly depends on the status interest of professional bodies. The social closure of career lines takes place particularly via the official acknowledgement of professional training and furthermore, via the legal protection of professional titles (Heidenreich 1999). Prestige as much as organisational autonomy or material position can thus be used by professional groups in maintaining their exclusive role and jurisdiction within the labour market. If the professional segment of the graduate labour markets exhibits a high degree of social closure for others, career mobility after entry should occur predominantly within the same professional group, while changes of the segment are less likely.

The theoretical discussion of OLM and ILM segments leads to specific forms of matching processes after graduation and further career mobility, depending on whether the social closure of professional and public labour market segments is closely linked to the higher education system or not.

H3.1: In graduate labour markets strongly segmented into public and professional sectors, selection processes at the "ports of entry" are based on specific higher education credentials.

H3.2: In graduate labour markets strongly segmented into public and professional sectors, labour market mobility predominantly occurs within the sector of initial employment, while cross-sector mobility remains low.

H3.3: In graduate labour markets strongly segmented into public and professional sectors, labour market mobility within these sectors mainly depends on internal rules (such as seniority or work experience) rather than higher education credentials.

If both forms of internal labour market segmentation are combined, the following classification of graduate labour markets is obtained (see Figure 2). In the private sector, labour market allocation and promotion should be less influenced by institutionalised rules, while market mechanisms associated with the external market are predominant. However, also in the private sector stronger or weaker firm-internal labour markets may also be present, depending on the size of the firm. Firm-internal job ladders are only likely to exist in larger firms, while smaller firms do not have enough hierarchical levels to develop rules and procedures for internal promotions (Blossfeld and Mayer 1988). However, even in large firms of the private sector, recruitment procedures and promotion strategies should be less institutionalised and formalised than in the public or the professional segments of the graduate labour market. Thus, contrary to studies examining the labour market as a whole (Blossfeld and Mayer 1988; Dekker et al. 2002), this analysis of graduate labour markets attributes labour market segmentation less to the size of firms, but rather to specific forms of employment or occupations associated with higher education.

Figure 2: Segmentation of graduate labour markets

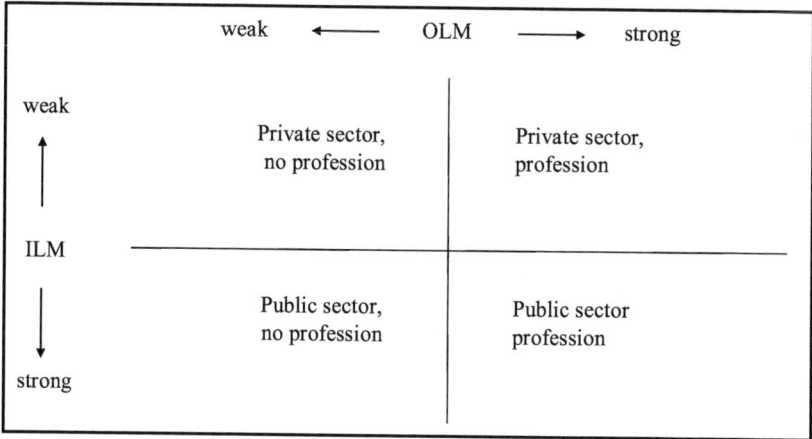

The other three labour market segments exhibit varying degrees of internal closure, depending on the predominant type of internal labour market. Public service professions are assumed to form the most exclusive sector, which combines a strong ILM with a strong OLM. The borders of each labour market segment are defined by the distinctiveness of education qualifications required for entry-level jobs. Graduate labour markets are strongly segmented along professional and public lines if both sectors require specific forms of higher education, and accordingly, if higher education is tightly coupled to a specific segment. Overall one can say that all these features – ILMs, OLMs, a large public sector and a strong system of professions – offer a high degree of job security within the respective segments of the labour market, since they are associated with specific entry positions and subsequent careers at least partly protected from market competition. All of these segments shall be found in different countries; however, cross-national variation will occur due to the prominence each segment is given in the respective graduate labour market.

Labour Market Regulation and the Strictness of Legislation

In addition to the distinction between external, internal and occupational segments, national labour markets also vary according to how flexible firms can adapt their labour offers and respond to changes of the market environment. Institutionally, a lower or higher degree of labour market flexibility is commonly believed to result from specific forms of labour market regulation, which serves to define the conditions under which employers contract labour and thus constitutes a key determinant of job structures and job vacancies in the labour market (Rubery and Grimshaw 2003). Comparing the concepts of labour market segmentation and labour market regulation, it is important to note that the degree of labour market regulation affects employment contracting and career mobility mainly in the external labour market of a country, while internal or occupational labour markets are less affected due to the existence of market-protected career ladders and mobility structures.

But just as in the case of labour market segmentation, the concept of labour market regulation suggests that employment contracts and conditions are not merely the result of individual bargaining processes between those seeking and offering labour as neoclassical economic theory would predict. It rather suggests that the process of contracting is strongly influenced by the national institutional framework, not the least since unions, collective bargaining institutions, or state legislation empirically tend to influence job conditions and matching processes. In systems with strict or inflexible labour market regulation, employers cannot easily adjust employment conditions to an individual's productivity and have lower control over terminating the employment relationship, while it is the other way around in more open systems (Sorensen and Tuma 1981; Tuma 1985). A country's unemployment protection legislation and employment protection legislation are the empirical indicators commonly used to measure the strictness of labour market regulation. In a nutshell, employment protection legislation, which is to say protection against layoffs, increases the probability of staying in the same firm. Unemployment protection legislation, which is to say, income protection during unemployment, promises a higher rate of return on a specific skill investment (Estévez-Abe et al. 2001: 150). Both forms of labour market regulation are likely to influence graduate career mobility, albeit, in a different direction and by different mechanisms.

The strictness of employment protection legislation (EPL) generally tends to influence the duration of mutual commitments of employers and employees and the stability of work relations. EPL defines these constraints as legally binding obligations, where contracting parties can seek juridical enforcement in case they disagree about certain conditions. The degree of employment protection legislation influences how easy it is to hire and fire employees, how quickly job offers can be adjusted to new conditions, how willing employees are to accept these new terms, and how strongly the form of employment contract can be individualised. In highly deregulated systems employers' are free to hire and fire in order to adapt their firms' workforce more easily to changes in product markets, technologies or corporate restructuring. At the same time, a high degree of freedom to adjust job offers to new conditions allows an immediate reaction to changes in employment circumstances and in the overall economic situation. Furthermore, if employers have the freedom to influence the form of employment contract, it is easier for them to respond to the high uncertainty of pace and direction of economic change, such as the outdatedness of certain skills. Strict employment protection legislation, on the other hand, essentially serves to stabilise existing employment relationships by restricting employers' rights to terminate the contract at will and by restricting the use of short-term or temporary contracts.

Since the degree of employment protection legislation affects all workers and employees to the same extent, no adaptation of this concept to graduate labour markets is necessary. Labour market protection influences both the ease with which graduates can be laid off as well as the ease with which unemployed workers are reabsorbed back into employment. Therefore, one can expect that stricter EPL is likely to lower job mobility rates among higher education graduates since it restrains employer-initiated labour turnover and makes it less likely that graduates will be laid off even during economic downturns. Consequently, once graduates have found their first job, employment relationships will be more stable and fewer job shifts will occur.

H4.1: The stricter labour market regulation, the more stable initial employment positions after graduation.

In particular, unemployment protection legislation influences the way unemployment impacts on further career development in relation to occupational mobility. A high degree of unemployment protection normally goes hand in hand with protection from income reduction due to unemployment and reduces the uncertainty over wage levels throughout one's labour market career (Estévez-Abe et al. 2001; Gangl 2002b). High replacement ratios and longer benefit duration permit the unemployed enough time to find another job that matches their skills, especially if they are permitted to turn down jobs that are outside their core competencies. This ensures that their reemployment will generate the same occupational

62

outcomes as before, simultaneously reducing occupational mobility. Therefore, generous systems of unemployment benefits may prolong the period of adjustment, encouraging the unemployed to engage in a long period of job search instead of settling for one of the jobs on offer. In systems with low unemployment protection, employers are free to adjust job offers to new economic circumstances and unemployed job seekers are likely to adjust their expectations downwrds, in line with the new set of job offers.

H4.2: The stricter labour market regulation, the lower the occupational mobility occurring after phases of unemployment.

Overall, the direct effect of labour market regulation on job mobility patterns should be to subdue involuntary occupational mobility and to stabilise employment relationships. But taken together, the degree of labour market regulation is also said to influence status mobility patterns (Gangl 2002b). By lowering labour market turn-over and by insuring that occupational positions are maintained even after phases of unemployment, strict labour market protection reduces the associated risk of downward mobility. However, this rather positive outcome of a strict regulatory framework also has its downside. Just as it reduces the risk of downward mobility, it is likely to reduce upward mobility, too. In this regard, Gangl (2002b) has argued that a high degree of labour market regulation has an indirect effect on mobility by lowering overall vacancy levels in the labour market and thus shortening mobility chains. Upon entering the labour market, graduates continue to acquire human capital, since job experience will continuously add to their productive capabilities. In less regulated labour markets, this skill enhancement should result in upward mobility, be it firm-internal or in a different company, to achieve better matches of individual skills and job requirements. However, since stricter legislation is likely to shorten mobility chains, graduates are less likely to experience upward mobility even after human capital increases in highly regulated labour markets. While being effective in protecting individuals' current positions, a high degree of labour market regulation might be unfavourable to career mobility dynamics because any reduction in overall labour market turnover implies reduced opportunities for upward mobility.

H4.3: The stricter labour market regulation, the lower status mobility among higher education graduates, both upwards and downwards.

Overall, labour market regulation should influence the stability and the quality of career mobility during the transition from higher education to work in external labour markets. In less regulated labour markets, graduates are likely to experience unstable career mobility with high degrees of occupational mobility after spells of unemployment as well as upward and downward mobility. In other words, rigid labour markets, while providing a higher guarantee for long-term employment, maintenance of occupational outcomes after unemployment, and less downward mobility, should also be likely to inhibit upward mobility.

3.2.3 Political Economies, Institutional Complementarities and the Transition Process

The discussion of the various institutional spheres has demonstrated how stratification, (standardisation), occupational specificity, labour market segmentation, and labour market regulation might influence the matching of graduate skills to jobs and as such the individual transition from higher education to work. By systematically applying these concepts to graduate career trajectories, it will be possible to explain the country-specific transition patterns graduates follow after finishing higher education. Yet, what all these approaches fail to make clear is whether and how the different institutional spheres interact with each other, and whether they are linked in any particular way. The general aim of this study is not only to obtain a large variety of more or less distinct labour market outcomes, but to identify how country-specific transition regimes are systematically produced by the institutional coupling between higher education systems and graduate labour markets. In this regard, the Varieties of Capitalism approach (Hall and Soskice 2001), popular in political sciences, offers helpful insights. Even though the theory on Varieties of Capitalism does not explicitly refer to individual career mobility, it provides a systematic approach to understanding the coupling between different institutional spheres. The application of the concepts developed in this strand of theorising can therefore help to explore the institutional embeddedness of career trajectories between higher education and work.

The Importance of Institutional Complementarities for Linking Institutional Spheres

Instead of focussing on the impact of institutions on individual life courses, the Varieties of Capitalism approach (see Hall and Soskice 2001 for the following) takes the point of view of individual firms, analysing how different institutional environments influence the way they solve their coordination problems in five different institutional spheres: vocational education and training, employee relations, industrial relations, inter-firm relations, and corporate governance. The main argument holds that differences in the institutional framework of the political economy generate systematic differences in corporate strategies. The core distinction is drawn between two ideal types of political economies, liberal market economies (LMEs) and coordinated market economies (CMEs). In LMEs, firms coordinate their activities primarily via hierarchies and competitive market arrangements, whilst firms in CMEs depend more heavily on non-market relationships, such as networks, collaboration, and trust. The notion of institutional complementarities is central to this approach, since the presence of institutional complementarities between these five different institutional spheres reinforces the overall differences of the political economies. According to Hall and Soskice (2001), two institutions are complementary if the presence (or efficiency) of one institutional sphere increases the returns from (or efficiency of) another (Hall and Soskice 2001: 17).

The institutional complementarities between VET systems and labour markets of different political economies identified by this theory are of particular interest for this study. According to Varieties of Capitalism, in the sphere of vocational education and training, firms are confronted with the problem of securing a workforce with suitable skills, while workers face the problem of deciding how much to invest in general or specific skills. Firms in CMEs, on the one hand, rely on a *high-skill* equilibrium with *high skill protection.* They employ production strategies that are based on high-quality products, which require a highly skilled labour force with substantial work autonomy, and consequently depend on a training system that provides workers with such skills. The matching problem in CMEs is solved by a publicly subsidised VET system that is supervised and coordinated by industry-wide employer associations and trade unions. This high level of skill protection ensures both that the training fits the firms' skill requirement and that free-riding on the training provided by others is limited.

Firm behaviour in LMEs, on the other hand, is based on a *low-skill* equilibrium with *low skill protection.* The production strategy employed aims at standardised mass products and relies on highly fluid labour markets with high job turnover, which quickly have to respond to changes in consumer demand. This encourages employees to invest in general skills transferable across firms and industries, and training is normally provided by formal education. At the same time, firms are reluctant to invest in standardised apprenticeship schemes imparting occupation-specific skills since they have no guarantee that employees will stay long enough to make training costs pay off, or that other firms will not simply poach their apprentices. Due to this lack of skill protection, companies in CMEs do a substantial amount of in-house training which provides employees with firm-specific skills that cannot easily be transferred from one firm to the next.

Even though Hall and Soskice do not consider individual labour market transitions and their relation to different political economies, one could argue that country-specific transition regimes from VET to work are a result of institutional complementarities between education systems and labour markets. The specific form of institutional complementarities in CMEs, which is based on high skill protection, is the prerequisite of the tight coupling between vocational training systems and labour markets. In this regard the organisation of a standardised and industry-wide apprenticeship system, where collaboration between employer organisations, trade unions and national governments guarantees that quality and quantity of vocational skills closely match labour market demands, can be considered an institutional basis for a smooth transition from vocational education to employment. The absence of a standardised vocational education and training system in LMEs in combination with market-led labour market matching and training-on-the-job are indicators of a low skill protection regime, which makes skill investments more risky and results in a loose coupling of systems. Labour market integration of young people is more turbulent and flexible, as it depends on market forces and discretionary employer recruitment. Table 2 summarises this line of argument by bringing together the theoretical concepts of the Varieties of Capitalism thesis and vocational education to work transition research.

Table 2: The institutional determinants of VET transition patterns in political economies

	CMEs	LMEs
Secondary schooling (Allmendinger 1989)	high degree of stratification in secondary schooling +	low degree of stratification in secondary schooling +
Vocational education (Kerckhoff 2001, Müller and Shavit 1998)	importance of occupation-specific skills +	importance of general skills +
Labour market segmentation (Marsden 1990, 1999)	occupational, sectoral labour market segmentation (OLM) +	internal, enterprise labour market segmentation (ILM) +
Labour market regulation (Estévez-Abe et al. 2001, Gangl 2002b)	strict labour market regulation and legislation ↓	weak labour market regulation and legislation ↓
Education-occupation link (Maurice et al. 1986)	qualificational space, tightly coupled ↓	organisational space, loosely coupled ↓
Institutional complementarities (Hall/Soskice 2001, Estévez-Abe et al. 2001)	specific skill equilibrium, high skill protection ↓	general skill equilibrium, low skill protection ↓
Patterns of labour market entry	smooth, late, integrated labour market entry	turbulent, early, stop-gap labour market entry

In brief, CMEs provide more institutional support for the strategic interactions required to realise the value of co-specific assets, primarily in the form of industry-specific training of standardised apprenticeship systems. The more fluid markets of LMEs provide economic actors with greater opportunities to move their resources around in search of higher returns, encouraging them to acquire switchable assets, such as general skills. Since in Varieties of Capitalism research, political economies are conceptualised as institutional complementarities between different economic spheres, higher education systems can also be understood as a complementary in national production systems. This should result in specific institutional complementarities between higher education and labour markets, which are likely to influence the labour market careers of higher education graduates in a similar manner and constitute the basis of national transition regimes. Therefore, the nature of institutional complementarities in different political economies can be considered the major cause of similarities and differences in graduate employment across Europe. In the existing literature on the transition from higher education to work, this institutional linkage has not been made explicit yet. The following empirical investigation explicitly aims at establishing the institutional complementarities between higher education and labour markets in LMEs and CMEs. It remains to be seen whether these institutional complementarities between higher education and work follow the same logic as the complementarities between vocational education and work and, in turn, entail analogous transition patterns.

3.2.4 Assessing Continuity and Change in Different Political Economies

A last comparative aspect of the transition from higher education to work is related to continuity and change. As indicated in the introduction, changes at the macro level are predominantly related to higher education expansion and the changing structure of labour markets. At the micro level, the ongoing ageing process throughout the life course and its connection to historical time, mainly in the form of cohort and period effects, is a key influence on individual labour market entry and career mobility. The major purpose of this last section is to link these two levels of analysis in a dynamic way to develop a theoretical model that takes into account the importance of time for institutional and individual development. This should lead to a more encompassing perspective on observed similarities and differences of graduate employment in different political economies.

At the institutional level, issues of continuity and change have been mainly addressed by arguments of institutional convergence and path dependency. Regarding convergence, for example, it has been argued in the field of research on higher education institutions that over time, national university systems have been becoming more and more alike due to the experience of common difficulties. Theorists proclaiming convergence start with the observation that massive changes in the institutional environment of higher education, such as the higher education expansion of the last decades in combination with structural changes stemming from globalisation, Europeanization and the rise of a knowledge-based society, create problems that countries have to respond to (Altbach and McGill Peterson 1999; Sporn 1999). All higher education systems have been subject to the same, or similar, pressures – to widen access and increase participation, to operate more efficiently, and to develop more relevant teaching and research programmes. As a result, countries should pursue similar reform strategies, and their higher education systems should become more and more alike (Scott, D. K. 2002). Based on the analysis of institutional development, similarities of graduate employment across Europe could, thus, be explained by converging structures of higher education systems. The Bologna Declaration on the European Space of Higher Education (CRE 2000) seems to be the logical consequence of this line of argument: The introduction of the same degree structure in all signatory countries is expected to serve convergence and standardisation of institutions as well as transition regimes.

However, the convergence argument neglects the country-specific historical development of institutions (Ebbinghaus 2005; Hall and Soskice 2001; Mayer 2001; Streeck and Thelen 2005). The notion of path dependence offers a promising possibility for a more general explanation in this regard. Two major reasons are often given to justify the existence of path dependency. The first argument for the existence of path dependency claims that once a country or region has started down a certain path, it is likely to stay on it in the future, since initial choices are not easily reversed, and paths cannot be left without large costs (see Ebbinghaus 2005 for a discussion). This notion of path dependency refers to those particular sequences which have self-reinforcing properties (Pierson 2004). Institutions are path dependent because of increasing returns encouraging processes where "each step along a particular path produces consequences which make a path more attractive for the next round" (Pierson 2004: 5). Through these processes, institutions provide resistance to pressure that might otherwise force actors off a particular path. As a result of these increasing returns, inefficient institutions may well persist over time. Thus the path dependency of institutional arrangements tends to be highly stable over time and does not allow for abrupt changes.

The second argument for the existence of path dependence refers to institutional complementarities. Hall and Soskice (2001) claim that although firms attempt to sustain or restore the forms or coordination on which the broader political economy has been built, these efforts may entail changes to existing institutions or practices in the economy. Institutional complementarities are assumed to play an important, but ambiguous role in these processes of adjustment (see Amable 2000: 656-660). The basic hypothesis of institutional complementarities in this regard is that they generate disincentives to radical changes, since firms attempt to preserve arrangements in one sphere of the economy in order to protect synergies with institutions that are of value to them. Thus, several institutions taken together reinforce each other so that they form a coherent and stable but not everlasting structure, while another combination of these institutions would be unstable. The coherence of a national political economy – defined as a set of interrelated national institutions – is thus the expression of complementarities between specific institutional arrangements.

A given set of institutions can either reinforce each other over time (which explains the emergence of a particular structure of institutions), or they tend to weaken the coherence of the structure over time (which explains why institutional structures, national models, or political economies are not eternal). Thus, in contrast to the first argument for the existence of path dependency, which stresses the spontaneous evolution of an institution and its subsequent long-term entrenchment, the existence of path dependent institutional complementarities can explain both institutional stability and change. The complementary connection of different areas of the economy can provide institutional stability through coherence over time. This also means that institutional changes in one sphere might have global effects for the whole system, since every complementary relationship with other institutions will be undermined and the stability of the whole system could become at risk (Hall and Soskice 2001). In this regard, the notion of a hierarchy among institutions is crucial. Institutional hierarchy points to the relative importance of one or a few institutions for the coherence and dynamics of the institutional architecture of the whole system. The circumstance in which such a hierarchy emerges also depends on history. For explaining the dynamics of institutional change, the existence of an institutional hierarchy stresses that only the transformation of a hierarchical superior institution affects the evolution of others by destabilising the coherence of the whole institutional architecture and by threatening the positive complementarities existing between institutions (Amable 2000).

Since country-specific transition regimes can be considered a result of institutional complementarities between higher education systems and labour markets, this line of reasoning is of immediate relevance to the analysis of institutional stability and change and its relation to the transition from higher education to work. Following from the argument above, the overall assumption is that institutional complementarities between higher education and the world of work are rather stable over time. This stability leads to a coherent transition regime from higher education to work. For the field of vocational training, the notion of a coherent national system can be used as an explanation for the question why the introduction of a more standardised vocational training system in liberal market economies has failed so far. Since it is not complementary to the national system of production and the structure of its labour market, employers do not have incentives to make use of a standardised vocational training.

This points to the fact that, on the one hand, changes in one institutional sphere – be it the higher education system or the graduate labour market – do not necessarily lead to a change of the whole transition regime. These changes might influence individual transition patterns in the form of period or cohort effects, but do not imply that the coherence of the whole system is in danger. Thus, in contrast to the convergence hypothesis, the convergence of life course regimes does not unavoidably follow from similar national strategies of reforming higher education. On the other hand, the existence of institutional hierarchies also raises the prospect that institutional reform in one sphere of the economy could snowball into changes in other spheres as well. In the field of vocational training, the labour market in LMEs seems to be the hierarchically superior institution, while it is rather the standardised vocational training system in CMEs that has stronger effects. In general, it is claimed that in negotiated economies adjustment processes to external shocks are often slower than in economies coordinated primarily by the market (Hall and Soskice 2001). In brief, for analysing continuity and change in the transition from higher education to work it is important to reflect on the coherence of the national system as well as to assess the hierarchy of institutions. But even if single institutional features of higher education systems or graduate labour markets change, the overall institutional complementarities and the resulting transition regimes should be rather stable over time.

3.3 Embedding the Transition from Higher Education to Work into Varieties of Capitalism

The point of departure in the previous sections was the claim that an empirical investigation of graduate employment has to include an analysis of the institutional set-up of educational systems and labour markets, as these institutions shape labour market career patterns by affecting both employee and employer action on the labour market. Based on the theoretical concepts of vocational education to work transitions and the Varieties of Capitalism literature, it can now be argued that country-specific transition patterns from higher education to work depend to a large extent on the coupling between higher education systems and labour markets, which is a result of institutional complementarities of different political economies. The question is whether the institutional complementarities between higher education systems and labour markets follow a logic similar to that for vocational training and labour markets, which, as a consequence, entail Varieties of Capitalism specific patterns for the transition from higher education to work.

Similar patterns of the transition process could follow from the fact that both vocational training and higher education are situated in the same political economy and should therefore exhibit similar complementarities to the labour market. As a consequence, the transition from higher education to work, too, should be less institutionalised in LMEs, which means that human capital has to be acquired and invested according to market rules. The pathways into the labour-market are likely to be much more flexible, while in CMEs all steps seem to depend on occupation-specific certificates, which are unavoidable prerequisites for progression. In order to get a clearer picture of what the institutional complementarities between higher education and work might look like in different political economies, it seems useful to study the impact of institutional elements on individual labour market entry and career mobility. The application of the theoretical concepts of stratification, occupational specificity, labour market segmentation, and labour market regulation to the transition from higher education to work are thought to give first insights of how cross-national institutional variations matter. While stratification should mainly impact status differences between various types of higher education institutions, degrees, or fields of study, occupational specificity is likely to influence the match between higher education credentials and initial employment positions as well as the occupational mobility occurring thereafter. Labour market segmentation points to the fact that higher education credentials should form the prerequisite for entry into public or professional segments of the labour market, where further career development proceeds in a way that is rather sheltered from the market. A high degree of labour market regulation is supposed to result in early labour market experiences of high stability and continuity, preventing downward status mobility, but also inhibiting upward movements.

By analysing how these institutional features impact individual life courses in different countries, it should be possible to establish a broader picture of cross-national similarities and differences in graduate employment. If the different institutional spheres have effects similar to those for VET to work transitions, institutional complementarities between higher education and labour markets are also likely to follow an analogous logic. Therefore, in a first step the impact of each institutional sphere has to be studied separately. In a second step, the combination of these institutional effects will allow for constructing institutional complementarities between higher education systems and labour markets to be related to the wider political economy. So far, it remains an open question what the institutional complementarities and hierarchies of higher education systems and graduate labour markets look like in different political economies. Therefore, in order to establish a general theoretical framework, it is necessary to empirically study both, the set-up of higher education and labour market institutions *and* individual transition processes from higher education to work in CMEs and LMEs.

4. Analysing Graduate Employment Trajectories – The Methodological Approach

The previous chapter identified four institutional spheres that are likely to structure the individual transition from higher education to work and thus explain cross-national patterns of graduate career mobility. In order to examine the different social mechanisms of graduate employment empirically, two country cases representing two varieties of capitalism will be analysed in order to grasp similarities and differences in the transition process in relation to the respective institutional framework. In a first step, each of the institutional spheres considered in the previous chapter and their effect on the transition from higher education to work is considered separately to examine if those institutional spheres are important for graduate career trajectories. The second analytical step focuses on the interplay between higher education and labour market institutions and aims at formulating more general theoretical mechanisms. The goal is to get an idea of the overall transition patterns and to relate them to specific institutional complementarities. This way of approaching the research problem strongly corresponds to the societal analysis developed by Maurice et al. (1986). But before a more detailed description of the methods used in this study is given, the motives and means of cross-national comparisons are discussed in more general terms.

4.1 Motives and Means of Cross-National Comparisons

What is to be gained from making cross-national comparisons? On the theoretical level, comparisons may provide a framework for explaining diversity between countries (Ragin 1994). Understanding a given social phenomenon is greatly increased when analysed with all its observable variations in different social contexts. For example, it has been shown for vocational training that, although certain tasks such as training and recruiting employees is essential for all modern political economies, they can be handled in a variety of ways and with differing results. This study aims at exploring patterns of diversity related to the transition from higher education to work by unravelling the causal conditions connected to different institutional environments. At a more practical level, cross-national comparisons increase our understanding of social phenomena by interpreting their historical and cultural significance. It might even be possible to learn from more efficient and effective institutional set-ups and the ways in which they structure individual careers. In the present study, however, the emphasis is on explaining higher education to work transitions in the theoretical term rather than on identifying practical applications.

The literature review given in the introductory chapter highlighted that previous studies on the connection between higher education and the world of work have been conducted either at the institutional or at the individual level and were focussing predominantly on the higher education system. In contrast, this study investigates the institutional impact of both higher education systems and graduate labour markets in order to demonstrate that "institutions matter" for the individual transition from higher education to work. There are different ways in which researchers may pursue a question such as "How do national institutions shape transition processes and outcomes?" At root, they reflect the different possible purposes of country comparisons: to identify universal laws or patterns, or to elucidate national uniqueness (Korsnes 2000; Maurice 2000; Ragin 1987; 1994).

The former is associated with the *universalistic approach* that aims at replacing countries by variables (Ragin 1987) and at identifying a set of laws which not only transcend national differences but also explain them. Typically, it involves an extensive comparative design using large samples of countries in order to distinguish empirically alternative country-level explanatory variables. It would be tempting to answer the research question of this project by reducing differences in the national institutional set-up to a series of dimensions or variables, which explain why transition processes and outcomes vary across countries without the need to refer to idiosyncratic national features. For studying the transition from VET to work, the dimensions of stratification, occupational specificity, labour market segmentation and labour market regulation have already been applied as a universal set of variables. Recent research into this transition process uses these concepts without further investigation of national idiosyncrasies (Brauns et al. 2000; see for example Gangl 2002a; Müller and Gangl 2003). For this study, such an approach cannot be considered appropriate; however, so far, no thorough investigation of the institutional framework along those dimensions has been conducted. The theoretical concepts cannot be demarcated as clearly as it can be done for the level of vocational training, but have to be adapted instead. Empirical data on the transition process from higher education to work provide evidence for the adequacy of these concepts in some respect, but at the same time cast doubts on a one to one transferability. For this reason, a more in-depth study of the institutional set-up of the higher education and labour market systems is required to further conceptualise the transition process.

Another possibility of cross-national comparisons is the *particularistic approach* which typically uses a small sample of countries for interpretive comparisons in order to highlight qualitative differences in concepts and institutions. In contrast to the variable-oriented approach, this strategy aims at discovering the unique logic which governs social processes within each country (Ragin 1987). According to this tradition each transition system comprises a unique set of structures, concepts and relationships which defy any attempt to generalise or classify across countries and thus emphasise the incomparability of each society. Even phenomena which appear to be general, such as entry to the labour market or the institution of higher education, have different significance in terms of their national logic, and the task of research is to explore differences between superficially similar concepts. Since the aim of this project is to develop a theoretical framework for cross-national comparisons of higher education to work transitions in more than one or two countries, a cultural perspective would be limited to understanding national idiosyncrasies and would not allow the research questions to be adequately addressed. However, focussing on national idiosyncrasies provides a valuable starting point for the institutional analysis to gain a better idea of possible influences on the higher education to work transition.

In general, the contrast described above is a matter of emphasis and there are few pure examples of either strategy. Many researchers have adopted an intermediate position (see for example Ebbinghaus and Manow 2001; Hall and Soskice 2001; Maurice et al. 1986; Shavit and Müller 1998). They recognise the existence of distinctive national 'logics' but also try to develop common cross-national concepts to describe them and cross-national theories which at least partially explain them. Taking this intermediate position, the research problem is approached by using the theoretical and methodological tools provided by the societal analysis of Maurice et al. (1968) and Maurice (2000). This comparative strategy of research can be described as a case-oriented approach that combines deductive analysis with concept formation, and aims at a relational construction of the social embeddedness of economic action and actors. Its characteristic is the use of intensive comparisons, which test a range of predicted contrasts or similarities across a small number of theoretically sampled countries. This approach is especially valuable in the absence of an already well-established theoretical framework for analysing the institutional embeddedness of transition processes. Such an approach compensates for the lack of degrees of freedom at the country level by including more qualitative measures and by making multi-level comparisons. The intensive approach is therefore dependent on detailed comparable data, and on a strong conceptual and theoretical foundation.

Societal analysis is based on various methods, including statistical analysis as well as more qualitative case studies. However, the approach suggests that the classical tradition of statistical analysis seeks to neutralise variables (such as "job" or "higher education") in order to make them comparable, even though the underlying national definitions might vary substantially and therefore cannot be compared that easily. Contrary to this mainstream thinking, societal analysis acknowledges the social construction of seemingly universal concepts, which gives them their national specificity and historicity. The principle of comparability is no longer regarded as a problem to be overcome in comparative research, but becomes the object of analysis itself (Maurice 2000). In order to compare societal constructions, which in the first place are not comparable, societal analysis proceeds in two steps: first, it compares separately different dimensions of each country case to identify the particular meanings of societal constructions; in the second step it shifts the emphasis to a higher level of abstraction which concerns the interrelatedness of these dimensions and their articulation in national configurations. Based on this abstraction, it seeks to construct inductively a common point of reference, which, in turn, will give meaning and significance to the comparison of what at first appeared to be incomparable.

This study follows a similar strategy. Two theoretically selected country cases are analysed separately along the dimensions of stratification, occupational specificity, labour market segmentation, and labour market regulation to examine if and how the institutional framework translates into career outcomes. Such an emphasis on the institutional environment of various societal systems strengthens the notion of path dependency and implies certain limitations on transferring elements from one society to another. After this initial analysis, a more common point of reference is constructed by identifying overall transition regimes and linking them to specific institutional complementarities crucial for the analysis of political economies. For the field of vocational education, Hall and Soskice (2001) identified different skill equillibria and the degree of skill protection as particular forms of institutional complementarities that link the VET system with the labour market in a country-specific manner. This study seeks to develop a similar framework for the comparison of the transition from higher education to work.

Based on this logic, the study follows several stages in its comparative analysis, closely following the three steps as proposed by Ragin (1994): First, an analytic frame has to be chosen, which is usually developed from existing social science literature, but might also build on empirical evidence. Second, cases are selected which are deemed to be comparable and to be part of a meaningful, empirically defined category. Third, patterns of diversity are analysed empirically, aiming at understanding how different configurations of causes produce different outcomes across the range of cases (Ragin 1994: 112f.). This study incorporates all of these steps. The theory chapter has already developed the analytic frame for analysing cross-national patterns of the transition from higher education to work. In the following, the country selection will be described in more detail in order to outline why Germany and Britain are considered useful cases for analysing how higher education and labour market institutions shape early career outcomes. After a detailed description of the methods applied, the study will proceed with an empirical examination of the diversity of graduate career trajectories.

4.2 The Country Cases: Germany and Britain

For this study, two countries have been selected that are comparable in many ways while differing as much as possible in terms of the institutional set-up of their higher education systems and labour markets. The number of cases has deliberately been kept small in order to maximise the specificity of each societal case. In contrast to variable-based comparisons that aim at testing general theories by means of replacing countries by variables, this study seeks to approach the research problem by combining causal analysis, interpretative analysis and concept formation. Germany and Britain are chosen as country cases for the empirical analysis, since they represent the two varieties of capitalism: Germany as CME and Britain as LME. Following from the theoretical discussion it is likely that within these countries, the institutional embeddedness of graduate employment can be studied. The comprehensive data on graduate employment and the theoretical concepts that already exist as a result of previous studies on VET to work transitions also provide a strong argument for selecting these two countries.

As has been shown in the introduction, both countries reveal considerable similarities and differences in labour market outcomes and employment patterns of higher education graduates. It is assumed that these variations can be systematically linked to differences of higher education and labour market institutions, which finally will allow for the construction of more general institutional complementarities. To analyse the interplay between higher education institutions, graduate labour markets and resulting transition regimes, this study requires a time frame that allows for the institutional framework to emerge and develop its impact.

As stated in the second chapter, this study is conducted against the background of changes that came to the forefront in the late 1970s and early-1980s when structural adjustments stemming from higher education expansion as well as the changing nature of labour markets began to have a combined impact on graduate labour market careers. The central hypothesis in this study is that in both countries, this combined impact leads to country-specific transition regimes from higher education work. Therefore, the beginning of the 1980s is the starting point of this research project. To choose where this study should stop in terms of its timeframe is slightly more difficult. The choice was made to study higher education and labour market institutions in association with the respective graduation patterns until 2000.

There are two reasons for choosing this particular year. First, eschewing the very recent past reduces the danger of overestimating recent changes relative to earlier changes. The other reason to end in 2000 is more pragmatic. In 1999, with the Bologna Process, a major new reform agenda was initiated within the European Union that aimed at changing the institutional structure of universities across Europe substantially. The Bologna Declaration represents the attempt to formulate a common European answer to common European problems of higher education, particularly by introducing common degree systems. With that step, the signatory countries agreed on major reforms of their higher education systems to be completed by 2010. While earlier changes of higher education institutions were at least partly a result of choices within the respective countries, the Bologna Declaration meant that in all higher education institutions, an externally imposed new structure was implemented. To prevent this turning point in higher education policies from interfering with developments of previous decades, both institutional data and the individual graduation year end in 2000, at a point before a rising number of graduates trained within the reformed systems entered the labour market. Thus, the country-specific paths of higher education systems and graduate labour markets end with the beginning of Bologna.

At the institutional level, the time period from 1980 to 2000 poses no problems in terms of comparability between Germany and Britain. In both countries, governments with a conservative agenda (the British Conservatives with Margaret Thatcher and John Major as prime ministers and the Christian Democrats with Helmut Kohl as chancellor) dominated most of the period politically. Both countries are highly developed capitalist industrial societies, displaying substantial similarities in terms of industrial development, endowment with natural resources, IO membership (EU, OECD, NATO, etc.) as well as in political and cultural heritage. Especially their common membership in the European Union has not only served to homogenise many political and economic activities, but has also presented the two nations with similar economic and social concerns and opportunities, which have increasingly become comparable constraints. The introduction made clear that policy changes in both countries were the result of similar economic problems and similar political ideologies.

Yet, a closer investigation of higher education systems and labour markets in Germany and Britain in the empirical chapters of this book will reveal that by the end of the 1990s, relatively little convergence towards a common European type of both higher education systems and graduate labour markets had occurred. Moreover, even superficially common structural arrangements hide enduringly distinctive national ways of thinking about and organising the transition from higher education to work. The unique character of German and British higher education and labour market systems is reflected in the wider political economy and is a result of its historical development and present state.

The institutional analysis, therefore, aims at determining these path-dependent differences. Based on the theoretical concepts of stratification, occupational specificity, labour market segmentation and labour market regulation, the institutional infrastructure of higher education systems and graduate labour markets of each country are analysed with a particular focus on developments in the 1980s and 1990s. The comparison will be based on secondary analysis of academic literature on the relevant topics as well as on official documents (for example legislative bills, statutes and opinion papers) and national statistics released by the respective political institutions, such as employment and graduation statistics. Emphasis will be placed on a broad description of general national differences rather than on a detailed analysis of particularities within each institutional sphere. This might lead in part to an oversimplification of institutional arrangements by levelling out variations within each country. At the same time, such an approach is necessary to illustrate cross-national diversity more clearly. Empirical findings will be linked to theoretical considerations to formulate more country-specific hypotheses about individual transition patterns.

4.3 Quantitative Data Analysis of Individual Transitions from Higher Education to Work

Building on the findings of the institutional analysis, a quantitative longitudinal data analysis of individual transitions from higher education to work is conducted in order to relate the institutional infrastructure to life course outcomes. For studying higher education graduates' career development at the individual level, this study examines their life courses empirically, following them from graduation to their first professional placement and the subsequent course of their career development. In the following sections, the data-sets to be used will be described in detail and the modelling strategy to be applied will be explained.

4.3.1 The Data Sources: German Socio-Economic Panel and two British Cohort Studies

The analysis of the individual transition from higher education to work is carried out based on the German Socioeconomic Panel (SOEP) and two

British cohort studies, namely the National Child Development Study (NCDS) and the British Cohort Study 1970 (BCS70). These studies are large-scale, multi-purpose surveys that collect information on different areas of social life, such as education and employment, household formation and dissolution, or fertility.

The SOEP is a longitudinal survey of private households in Germany, issued by the SOEP Group of the German Institute for Economic Research (DIW) in Berlin (Haisken-DeNew and Frick 2005). It is conducted as a panel survey, i.e. the same individuals are re-interviewed on an annual basis on a large variety of topics, including information on labour market positions, educational attainment, attitudes or family status. The longitudinal development of labour market mobility is measured in two different ways. Information on labour market states, positions and industries are gathered as panel information on a yearly basis at the time of the interview. Furthermore, labour market careers are measured retrospectively with calendar information on periods of education, employment, unemployment and periods out of the labour force, which occurred between two successive panel waves. These spell data are measured in discrete time intervals on a monthly basis for each respondent since his or her entry into the sample.

Starting in 1984, the SOEP represents the residential population of the Federal Republic of Germany in 1984 including West Berlin, and later the German residential population of the former German Democratic Republic in June 1990, including East Berlin. All SOEP samples are multi-stage stratified random samples which are regionally clustered (Haisken-DeNew and Frick 2005). In the West German sample, selected foreign groups were oversampled. Furthermore, the sampling probability for the Eastern sample is bigger than the probability for the main sample in West Germany. Those different sampling probabilities were chosen to make sure that the number of cases for the different groups in the sample are large enough for analysis (Haisken-DeNew and Frick 2005). The study at hand takes account of all respondents with a higher education degree who graduated in the years 1984 – 2001 while surveyed by the SOEP, meaning that a total number of 878 graduates were included in the calculations.[8]

---

8   This means that all SOEP samples have been used. Sample A „Residents in the FRG" covers persons in private households with a household head who does not belong to the main foreigner groups of „guest workers". Sample B "Foreigners in the FRG" covers persons in private households with a household head from Turkey, Greece, former Yugoslavia, Spain or Italy. Both were drawn in 1983. Sample C "German Residents in the GDR" was drawn in 1990 and covers persons in private households where the household head was a GDR citizen. Sample D "Immigrants" started in 1994/95 and consists of households in which at least one household member had moved from abroad to West Germany after 1984. In 1998, a new sample E "Refreshment" of the population of private households in Germany was selected independently from the ongoing panel, following the same selection scheme also used for the selection of sample A. Sample F "Innovation" – also selected independently from all other samples – again was drawn from the population

Data for Britain are drawn from the National Child Development Study (NCDS) and the 1970 British Cohort Study (BCS70), which are both conducted by the British Joint Centre for Longitudinal Research[9]. Even though the most common British data-set used for comparisons with the SOEP is the British Household Panel Study (BHPS), it is not used for this study, since it does not contain sufficient information on higher education obtained by its respondents. The cohort studies, in contrast, provide contemporaneous information on higher education achievements as well as detailed information on early labour market careers and mobility developments (see Bynner et al. 2001). The NCDS is a panel study of all the children born in the first week of March, 1958 (n=17.634). Six follow-up surveys were carried out, when the children were of age 7, 11, 16, 23, 33 and 42 years. For the analysis at hand, data from sweeps 3 to 5 are used. The employment history in the NCDS is drawn from the retrospective responses given by individuals in the fifth wave of the survey. The BCS70 began in 1970, when data were collected about the births and families of babies born in England, Scotland, Wales and Northern Ireland in the week of April 5th-11th, 1970 (n=16.571). To date, there have been five attempts to gather information from the full cohort, at ages 5, 10, 16, 26 and 29-30 years. For the current analysis, sweeps 3 and 5 are used, with the last one providing detailed information on the education and work history since age 16. In order to achieve a period of labour market entry that is more or less comparable with the German data-set, both cohort studies were pooled. The final data-set covers 3805 individuals graduating in the period between 1979 and 1997.

Sampling Strategy and Panel Attrition

Even though both data sets are conducted as panel studies, there are important differences to be taken into account when analysing them comparatively. While the SOEP is a representative sample of the German

---

of private households in 2000, following more or less the same procedure as for sample A and E (Haisken-DeNew and Frick 2005). Despite knowing that the use of sample A-F leads to an overrepresentation of certain groups (for example foreigners in sample B or immigrants in sample D), the whole sample is chosen to have a sufficient number of cases for each of the surveyed years. Only sample G "Oversampling of High Income", which was drawn in 2002, is excluded as the available work history of likely graduates within this sample is too short for the respective quantitative modelling.

9   The Joint Centre for Longitudinal Research comprises the Centre for Longitudinal Studies (CLS), Institute of Education, University of London; the International Centre for Health and Society (ICHS), University College Medical School, London; and the National Centre for Social Research (Natcen). Natcen was responsible for assisting in the development of instrumentation, the development of CAPI programmes, the conduct of fieldwork, initial data coding and editing, and some documentation. The British Office for National Statistics was responsible for the co-ordination of funding on behalf of various government departments.

population and therefore covers a broad range of age groups, dates of the NCDS and BCS70 only refer to two birth cohorts born in 1958 and 1970 respectively. Estimations based on such a cohort design represent only the cohorts included – in this respect, the parameters are cohort-specific, and their implications might be specific for these cohorts rather than a country's whole population. Therefore, the sample design of the SOEP is, compared to the cohort design of NCDS and BCS70, clearly the more appropriate basis for estimating population parameters, and the selection of cohorts is a strategic and far reaching decision.

Apart from mere practical reasons, namely the availability of sufficient information on higher education, the strongest arguments for choosing the two British cohorts are the type of analysis conducted and their comparability with the German data set. The main goal of statistical modelling in this study is not to obtain descriptive population estimates, but rather causal interrelations between variables in order to examine the relation between institutional environments and individual career trajectories. These relations should be similar for different cohorts living in the same institutional environment, and, as it has been argued in the theory chapter, should also be rather stable over time. In addition, the inclusion of both cohorts allows for investigating a similar period of labour market entry as that covered by the German sample, namely the 1980s and 1990s. This would not have been the case for the BHPS, which only covers the 1990s. Another major difficulty that arises from comparing such different sample designs lies in the differentiation between period and cohort effects. In the German sample, it is easier to include parameters that clearly distinguish both, while in Britain, it is more difficult to relate changes to any of these two effects (Scott, J. and Alwin 1998).

Despite the apparent advantages of the German data set, the panel design as used by the SOEP has to solve considerable problems with population representation as well. Due to panel mortality and attrition, the sample size decreases wave by wave. This can lead to severe problems for making reliable population estimates over time. There would be no problem in the case of random non-response; however, there is little reason to expect that this is the case (Haisken-DeNew and Frick 2005; Scott, J. and Alwin 1998; Solga 2001). Hence, modelling occupational mobility in the SOEP over time might be biased since occupationally mobile respondents may be more likely to drop out of the panel due to residential mobility connected to new jobs. In addition, the multi-time measurement of information in the panel design carries the risk of changing measurements of occupational mobility, which might lead to biased comparisons over time or might even make comparisons impossible. As far as sample attrition in the cohort studies is concerned, it has been possible in both cohort studies to closely monitor the evolving rate and pattern of non-response. While it is clear that various biases have emerged, these appear to be rather small and, moreover, they seem to be much the same from one study to the other. For both cohorts, sample attrition is most apparent among those with minority ethnic status, with disadvantaged class backgrounds, with teenage or single mothers, and with low levels of educational attainment (Plewis et al. 2004).

One way of dealing with the problem of sample attrition is the use of sample weights. However, in the case of panel data, conventional sample weights are not appropriate. Instead, longitudinal attrition-adjusted sampling weights are needed. One important criticism regarding those weights is that they implicitly assume independent censoring, i.e. that individuals who drop out behave in the same way after their last interview as they did before (Hill 1997). To the contrary, it is quite likely that panel drop-out is related to an important life change taking place, such as a finishing university or becoming unemployed, which led to a change in the person's behaviour. Consequently, longitudinal weights are not the best way of dealing with the problem of panel attrition.[10]

In addition to these more practical reasons against the use of sample weights to account for panel attrition, the modelling strategy applied in this study (see next section for more details) has an important advantage in dealing with this problem. It has been shown that weighting problems only occur for models using continuous time, while this problem does not occur in event history analysis if the models are specified for discrete time (Hartmann 1997). Hartmann's (1997) analysis of marital stability indicates that it is possible to estimate discrete time models, such as logit models or cloglog models (Allison 1984; Jenkins 2004) without including sample weights and nevertheless obtain unbiased parameter estimates. He shows formally that the odds ratios in discrete time models are the same, whether or not sample weights are applied. Only for the estimation of standard errors sample weights have to be applied. Since all estimations made in this study make use of discrete time models, and furthermore, the major focus is on transition patterns, i.e. the direction of effects, rather than on absolute values of parameters or standard errors, it does not include sample weights in its models.

Survey Design

Another important difference between the SOEP and the NCDS/BCS70 is in the way of gathering information. Even though all surveys are conducted in form of a panel, the time interval between the different waves (SOEP) or

---

10 Applying the SOEP standard panel weights did not seem plausible, either, as these are designed to apply to the population as a whole, and not only to higher education graduates. In addition to the reasons mentioned, the construction of graduate-specific weights is very difficult due to a lack of representative data for the respective period in Germany.

sweeps (NCDS/BCS70) differs substantially. While, in the SOEP, panel information is collected on a yearly basis in combination with retrospective questions on education and labour market mobility of the past 12 months, sweeps of the two British cohorts cover a much longer period, lasting from four to ten years. Thus, even though NCDS and BCS70 are panel studies, their data collection closely represents those of retrospective life history studies. Both types of survey design have their distinct advantages and disadvantages.

A problematic issue in terms of education and labour market mobility measures stemming from the SOEP panel design is the difficulty of capturing duration dependence. Even though event histories are gathered on a monthly basis through retrospective questions, the collected data only reflects changes in labour market states (such as changes between education, full-time employment, unemployment, or family leave), while more precise information on type of education, type of job, occupational position, or industrial sector of employment is only gathered on a yearly basis. As a consequence, it is quite complicated to rearrange the discontinuous information about status, events and transitions – given in the several waves – into a continuous flow of life histories. The most serious problem stemming from this survey design is the fact that there is not enough information about shifts between occupations and industries that may have occurred between two panel waves while being full-time employed in the retrospective calendar. As a consequence, estimates of labour market mobility based on the SOEP might be biased since the study tends to underestimate the mobility observed. At the same time, the panel design carries the risk of overestimating labour market mobility due to non-randomly missing information on job titles and the risk of inconsistency in the frame of reference and the meanings of instructions between several panel waves (Solga 2001).

In contrast to the "pure" panel design used by the SOEP, data on education and labour market mobility in the two British cohort studies is collected through retrospective life histories that go backwards from the current state to the date of the previous sweep, and sometimes even further. (The labour market history of NCDS sweep 5 conducted in 1991, for example, covers every month since January 1974, even though another sweep was conducted in 1981). According to Elder (1992), a life history is "a lifetime chronology of events and activities that typically and variably combine data records on education, work life, family, and residence (Elder 1992: 1122). Thus, instead of yearly records of mobility variables provided by the SOEP, the cohort studies allow continuous records for several life domains to be collected. The strength of this design is that for each point in time the status in the life domain as well as relevant covariates can be captured more precisely. However, since respondents are asked to recall the "continuous" history of events and transitions on a monthly basis, there are restrictions for estimating unbiased parameters across time as well, namely recall error and missing information because of memory (Solga 2001). Both problems stem from the fact that remembering is a constructive process, since memory is inevitably open to a range of distortions and reinterpretations in the light of subsequent knowledge and experience (Scott, J. and Alwin 1998). Sometimes, measures of past events and transitions are unavailable both because of memory lapse and because the information is only available at the time. Furthermore, individuals can misclassify episodes or events or recall them inaccurately due to errors in their recollections of timing or dating of events. It is stated in general that the longer the recall period, the greater the concerns about the reliability of retrospective data. Regarding labour market mobility, retrospective designs involve the risk of underestimation, since recall errors may smooth out the true extent of mobility due to unreported job changes (Solga 2001).

In summary, all data sets used in this study have their respective advantages and disadvantages, be they related to sampling strategy or survey design. Nevertheless, their applicability and comparability has already been proven in numerous studies. For the research problem at hand, a comparison of SOEP, NCDS and BCS70 is considered the most appropriate way of exploring the institutional embeddedness of the transition from higher education to work.

4.3.2 The Method: Event History Analysis

In order to statistically model labour market entry and early career development of higher education graduates in both countries at the individual level, discrete time piecewise constant exponential models of event history analysis have been employed (Allison 1984; Blossfeld and Rohwer 1995). By means of event history analysis (also referred to as survival analysis), we may examine how the probability of an event progresses longitudinally, i.e. over time, and furthermore, how this probability varies according to relevant covariates. Cross-sectional designs (which only estimate the overall probability of an event without making reference to the duration at all) and longitudinal panel designs (which merely observe changes in labour market states between two points in time and accordingly only take the initial and the final stage of a certain period into account) are less appropriate for studying mobility processes than event history analysis. With this modelling strategy, all relevant changes of the condition during a time period as well as the timing of events can be considered. This is particularly important for analysing career trajectories, since not only the quality of the matching process matters, but also the time it takes to obtain such a matching job.

Although continuous-time survival analysis is frequently used in many settings (see Blossfeld and Rohwer 1995), discrete-time survival analysis is often more natural in social and behavioural science applications where time is likely to be measured discretely (Allison 1984). This study also makes use of discrete-time models instead of continuous-time models. The major reason for this strategy lies in the fact that time in the SOEP is coded discretely, namely on a monthly rather than on a more detailed basis, and only discrete time modelling makes it possible to take into account the fact that the exact exit times are not known. We only know that they fall within a certain interval of time (Jenkins 2004). A rather practical advantage is the fact that discrete-time models can easily accommodate time-varying covariates, and, as already stated above, produce unbiased estimates even if sample weights are not included in the models.

The central concept for describing the timing and duration of transition processes with event history analysis is the hazard rate. According to Allison (1984), the hazard rate describes "the probability that an event will occur at a particular time to a particular individual, given that the individual is at risk at that time" (Allison 1984: 16). In the present study, the simplest form of a hazard rate is the probability of getting a first job within a particular month after graduation for those who have not yet had a job. Allison (1984) stresses that the hazard rate is an unobserved variable; however, since it controls both the timing and occurrence of events it is the fundamental dependent variable in event history models. In discrete time models, the exact point of time of the transition is unknown; instead, the interval hazard rate $h(a_j)$, i.e. the probability of exit in the interval $(a_{j-1}, a_j]$ is defined as[11]

$$h(a_j) = \Pr \left(a_{j-1} < T \leq a_j \mid T > a_{j-1} \right)^{[12]}$$

with T defined as a discrete random variable that indicates the time period or interval when the event occurs. Another distributional representation of event time is the survivor function. The survival probability at time period j is defined as the probability of not experiencing an event (i.e. the probability of "surviving" through time period j). In discrete time, the survivor function at the time demarcating the start of the jth interval is defined as

$$S(a_{j-1}) = P \left(T > a_{j-1} \right)$$

while the value of the survivor function at the end of the jth interval is

$$S(a_j) = P \left(T > a_j \right).$$

---

11 The formulas for describing discrete-time event history models are taken from Jenkins 2004.

12 The value of the discrete hazard rate differs from the continuous hazard rate in that the former is a (conditional) probability with values between zero and one, while the latter may be greater than one, since it is not a probability, but refers to the exact exit time rather than an interval (Allison 1984; Jenkins 2004).

A final important feature of event history analysis is the concept of right censoring, which occurs when it is unknown whether an individual experiences the relevant event because the observation period ended beforehand. This might be due to panel attrition, i.e. the individual does not take part in the survey any longer, or due to the conclusion of the observation period. Event history models can take this fact into account by calculating both the likelihood of individuals experiencing an event while at risk and or those who are right censored.

As there is no single shape for the hazard function that is appropriate in all contexts, the analysis of event history data requires some model assumptions on how hazard rates vary with time. A model that does not impose too many restrictions regarding the shape of the hazard function and that, furthermore, has already proven its validity for studying education to work transitions is the piecewise constant exponential (PCE) model (Bernardi et al. 2004; Falk et al. 2000; Hillmert 2001). Its flexibility stems from the possibility of allowing hazard rates to vary between different time periods (Allison 1984; Blossfeld and Rohwer 1995; Jenkins 2004). Thus, with the discrete time PCE model any variation in the hazard between any numbers of time intervals can be estimated. Furthermore, PCE models do not require a hazard-related proportionality assumption (Jenkins 2004) that is commonly used in entirely non-parametric survival models, such as the Cox proportional hazards model. An important question in this regard is how to define the number and length of time intervals in between which the hazard is likely to vary most extensively. Previous studies on the transition from school to work have shown that differences of the hazard rate for finding a job are especially pronounced during the first year after graduation (Bernardi et al. 2004; Falk et al. 2000; Hillmert 2001). Furthermore, Jenkins (2004) suggests that the decision of whether the hazard function generally increases or decreases with survival time should be based on the data, rather than specified *a priori*. Taking both positions into consideration in order to avoid a random setting of time intervals, the bands of the time intervals in this study will be smaller during the first year and will be derived from the descriptive analysis of the survivor function.

In order to derive an estimate of parameters describing the continuous time hazard, whilst taking into account the nature of the banded survival time data, calculations are based on the *logistic hazard function*, which is a straightforward way of analysing discrete time data with piecewise duration dependence (Allison 1984; Jenkins 2004). The logistic hazard model assumes that the relative odds of making a transition in month j, given survival up to end of the previous month, is summarised by an expression of the form.

$$h(j, X) = [1 + \exp(-\alpha_j - \beta X_{i(j)})]^{-1},$$

where $h(j, X)$ is the discrete time hazard rate for month j, X are the effects of the covariates[13] and $\alpha_j = \text{logit}[h_0(j)]$. In principle, α_j may differ for each month. In the PCE model, the duration dependence specification assumes that groups of months have the same hazard rate, but the hazard differs between these groups. The major advantage of this modelling strategy lies in the fact that it can be estimated by means of normal logistic regression once the data has been converted to a person-month format (Jenkins 2004). As a consequence it is possible to estimate single event models by using the logistic regression function and to estimate competing risk models by using the multinomial logit function as provided by standard statistical software packages. For the current study, all event-history estimations have been carried out with STATA 10.0.

By applying this modelling strategy to the German and British data sets it will be possible to analyse the transition from higher education to work, making use of the timing and nature of events occurring during the first five years after graduation. The last section of the methods chapter will give a detailed description of the variables used for this task and of the way in which the most important theoretical concepts have been operationalised in this study.

4.4 Operationalisations of Concepts and Variables

In the previous chapter, several theoretical concepts were moulded into one theoretical model (see Figure 1 on p. 42). For the empirical investigation of this model, three types of variables need to be operationalised:

— Dependent variables: quality and duration of the matching process,
— independent variables: higher education and labour market institutions, and
— control variables at the macro and micro levels.

All of these variables and their operationalisations will be discussed in the following. A description of the distribution of the most important variables in both data sets is given in Appendix A.

---

13 By dropping the j subscript from X, the effects of the covariates are constrained to be equal across all time periods. This is referred to as the *proportional odds model* because the hazard ratio for the event corresponds to the proportional hazard assumption with a baseline hazard common to all individuals and an individual-specific scaling factor based on the covariates with constant effects across all time periods. Such a model can, however, not be applied in the present study, since not all covariates included fulfil the proportionality requirement (for further explanations and tests of the proportionality criterion see Allison 1984, Jenkins 2004).

Dependent Variables: Duration and Quality of the Matching Process

The *explanandum* of this study is the national transition regime from higher education to work, which is defined as a nationally coherent pattern of career mobility among higher education graduates. Since this term refers to a theoretical concept rather than an empirical observation, its operationalisation has to identify dimensions that, taken together, make up a country's transition regime. The theoretical discussion has shown that both duration and quality of the matching process are decisive for measuring transition patterns after leaving higher education. The results of research on vocational education and training already indicated that in liberal market economies, labour market entry generally associated with a short transitional duration from education to work, coupled with high job turnover, frictional unemployment, and a pattern of intensive job hopping between low quality jobs. Transitions within coordinated market economies, in contrast, are marked by longer transitional durations (at least if vocational training is included as part of the transition process), going hand in hand with a "productive" matching process between job applicants and jobs, where a high-quality match is achieved rather easily, unemployment remains low, and initial positions are generally stable. Thus, in order to operationalise the transition regime from higher education to work, it is important to look at both the duration of transition periods and the quality of the labour market match.

To study the duration of the matching process in more detail, the career development of higher education graduates is examined by following them from graduation to their first occupational placement and the subsequent course of their career during the first five years (or 60 months) after graduation. The main reason for this focus is the assumption that at the beginning of a career, the relationship between educational credentials and labour market outcomes can be grasped in its purest form. Later career developments will depend on many other factors which, if not properly controlled for, may distort the effects of higher education. By means of event history analysis, it is possible not only to study the duration of any kind of spell experienced by higher education graduates during this phase, but also any kind of changes taking place. In this regard, it is important to note that work histories are observed directly after leaving higher education for the first time, while jobs or spells of unemployment that took place before graduation are not taken into account. The duration of transition phases is calculated in months, since this is the most detailed time measurement available in the SOEP.

Regarding the quality of the matching process, three different labour market outcomes are taken into consideration. The first refers to different spelltypes a graduate can experience after leaving higher education, namely spells of employment (full-time or part-time), unemployment, further (higher) education, parental leave and homemaker, and a residual category of other spelltypes. The latter comprises spells without information given by the respondent on the life phase, but also more specifically military service in Germany, the so-called "gap-year" in Britain, or times out of the labour force due to sickness. Employment and unemployment status in both datasets are measured according to international standard definitions (see Hussmanns et al. 1990) with the exception that participation in formal education and training is given priority status compared to the ILO classification. As such, working students, but also apprentices or individuals in similar training environments are not considered as part of the active labour force.

The second type of quality criterion is the type of occupation obtained after graduation, which is coded by using the 1988 International Standard Classification of Occupations (ISCO-88) (see Elias 1997). This occupational classification has been designed and constructed around two key concepts: the concept of the job and the skills required for competent performance in the job. The former is defined as the set of tasks or duties designed to be performed by one person, while the latter refers to the ability to carry out the tasks and duties of a particular job. According to Elias (1997), the application of occupational classifications such as ISCO-88 to national occupation schemes remains a difficult process since it is subject to a fairly low level of reliability. In addition, the validity of cross-national comparison may also be affected by misinterpretating of the international standard within a national context. Elias (1997) stresses that most errors of misinterpretation stem from either a simple misunderstanding of the conceptual basis of ISCO-88 or from problems associated with the fact that national classifications may group occupations by criteria other than skill level and skill specialisation. However, international comparability can be improved by aggregating national data which have been classified to ISCO-88 data. Coding/recoding studies indicate that the major group level of ISCO-88 represents a useful level at which to undertake comparative analyses of occupational data, a strategy which was largely followed in this study as well.

A third quality measurement is related to the achieved status or class of any type of occupation or employment. Class definition is not trivial in cross-national comparisons, since high and low status jobs are historically and culturally constructed and therefore not easily transferable from one country to another. Thus the mere self-description of respondents will not necessarily produce comparable data (Brauns et al. 1997a). However, the class scheme developed by Erikson, Goldthorpe und Portocarero (1979) (EGP) provides a useful attempt to classify the class positions held by individuals for comparative analysis. This scheme not only takes into account the actual occupation an individual holds, but also further information about the work situation, such as the form of the employment contract, employer-employee relationship, firm size, number of employees etc. (Erikson, Robert and Goldthorpe 1992). With this additional data, it becomes possible to construct an occupational class scheme that is more suited for comparisons than mere occupational information (Brauns et al. 1997a). Within the seven-class version of the EGP scheme, the so called high service class I (higher-grade professionals, administrators, and officials; managers in large industrial establishments; large proprietors) are of special interest for measuring high-quality positions of higher education graduates (see Appendix B for more details of the EGP class scheme).

Stratification

In order to operationalise the concept of stratification, the study will examine how the proposed institutional dimensions – types of institution, degrees, and fields of study[14] – stratify the transition rates of higher education graduates to employment in both countries. At the same time it analyses the distribution of overall status returns of initial employment positions as measured by the EGP class scheme in order to account for the selectivity of secondary schooling and the impact of higher education expansion.[15] To do so, the institutional analysis of stratification simply considers the structural set-up of a higher education system and determines whether its various dimensions are differentiated vertically or horizontally. It will look at the institutional differentiation of national higher education systems and describe the kinds of degrees awarded, existing types of higher education institutions, and the fields of study available. Furthermore, the study will describe structural changes that have taken place, particularly during the 1980s and 1990s. To get an impression of the degree of higher education expansion and of how

---

14 Unfortunately, both data sets do not contain any information on the specific higher education institutions a graduate attended. Thus, the influence of institutional reputation cannot be analysed. In order to overcome these shortcomings of the data sets, results of other empirical studies are quoted in the institutional chapter to give at least some impressions of likely impacts.

15 Like the present study, previous research analysing the stratification of secondary schooling looked at the number of tracks existing at this educational level and their impact on labour market outcomes. For example, according to Müller and Shavit (1998), the degree of stratification in secondary systems is low in weakly stratified countries with a prevalence of comprehensive schools, while systems with a medium degree of stratification differentiate between academic and vocational routes in secondary education, and highly stratified systems represent an extreme form of stratification with very early differentiation among a plurality of secondary tracks. In their estimations, employment in various EGP classes has proven to be the most robust indicator to capture country differences in stratification (Müller and Shavit 1998: 26). While Müller and Shavit used cross-sectional data, Bernardi et al. (2004) applied event-history models to analyse the effects of educational stratification by estimating the differences in entry rates by qualification in stratified educational systems. This approach is adopted in this study as well.

participation in higher education changed during this time period, it will also give a quantitative account of the size of graduation cohorts. Furthermore, pathways into higher education are examined to get an idea of the stratification of secondary education. Based on these insights, the study will be possible to formulate more refined country-specific hypotheses on the overall status outcomes of initial employment positions as well as on the stratification of labour market outcomes between the various tracks in higher education.

At the individual level, the concept of stratification is operationalised by estimating the transition rates to various forms of employment and controlling for the discussed dimensions of institutional differentiation, i.e. by looking at which kind of higher education institution a graduate attended, which degree he/she received and in which field of study she/he has been enrolled. A high vertical stratification of these dimensions should lead to a stronger dispersion of the transition rates. To differentiate between different types of higher education institutions, university institutions are contrasted with non-university institutions. To measure different forms of higher education degrees, the Casmin educational classification is applied. In contrast to other, particularly economic comparative approaches on educational attainment that rely primarily on continuous educational scales such as 'years of schooling', Casmin is a certificate-oriented classification schema which has proved to be highly valuable in comparative stratification and labour market research (see in particular the work of the Mannheim Centre for European Social Research (MZES)). The Casmin scheme is constructed by distinguishing educational credentials according to hierarchical level (length, quality and value of education) on the one hand, and according to whether they imply general or vocationally oriented education on the other (Brauns and Steinmann 1997; Shavit and Müller 1998 for more details).

For the British case the more refined Casmin levels of general lower level tertiary degrees (3a_gen = Diploma, Certificate of Higher Education), first degree qualifications (3b_low = BA, BSc) and post-graduate degree qualifications (3b_high = MA, MSc, MBA, PhD, Postgraduate Certificate) are used. Since the German higher education system was less differentiated during the period of observation, the basic Casmin levels of lower tertiary education (3a = *Fachhochschule*-degree) and upper tertiary education (3b = *Diplom, Magister, Staatsexamen*) are taken into account (see Brauns and Steinmann 1997 for more details). A further differentiation between different types of university degrees, which cannot be captured by the Casmin scheme, was implemented as well: the difference between academic (*Diplom, Magister*) and state (*Staatsexamen*) examinations. Fields of study are coded in six categories, closely representing the classification used in OECD publications (OECD 2004b): Education; Humanities and Arts (including

Services); Social Sciences, Business and Law; Sciences (including Agriculture); Engineering, Manufacturing and Construction; Health and Welfare.

Occupational Specificity

In order to operationalise the concept of occupational specificity for higher education systems at the institutional level, the next chapter analyses the various dimensions of institutional differentiation with reference to the applicability of knowledge for the labour market and the incorporation of practical training. In addition, selected degrees and fields of study and their relation to the labour market are analysed in more detail to exemplify variations in occupational specificity at the institutional level, such as professional training, training of engineers, or the training of civil servants. In this regard it is also important to examine the general principles that underpin higher education systems in both countries.

The modelling of occupational specificity at the individual level mainly focuses on the relation between higher education subjects and the occupation obtained after graduation. To determine the occupational specificity of a subject and the resulting fit between the subject studied and the job found on the labour market, fields of study are matched to three-digit ISCO88 coded occupations (see Table 3).

Table 3: Matching fields of study and occupations

Field of Study	Matching ISCO-88 Codes
Education	230, 231-235, 330, 331-334
Humanities/Arts	230, 231, 232, 243, 245, 246, 347, 348
Soc. Sc., Business, Law	110, 111, 121-123, 130, 131, 230-232, 241, 242, 244, 247, 341-344, 346
Sciences, Agriculture	211, 212, 221, 230-232, 315, 321
Engineering	213, 214, 311-315
Health/Welfare	222, 223, 322, 323

An occupation-specific job match is defined as congruence between the first occupation held and the higher education field of study. The idea is simply to identify the proportion of graduates employed in an occupation matching their field of study in the first job after graduation and how long it takes to obtain such a job. In this way, it is possible to construct a measure for how well education and labour market structures correspond with each other on the basis of educational and professional classifications. A higher degree of occupational specificity of higher education systems means that a larger proportion of individuals in matching occupations as compared to individuals working outside their field of study. At the same time, transitions rates to a matching occupation are supposed to be much higher in occupation-specific systems. The basic criterion for assigning occupational codes to a field of study is the assumed congruence of skills acquired through the subject and those needed in the job.[16] For example: the category of sciences includes

---

16   This operationalisation of the congruence between fields of study and occupations is largely in line with other studies examining the match or mismatch between educational credentials and labour market outcomes. For example, Wolbers (2003) uses a similar scheme to analyse the labour market effects of job mismatches among school leavers in Europe. Kivinen and Nurmi (2003) apply a comparable classification to determine the proportion of graduates employed in their 'own field' four years after graduation, as well as the proportion of those working in a close field and of those working in an entirely different one. However, this way of operationalising occupational specificity is necessarily a very crude way of assessing the match between educational credentials and labour market outcomes, since both the classification of fields of studies and the classification of matching occupations are very heterogeneous in their single categories. This becomes most apparent for the subject cluster "social science, business, law", which not only incorporates three broad subject categories, but also groups a strongly profession-specific subject such as law together with the more general subjects of social sciences. The large number of occupations matching this field of study group is not surprising, given the large variety of subjects included. A simple way out of this problem would have been to use a more refined classification of fields of study. However, this study had to make use of the broad subject clusters, not only because the low number of cases in the German data set might have caused problems for fitting multivariate models, but also because the older British cohort (NCDS) data-set only contained field of study information on such a broad basis. Another problem of this way of measuring occupational specificity is the assignment of occupations to fields of study based on the researcher's own subjective judgement of congruence, which might lead to biased assignments based on the researcher's nationality and background. Since the classification used in this study is very similar to those used by Wolbers (2003) and Kivinen and Nurmi (2003), researchers with both different study interests and different nationalities, the problem of subjective bias is considered low due to the high degree of correspondence of the single categories.
A more objective way of approaching the congruence between field of study and occupation and, furthermore, of incorporating national specificities of this relationship would have been to calculate an occupational dispersion index for each field of study held by graduates. This method has been applied by Dekker et al. (2002), who were interested in the opposite direction, namely the educational dispersion of single occupations. They computed the Gini-Hirschman dispersion index of the educational background of workers in the occupations concerned by means of the Dutch labour force survey. An application of this approach to the estimation of dispersion of occupations in single fields of study can be expressed as

$$OS_S = (1 - \sum (NW_{SO}/NW_S)^2) * (O/(O-1))$$

with OS_S = dispersion index of occupations in field of study s;
       NW_{SO} = number of graduates in occupation o with field of study s;
       NW_S = number of graduates with a higher education degree in field of study s; and
       O   = number of occupations.

This approach would most probably yield better estimates for assessing the match between fields of study and occupations in different national contexts. However, this study could not make use of such a measurement, again due to the broad subject clusters adopted, since the dispersion of occupations in each field of study category necessarily has to be rather high. However, in data sets where more refined information on fields of study is available, the

94

physicists, chemists, mathematicians, and statisticians (codes 211 and 212); the category of Health/Welfare includes health professionals (code 222), but also nursing and midwifery professionals (code 223), since both are taught as subjects at British universities. The following table summarises the ISCO 88 occupations that match a particular subject.

To determine the impact of occupation-specific training on occupational mobility taking place after initial employment, the study applies a competing-risk model that disaggregates job-shift rates within and between occupations. In particular, much of the analysis rests on a broad reclassification of the original three-digit ISCO-88 codes into eight broad occupational groups. This classification distinguishes between (1) management occupations, (2) professional occupations, (3) technicians and associate professional occupations, (4) clerks, (5) service and market sales personnel, (6) craft and related trades workers, (7) plant and machine operators, and (8) elementary occupations including skilled agricultural workers. It mostly represents the broad ISCO-88 occupational groups, which is a compromise between established practices, feasible data harmonisation, and a level of disaggregation that still permits meaningful statistical modelling, in particular with the smaller German sample. Any occupational mobility processes occurring below this particular level of aggregation could therefore not be taken into account.

Labour Market Segmentation

To operationalise the degree of labour market segmentation at the institutional level, professional and public labour market segments were analysed in relation to their historical development, entry level requirements, career mobility patterns, and the quantitative share of people employed in these segments for both countries. Special attention was paid to the country-specific legal definition, the importance of higher education credentials as entry certificates as well as the degree to which both segments are sheltered from market mechanisms. To analyse the importance of OLM and ILM segments for graduate career development at the individual level, the labour market of higher education graduates was divided into four exclusive segments along the axes of public/private and professional/non-professional, as suggested in the theory chapter. The operationalisation of the professional labour market segment was based on the ISCO 3-digit category 200 "Professionals", consisting of the sub-categories 210 "Physical, mathematical and engineering science professionals", 220 "Life science and health professionals", 230 "Teaching professionals", and 240 "Other professionals", such as business professionals (241) or legal professionals (242).

---

calculation of an occupational dispersion index for each subject is likely to produce a better measurement of the occupational specificity of higher education systems.

Measurement of public sector employment could not be based on a comparable indicator, but had to rely on the variables provided in both data sets. This necessarily results in a higher chance of bias in estimates based on country-specific differences in the definition and composition of public sector employment, since the coverage of public sector statistics is usually determined by national legislation and reflects the historical development and the evolution of the status of public institutions (Hammouya 1999; Rothenbacher 2001/2002). However, in absence of any standardised classification tool, no other possibility was available. In addition, the incompleteness of the data did not allow for the inclusion of some standard measures commonly used in labour market segmentation analysis in the models. For example, it would have been worthwhile to take into account firm size as an indicator of the existence of strong firm-internal labour markets in any of the four segments. Likewise, it was only possible to model segment mobility as between-firm mobility, while within-firm mobility could not be considered. While the SOEP would have included all necessary variables, they are not available in the British data sets.

Labour Market Regulation

For the operationalisation of labour market regulation at the macro level, unemployment and employment protection legislation were analysed for both countries, with a special focus on reforms that took place during the 1980s and 1990s. In addition, the development of unemployment and employment rates throughout the last 20 years were used quantitatively to assess the effects of the strictness of employment protection legislation. To operationalise the influence of labour market regulation on graduate career mobility at the micro level, several measurements were applied. In order to examine the stability of career development during the first five years after graduation, the mean duration of various spell types as well as the number of full-time and part-time jobs were calculated. The incidence of unemployment was analysed by estimating Kaplan-Meyer survivor function for the transition to unemployment, while the effects of unemployment for further career mobility were approached by comparing the occupational group of a job held before and after spells of unemployment. For this analysis, the eight occupational categories applied were the same as for the estimations on occupational mobility, namely management occupations, professional occupations, technicians and associate professional occupations, clerks, service and market sales personnel, craft and related trades workers, plant and machine operators, and elementary occupations including skilled agricultural workers. Upward and downward status mobility was operationalised by comparing the EGP classes of jobs held before and after job shifts and phases of unemployment. It would have been worthwhile also

96

to include other measures of labour market regulation into the models, such as type of employment contract (fixed-term vs. permanent) or self-employment. Unfortunately, the former could not be taken into account due to data limitations in the cohort studies, while the latter was dismissed because the number of self-employed individuals in Germany was too low.

Control Variables at the Macro and the Micro Levels

In order to account for changes in the macroeconomic environment that took place during the observed period, four main indicators were included in most of the models. Variations of labour market demand are operationalised roughly through annual unemployment rates for each country as well as annual changes of the gross domestic product. Both variables were obtained through the OECD Employment Statistics online data base and merged as time-varying covariates to the individual data sets for each year. In order to account for the degree of higher education expansion and thus competition at career entry, the size of birth cohorts and the annual age participation rate were included in the models. The first one was matched with the individual based on the year of birth for each respondent, while the latter was matched based on of the year of graduation. Even though it would have been worthwhile to include further indicators, such as the size of the public and professional sector or the strictness of labour market regulation, this approach could unfortunately not be realised since statistical information on country-level development was not available for either country for a period of more than 20 years.

In case when including all of these variables was not feasible due to problems with fitting models, graduates were divided into two graduation cohorts, the first consisting of graduates receiving their degree prior to 1990 and the second of graduates leaving the university in 1990 and later. This division controls for changes in both countries contrasting the 1980s with the 1990s, but also allows for considering changes stemming from German reunification. As will be shown by the institutional analysis, changes that are captured by this differentiation are variations in the size of the student and graduate population (as a result of educational expansion in both countries), changes in size of the public sector employment in both countries, changes in the regulation of the professional labour market (most pronounced in Britain), and changes of labour market regulation in both countries (again most pronounced in Britain). Of course, this way of assessing continuity and change is less accurate than including relevant macro variables into the respective models, since the different forms of social change cannot be disentangled any longer.

Control variables at the micro level consist of general socio-structural indicators such as gender, dependent children under the age of six, the parental socio-economic status/education, and nationality/ethnicity. Due to data restrictions and missing values, the parental socio-economic background as well as ethnicity had to be coded differently for each country. While, in Germany, parental socio-economic status is measured by parental educational attainment, namely whether the father possesses a higher degree at the time the respondent is 15 years of age, in Britain, parental background measures whether the father is occupied in EGP class I or II at the time the respondent is 16 years of age. Ethnicity in Germany is coded as German vs. Non-German, while ethnicity in Britain is coded as white vs. non-white. Despite knowing that these variables measure different socio-structural aspects in both countries and are thus of limited use for direct comparison, they have been included in order to control for within-country variations.

In addition, further indicators related to human capital and indicators of labour market experience were included in the models. Some of them are more general in nature, e.g. work experience, vocational education in addition to higher education, or the duration of unemployment spells. Others are related to higher education, but are not specifically captured by one of the institutional concepts. For example, a variable measuring graduation in East Germany controls for differences between West and East Germany after re-unification. The age of graduation was also controlled for since it differs strongly between the two countries. It was included in the form of age intervals (below 24 years, 24 to 29 years, 30 years and over) to allow for curvilinear age effects.

5. Higher Education and Labour Market Institutions in Germany and Britain

This chapter examines higher education and labour market institutions in Germany and Britain to explore how they might shape graduate careers. In order to analyse higher education stratification, an account is given of the legal basis and structural set-up of the German and British higher education systems, and explicates the educational pathways that are necessary preconditions for entry into higher education. The chapter then goes on to explain the importance of occupation-specific contents of higher education programmes for labour market entry by analysing training for occupations in general as well as specifically for professionals, engineers and managers in both countries. Also, it sketches in rather broad terms the different principles underpinning higher education in both countries and elaborates how these different principles have created country-specific cognitive frameworks for the relative importance given to occupation-specific and general higher education. The different segments of the graduate labour market are taken into consideration by looking at the way professions and the public sector are organised in both countries, with a particular focus on their social closure from external labour markets. In order to account for different modes of labour market regulation, the institutional analysis proceeds by examining how national systems of labour market protection are organised. A short historical overview on the development of institutional features is given at the beginning of each section. In addition, each institutional analysis is accompanied by a quantitative assessment of relevant indicators.

Instead of giving a mere descriptive account, the aim of this comparative analysis is to link the set-up of higher education and labour market institutions back to the discussed theoretical concepts in order to examine how national institutions might structure higher education to work transitions. This allows for making more explicit hypotheses about transition patterns for both countries, which will be tested afterwards by the quantitative analysis. But for now, the focus is on the more qualitative study of higher education and graduate labour markets in Germany and Britain.

5.1 Stratification in Higher Education: Vertical and Horizontal Institutional Differentiation

Stratification of higher education systems depends on their vertical and horizontal institutional differentiation in combination with the stratification of secondary education and the degree of a country's higher education expansion. The main assumptions connected with this concept are that the lower the percentage of a birth cohort that acquires higher education and the more vertically differentiated tracks exist, the more strongly are graduates channelled into particular sections of a stratified occupational structure. Different types of higher education institutions, degree levels, as well as fields of study have been identified as indicators of institutional differentiation within a higher education system (Teichler 2002a). The analysis of these institutional structures in Germany and Britain will demonstrate whether they are differentiated vertically or horizontally and, based on this differentiation, whether they are likely to stratify individual labour market outcomes. But not only does the structural set-up of higher education itself matter. The structure of secondary schooling and resulting pathways into higher education are important aspects of institutional stratification as well, since these strongly influence higher education participation rates. Before analysing the structural set-up of both levels of education in Germany and Britain in detail, this chapter gives an overview of the development of higher education expansion.

5.1.1 The Road to Mass Higher Education

The overall goal of higher education policies in Germany and Britain nowadays is to increase participation in higher education and thereby foster higher education expansion. The British Labour Party explicitly aimed at achieving an enrolment rate of 50 percent of those aged 18–30 by 2010 (DfES 2003). Even though it may not have such explicit figures in mind, the German federal government also stressed the importance of increasing the number of students in higher education (BMBF 2007). And indeed, both countries have experienced a massive expansion of higher education during the past decades.

Initially, higher education expansion in Germany and Britain was not merely a political process, but was mainly driven from below. Ongoing processes of democratisation, which enabled ever larger numbers of citizens to participate in society and to profit from the expansion of welfare programmes, lead to an increasing demand in education participation among all social groups (Klemm 2000; Müller 1998). The German saying "Send your child to better schools for a longer period of time" ("Schick dein Kind länger auf bessere Schulen") is a good example of the rising value of education (Klemm 2000: 150, own translation). While rising participation in education naturally started at lower educational levels, such as primary and secondary schooling, soon more and more children acquired upper secondary credentials, the necessary prerequisite for entry into higher education. As a consequence, demand for attending universities afterwards rose considerably. Given the relatively low number of university institutions in both countries at the beginning of the last century, education policy had to respond to the expansion of education. For the decades following the Second World War, German and British governments increasingly responded to the enormous education demands by increasing public spending as well as introducing new institutional structures.

First political attempts to accommodate the increasing number of students started shortly after the Second World War in Germany and Britain, even though the overall goals of higher education policy differed as a result of the respective post-war experiences (see Eurydice 2000). In Germany, the primary focus was on reconstructing and re-establishing German higher education after the end of the National Socialist era, while participation rates only played a minor role. The organisational and structural set-up of German higher education institutions was reinstated and in many respects replicated from the situation existing prior to 1933. Initially, the German Federal Government exerted no influence whatsoever on this development, since according to the principle of cultural sovereignty (*Kulturhoheit*) as reinstated in the Constitution the rebuilding of the higher education system was a matter for the *Länder*.[17] Since 1948, *Länder* policies on higher education were

---

17 The principle of federalism (*Föderalismus*) in Germany may be understood against the background of Germany's constitutional and state tradition. One of the fundamental elements of the Basic Law (*Grundgesetz*), besides the principles of democracy and the rule of law, is the principle of federalism (Article 20, Paragraph 1). Its major characteristic is that both the Federation and its constituent states, known as *Länder*, have the status of a state. One core element of this status is, according to the constitutional order laid down in the Basic Law, so-called cultural sovereignty (*Kulturhoheit*), i.e. the predominant responsibility of the *Länder* for education, science and culture. This element lies at the heart of their sovereignty and means in principle that each *Land* bears responsibility for its educational and cultural policy. On the other hand, the constituent states of the federal state bear joint responsibility for the entire state. This overall responsibility both entitles and obliges them to cooperate with one another and to work together with the Federal Government. Federalism and cultural sovereignty have a long constitutional tradition in Germany. Various models of state organisation developed within the framework of the federal order include the Holy Roman Empire of the German Nation (to 1806), the German Confederation (1815-1866), the German Empire (1871-1918) and the Weimar Republic (1919-1933). The founding fathers of the constitutional order established by the Basic Law created a federalist order in the newly-founded Federal Republic of Germany in 1949 not only in order to carry on a constitutional tradition, but also in order to make a conscious break with the National Socialist centralist state (1933-1945). In doing so, they particularly

coordinated by the Standing Conference of the Ministers of Education and Cultural Affairs (*Kultusministerkonferenz KMK*). This strong federal component in German higher education governance changed with the beginning of higher education expansion. University enrolment first began to rise appreciably in the mid 1950s, a trend that continued into the 1960s against the background of public concern about an imminent shortage of graduates and the call for the reduction of social and regional inequalities. The political response was to expand existing universities and establish new ones in structurally weak regions. A key impetus was provided by the Science Council (*Wissenschaftsrat*), set up in 1957, in which the Federal Government and the *Länder* worked together for the first time and which served to institutionalise the cooperation of academic and governmental actors in higher education.

In Britain, the first phase of higher education expansion started before the end of World War II, when more and more families from all class backgrounds demanded better educational opportunities. In response and as a first step towards higher education expansion, the Education Act (1944) proposed to educate and mobilise the working class by abolishing tuition fees charged in the British secondary school system. As a result, a far higher percentage of pupils attended upper secondary schools, which led to a vast increase in the number of qualified young people entering higher education. Only two years later, the Barlow Report (1946) worked in the same direction by recommending a doubling of university student numbers, especially in science subjects, to meet the country's need for scientific manpower. As a consequence, both government funding and student numbers were greatly increased in the immediate post-war period in Britain.

During the 1960s, both countries experienced a continuously growing demand for higher education participation. As a consequence, education policy more and more focussed on the expansion of higher education, which subsequently lead to the establishment of a binary structure of higher education institutions. In Germany, the post-war consolidation period was followed by a phase of active higher education development as a response to the increasing number of students. From around 1960 onwards, West German higher education institutions were under considerable pressure to change and modernise, which, in turn, initiated a phase of fundamental reform in the higher education sector. Public spending for the higher education system rose significantly. Between 1965 and 1980, the structure of the higher education system changed considerably, partly due to the introduction of new types of higher education institutions and partly due to the merging of existing ones. The constitutional provision for these reforms was fleshed out by the 1969 Higher Education Institutions Construction Act

---

returned the education system into the hands of the *Länder*. This federal order was also retained after the establishment of German unity in 1990 (Eurydice 2006).

(*Hochschulbauförderungsgesetz*), a law to promote the joint task of expanding existing institutions of higher education and building new ones in order to cope with rising enrolment rates (BMBF 1969). One of the most prominent reforms was the establishment of *Fachhochschulen* (technical colleges), which were introduced in 1970/71. The characteristic feature of course design as well as teaching and study organisation at this new type of institution was and continues to be a particular emphasis on the practical application of knowledge and an orientation towards labour market requirements. With the establishment of *Fachhochschulen*, German higher education moved towards a binary structure within its higher education system, consisting of universities and technical colleges (Eurydice 2000), a structure which remains in place until today.[18]

In Britain, the continuously rising number of higher education students created a pressure for change in the provision of higher education in the early 1960s, too. The subsequently established Committee on Higher Education made a comprehensive assessment of the present and future of British higher education. The resulting Robbins Report (1963) laid down the basic principles of higher education, which guided university development in subsequent years. Its main goal was to provide higher education courses to all those who wished to do so, as long as they were qualified in terms of their abilities and credentials (Robbins 1963). Moreover, it recommended further expansion, a broadening of both the regional spread and of the scope and diversity of university education. This was accepted by the Government, and additional funds were made available to the University Grants Committee (UGC) to meet the new targets. In the following years, new universities were created, and many technical colleges were upgraded to receive university status. However, just as in Germany, it was recognised that there was a growing need for vocational, professional, and industry-based training, which could not be fully met by the universities. As a consequence, the White Paper "A Plan for Polytechnics and Other Colleges", published in 1966 (DES 1966), aimed at establishing non-university higher education by introducing a new type of institution, the so called *polytechnics*. The subsequent foundation of 31 polytechnics in England, Wales and Northern

---

18 In addition to this primary institutional differentiation, the German university system consists of a range of institutions that also enjoy university status. Besides the traditional universities, there are universities of technology (*Technische Hochschulen* or *Technische Universitäten*) that specialise in the natural and engineering sciences, or schools that only offer a limited range of degree courses, for example theological colleges and *Pädagogische Hochschulen* (colleges of education). The 29 *Fachhochschulen* for public administration (*Verwaltungsfachhochschulen*) play a special role, which train civil servants for careers in the so-called higher level of the civil service. They are maintained by the Federation or by a *Land*, and their students have revocable civil servant status. However, the main differentiation in German higher education is between university-type institutions and technical colleges, as will be demonstrated in the following.

Ireland and of 14 new institutions in Scotland led to the development of a "binary system" of higher education provision in Britain too.

Overall, the development in both countries followed rather similar pathways with the binary structure being the major political reform following from the expansion of higher education and changing labour market demands. In the years to come, Germany and Britain experienced an enormous rise in the number of students, both in absolute and relative terms. Since the 1970s, the higher education sectors in both countries have witnessed an ongoing expansion in terms of growth in types and numbers of institutions, number of students, as well as increases in enrolment rates of a given age cohort. The following figure gives an account of the development of absolute student numbers enrolled in higher education in Germany and Britain since 1975.

Figure 3: Number of German and British students enrolled in higher education

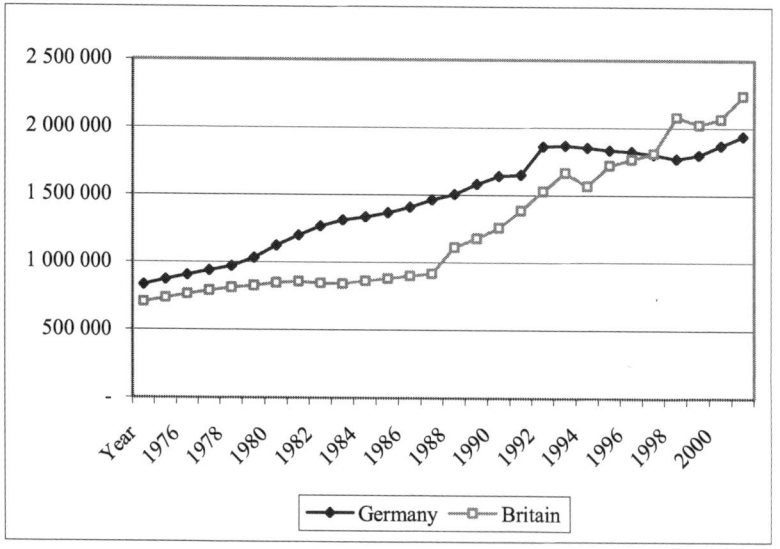

Number of students enrolled in higher education, full-time and part-time, undergraduate and postgraduate

Source: Calculations based on data from Statistisches Bundesamt, Eurostat, UK Universities Historical Data

In Germany, participation in higher education more than doubled between 1975 and 1990, from 836,000 to 1,578,000 students in total. After a dramatic increase in 1993 due to new entrants from the former GDR,[19] expansion in Germany slowed down. Until the late 1990s, enrolment figures slightly fell every year due to a drop in birth rates in the relevant age cohorts, but since 1997, they have started to rise again. The number of students participating in German higher education reached its peak in 2003, when, for the first time, 2 million students were enrolled (BMBF 2004). In Britain, the total number of students enrolled in higher education increased from 827,000 in 1980 to about 1.2 million in 1990 to about 2.1 million in 2000 (Elias and Purcell 2003). Full-time student numbers increased by almost 70% between 1989 (1113,000) and 1998 (1809,200). Today, one in three young people enters higher education, compared to one in six in 1989. Overall, both countries experienced a large growth in their number of students since the 1970s, but each experienced this to varying degrees. German higher education expansion was strongest during the 1980s, but has levelled off since the early 1990s. In contrast to the German development, British enrolment rates in higher education continued to rise considerably during the 1980s and even more strongly during the 1990s.

While these absolute numbers give some indication of the scale of higher education expansion in both countries, they mask the fact that the size of the population of young people differs between them. Instead of absolute numbers of students, participation rates by age cohorts (= age participation rate) are a better measure for comparing the degree of higher education expansion that took place in both countries. At the same time, only relative student enrolment rates can be taken as an empirical indicator of the degree of stratification related to the whole education system. Theoretical explanations have shown that a system with a low degree of stratification is characterised by a high proportion of students obtaining the highest number of school years available (Allmendinger 1989a). Figure 4 displays the participation rates in higher education of the 20-29 year-old population in both countries. It becomes clear immediately that differences between the two countries are even more pronounced than in the comparison of absolute student numbers. While in absolute figures, Germany exhibited a larger number of students enrolled in higher education for most years of the observation period, relative figures indicate that Britain's participation rate became much higher than the German one over the years. Until the late 1980s, the German education system was apparently slightly less stratified than the British one since a higher proportion of young adults was enrolled in

---

19   Higher education in the former GDR evolved under completely different conditions. It was based on a unitary and centrally controlled concept in the service of Marxist-Leninist party ideology and committed to serving the ends of a planned economy. Higher education in the GDR did not see the same unchecked expansion as in West Germany: the enrolment figures peaked in 1972 after the universities had been opened explicitly to server sons and daughters of workers and peasants, and distance learning courses had been introduced to reach many working people.

higher education. In 1991, the age participation rate was similar in both countries with around 13 percent of the respective age cohort participating in higher education. However, since then, British stratification has decreased at much higher rates than stratification in Germany, due to the strong expansion that took place in Britain during the 1990s. By the end of that decade, net enrolment rates as well as graduation rates were about ten percent higher in Britain than in Germany. National differences are also remarkable if enrolment rates at the beginning and the end of the observation period are compared. The variance in participation amounts to more than 20 percent in Britain, while the increase in Germany amounts to less than 10 percent. Today, one in three British students is enrolled in higher education, while in Germany it is little more than one in five.

Figure 4: German and British age participation rates in higher education

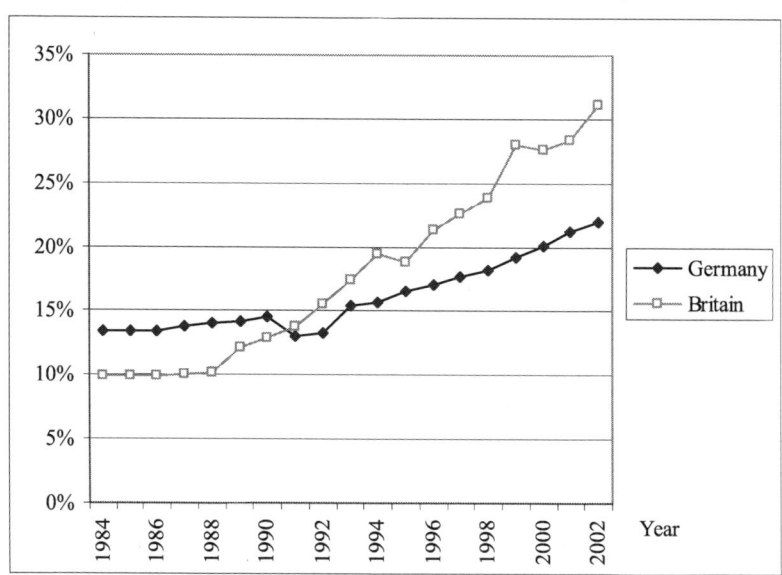

Students enrolled in German and British higher education as percentage of the 20-29 year old population

Source: Calculations based on data from Statistisches Bundesamt, Eurostat, UK Universities Historical Data

These figures can be taken as a first indicator that both countries have become less stratified during the 1980s and 1990; however, expansion in Britain has taken place at a much faster pace and to a much stronger extent than in Germany. Indeed, the rank order of the degree of stratification as measured by the number of students enrolled in higher education by cohort has changed during these two decades. Whilst in Germany, a slightly higher proportion attended higher education during the 1980s, higher education expansion in Britain was so strong during the 1990s that participation rates nowadays exceed those of Germany by far. Thus, British higher education has become much less stratified than higher education in Germany over the last two decades. Since higher numbers of students per age cohort increase competition among graduates, the steadily increasing age participation rates are likely to lower overall labour market returns after finishing higher education in Britain. This stratification effect should be observable in Germany as well; however, since the intensity and pace of higher education expansion was much weaker during the time of observation, effects should be less pronounced.

Overall, these historical specificities of higher education expansion laid the foundation for country-specific higher education policies during the 1980s and 1990s. The following passages describe the structural set-up of German and British higher education during these two decades, which was very different until the Bologna Process was initiated. The institutional analysis of type of institutions, type of degrees, and type of fields of study is accomplished by a description of pathways into higher education in both countries. Taken together, these insights will help to identify more precisely the degree of institutional stratification inherent in British and German higher education and to formulate further hypotheses about what labour market entry might look like.

5.1.2 Institutional Differentiation and the Stratification of Higher Education[20]

The legal basis of the structural set-up of higher education institutions differs fundamentally between the two countries. While Germany is marked by a strong legalism, where any change of the higher education sector has to be based on a new law, British higher education is less influenced by juridical bodies. Instead, university governance has always enjoyed considerable autonomy from government authorities. In Germany, the legal basis of any institutional feature of higher education is provided by the Framework Act for Higher Education (*Hochschulrahmengesetz*), which was first issued by the Federal Government in 1976, and the specific legislation on higher education of the *Länder*. The *Hochschulrahmengesetz* provides a systematic foundation for the German higher education system by describing the general objectives of higher education as well as the general principles underlying the system of higher education, such as organisation of study, teaching and research, admission procedures, as well as staff recruitment and staff

---

20   The following analysis was derived, if not stated otherwise, from Eurydice (2006).

decisions. Based on the general provisions of the Framework Act, the laws on higher education passed by the *Länder* cover the above-mentioned areas in detail in their own Higher Education Acts (*Hochschulgesetze*). Because of the more autonomous nature of higher education in Britain there was and is no single coherent body of legislation dealing with higher education policies and there have only been very few Education Acts to govern the higher education sector. In addition to such formal legislation, policy on higher education has often been signalled by so called White Papers, which are policy proposals by the Government that set out their intention to legislate. White papers often lead to the creation of new laws and tend to shape existing policy, but their content itself is not legally binding.

Institutional Differentiation by Type of Higher Education Institution

At first sight, institutional differentiation by type of higher education seems to be rather similar in both countries, since technical colleges have been established in addition to traditional universities in Germany and Britain as a response to the increasing participation in higher education. Although country differences exist in terms of names and structural organisation, both university-type institutions are more theoretically oriented and offer the full range of academic courses, while technical colleges offer more practically and vocationally oriented courses, usually in shorter programmes. These similarities notwithstanding, the type of institutional differentiation differs strongly between the two countries.

The German higher education system can be described as a dual system, consisting of universities and *Fachhochschulen* since the 1970s. As mentioned before, the strong expansion of higher education institutions is particularly related to the establishment of new *Fachhochschule* institutions, which today even outnumber universities (in 1998, 170 universities and equivalent institutions including colleges for music and arts and 185 *Fachhochschulen,* including those for administrative studies, existed in Germany). The major difference lies in the kind of knowledge taught at both types of institutions. Universities, on the one hand, place a strong emphasis on academic and scientific research – particularly basic research. The training of the next generation of academics is another distinctive feature of German universities, since they have the traditional right to award the doctorate (*Doktorgrad*) and a post-doctoral lecturing qualification (*Habilitation*). The distinctive feature of *Fachhochschulen*, on the other hand, is a particular emphasis on the practical application of knowledge and an orientation towards the requirements of the labour market. *Fachhochschulen* are characterised by a more practice-oriented bias in teaching as compared to universities, an integrated semester of practical training, and

108

professors, who,, in addition to their academic qualifications, have gained professional experience outside the field of higher education.

These differences in orientation towards the theoretical or practical applicability of knowledge might at first sight create a vertically differentiated system of higher education institutions in Germany. However, there are other indicators that point towards a low level of hierarchy between the two types of institutions. First of all, the juridical status of both types of institutions is rather similar. The general institutional organisation of universities and *Fachhochschulen* is governed by the same legislation, the Framework Act for Higher Education, which regulates mission, structures, admission procedures, personnel procedures, and financial issues (BMBF 2002). Due to the legal equivalence of German higher education institutions, the institutional differentiation at this level can be described as horizontal, despite the obvious differences in knowledge design. What is more, differences in institutional reputation, a strong indicator of vertical differentiation, can be considered low between German universities and *Fachhochschulen*. Especially over the past two decades, the social esteem of *Fachhochschulen* has become equal to that of universities, not only as a result of their increasing attractiveness for students, but also due to their effective occupation-specific programmes (Müller et al. 2002). Taken together, these factors point more strongly towards a horizontal differentiation among German higher education institutions, despite the differences in knowledge orientation. This can be taken as an indicator of a system with a low degree of stratification by type of higher education institution. As a consequence, there should be a low degree of stratification in the status of labour market outcomes between university and *Fachhochschule* graduates.

The institutional set-up of German higher education remained surprisingly stable throughout the 1980s and 1990s despite the ever increasing number of students. Even the peaceful revolution in the GDR in 1989 and the reunification process did not change the structure of German higher education institutions. After reunification, the autonomy of East German higher education institutions was restored along with freedom of research and teaching, ideologically encumbered faculties were overhauled, and wider access to higher education was introduced. In the following years, some East German institutions of higher education were closed or integrated into universities, new faculties were set up in the fields of law, economics and business, and social sciences, and *Fachhochschulen* were established as a new type of institution. Since then, East and West German higher education institutions have become very alike in their structure and organisation.

Only since the mid 1990s have the Federation and the *Länder* intensified their efforts to introduce reforms throughout Germany as a response to inadequate financial resources and staffing levels as well as the need to improve higher education management. This has involved, for example, a review of *Regelstudienzeiten* (standard periods of study) and examination requirements at both types of institutions in conjunction with improvements in teaching. One priority still is to expand *Fachhochschulen* and to make them even more attractive, for example by consolidating applied research work and technology transfer (Eurydice 2000), which again indicates a more horizontal differentiation between the two types of institutions. Furthermore, institutions of higher education are to be made more efficient by granting them further autonomy, allowing them to build an individual profile in a particular area and encouraging more competition. With the amendments of the Framework Act for Higher Education of 1998 and 2002, the *Länder* enjoy greater scope regarding their own decisions. However, substantial reforms of the binary institutional structure of German higher education have not been on the agenda of higher education reforms. Even the latest revisions of the German higher education system in the wake of the Bologna Process leave the horizontal differentiation between universities and *Fachhochschulen* largely untouched.

In contrast to the stability of German higher education institutions, British higher education has been marked by strong reforms during the same period. From the 1970s until the early 1990s, British higher education was provided by three main types of institutions[21]: universities, polytechnics, and non-university institutions of higher education. British universities are autonomous institutions, empowered by a Royal Charter or an Act of Parliament. This autonomy from state administration is particularly relevant for course design, since universities have their own degree-awarding powers and determine which degrees and other qualifications they offer as well as the conditions they apply. As a consequence of this organisational independence, British universities are diverse, be it in terms of size, mission, subject mix, and of course history. Generally, universities offer research opportunities as well as a wide range of courses at the undergraduate and postgraduate levels, catering more to labour market requirements, although the balance between these activities varies between institutions. Sometimes universities also offer specific professional qualifications and certain qualifications below degree level.

The second type of higher education institution in Britain was the polytechnic, which existed up until 1992. They were originally set up by charitable endowment to enable men and women of lower socioeconomic

---

21 An analysis of the institutional framework of Britain sometimes has to differentiate between England, Wales and Northern Ireland on the one hand and Scotland on the other, since the latter has followed a somewhat different pathway due to the existence of a distinct education system. To acknowledge this fact does not mean, however, that there are completely different types of higher education in these regions in Britain, but rather that certain aspects vary in their specific organisation, just as they might vary between German *Länder*. The most important variations will be stated separately.

status to advance their general knowledge and industrial skills on a part- or full-time basis. Thus, similar to their German counterparts, the specific focus of teaching and course design at polytechnics was on applicable knowledge. However, unlike German *Fachhochschulen*, they could offer the full range of academic qualifications up to doctorates and in general provided some programmes in traditional academic fields. The third type of British higher education institution are higher education colleges and university colleges – so called non-university higher education institutions, which are also characterised by an emphasis on vocational and professional courses. In contrast to university institutions, only a small number of university colleges and higher education colleges have the power to award their own degrees and qualifications. The majority of qualifications offered by non-university institutions are validated by external bodies such as universities or national accrediting bodies. If polytechnics had the right to award degrees, these rights were normally restricted to first degrees and taught (not research) master's degrees.

The differentiation between British universities and polytechnics points to the opposite direction compared to Germany. On the one hand, both types of higher education institution theoretically offered the same type of degrees. However, as regards institutional governance polytechnics did not have the same autonomous status as universities, particularly in relation to degree awarding powers, but were financed and regulated by local education authorities (LEAs). This legal differentiation between autonomous universities and externally controlled polytechnics created a higher education system which differed strongly in quality and quantity, for example as regards the degrees offered, the emphasis placed on research, financial resources, and the volume of public funding. Finally, the universities' reputation has traditionally been much higher than that of polytechnics (Chevalier and Conlon 2003). As a result, the make-up of the student body was remarkably different, since polytechnics showed a much higher enrolment of students with lower socio-economic backgrounds or from ethnic minorities, and of mature students (Booth 1999). These differences in institutional hierarchy and reputation can be taken as indicators of a vertically differentiated higher education system, which should lead to strong status differences in labour market outcomes of higher education graduates from universities and polytechnics.

British higher education policy, however, aimed at putting an end to this hierarchical binary structure as a response to mass higher education (Booth 1999). First changes in this regard were introduced by the Education Reform Act (1988), which removed polytechnics from the control of local authorities and provided them with more autonomous funding via the Polytechnics and Colleges Funding Council (PCFC), a Non-Departmental Public Body. Even more substantial reforms have been proposed by another White Paper in May

1991 named "Higher Education: A New Framework" as a response to the increasing number of students in higher education (DES 1991). Its main recommendation concerned the abolition of the "binary system" between universities and polytechnics, leading to the establishment of a unitary system in British higher education. The proposed reforms formed the basis of the Further and Higher Education Act (1992). With this act, polytechnics were given university status if they fulfilled certain criteria such as a specific range of courses offered and a particular distribution of students across curricular areas. When polytechnics met the requirements, they were allowed to include the word 'university' in their title and became legally independent, self-governing institutions, with the power to award their own degrees just like universities. By the year 2000, many of the former polytechnics had been granted university status. Today, 88 universities exist in England, Scotland, Wales and Northern Ireland, while there are only 62 non-university institutions (Eurydice 2006)

However, regarding the degree of institutional differentiation following from this reform, the binary structure still seems to be in place in the British system (Booth 1999; Eurydice 2000). Despite the upgrading of polytechnics and the creation of one unified sector for British higher education, some of these organisational differences between the 'old', or 'pre-1992' universities and the 'new', 'modern' or 'post-1992' universities[22] remain. Differences continue to exist, particularly with regard to mission and subject mix. Old

---

22   Within the "old" universities, there are two further lines along which universities are separated. The first one is related to the age of university institutions, which distinguishes between the traditional universities, most of which were established in the Middle Ages, and university institutions founded during the first wave of higher education expansion in the 1960s, which are often referred to as "new" universities. Due to this differentiation within the old universities, another term had to be found for former polytechnics. Therefore, the newest of the new universities, which attained university status only in 1992 by the Higher and Further Education Act, are called "modern" universities in order to differentiate them from the "new" universities. As a result, today three types of universities can be found in Britain today: traditional, new, and modern universities, which all differ in the criteria quoted above. In addition, a more informal divide exists among the old university institutions, one that is related to institutional reputation and research strength. A self selected informal coalition of 19 research intensive institutions formed, encompassing mainly the oldest and most prestigious higher education institutions, but also some of the new universities. This group of institutions is referred as the Russell Group. The members of the Russell Group universities are University of Birmingham, University of Bristol, University of Cambridge, Cardiff University, University of Edinburgh, University of Glasgow, University of Leeds, University of Liverpool, University of Manchester, University of Newcastle upon Tyne, University of Nottingham, University of Oxford, University of Sheffield, University of Southampton, University of Warwick, Imperial College, King's College London, London School of Economics and University College London (Chevalier and Conlon 2003). However, since the data sets used for Britain do not contain any information on institutional differentiation among the old universities, higher education stratification will be restricted to a differentiation between pre-1992 universities on the one hand and polytechnics and non-university institutions on the other.

universities still tend to provide more academic courses rather than professional training. New universities, in contrast, generally place greater emphasis on the practical application of knowledge and consequently offer a wider range of courses leading to the professional qualifications recognised by professional institutions. In addition, the amount and the resources of funding differ strongly between modern and old university institutions. Old universities generally obtain a much higher share of state allocated funds. For example, the former polytechnics received only 7 percent of resources allocated through the Research Assessment Exercise, which is one of the major funding sources for British universities today (Hillyard et al. 2003: 10) These distinctions, now working more informally, still reproduce the pre-1992 institutional hierarchies in reputation and standing. Overall, this hierarchy of institutions continues to create a strong vertical differentiation among both types of British higher education institutions. This strongly stratified British system has already been shown to have an impact on graduate earnings (Chevalier and Conlon 2003). In addition, labour market rewards after graduation should be strongly stratified between traditional universities on the one hand and former polytechnics and other non-university institutions on the other.[23]

Institutional Differentiation by Type of Degree and Field of Study

The types of degrees awarded in German and British higher education vary even more between the two countries than the types of higher education institutions. But again, institutional differentiation follows a similar pattern as above, with German degrees exhibiting more horizontal demarcations, and British degrees clearly being vertically structured. In addition, both higher education systems are differentiated horizontally, mainly along faculties or

---

23 Somewhat different to England and Wales, four different models of governance in the higher education sector existed in Scotland until 1992, each reflecting different founding origins. But despite these differences, the main institutional differentiation between traditional universities and polytechnics/non-university institutions can be found there as well. The four 'ancient' universities (University of Aberdeen, University of Edinburgh, University of Glasgow, St. Andrew's University) were founded as legally autonomous governing bodies by the Scottish Universities Acts in 1858 and 1889 and are best comparable to the traditional English universities. Another four Scottish universities (Dundee University, University of Stirling, Strathclyde University, Herriot Watt Edinburgh) were established by Charter during the 1960s and most closely resemble the new universities in England. Both types of institutions enjoyed university status and thus institutional autonomy from their beginnings. Designated institutions, on the other hand, were similar to English polytechnics. They are governed in accordance with Orders of Council made under Section 45 of the Further and Higher Education (Scotland) Act 1992 and only then received university status. Very much like English non-university institutions, the Scottish colleges of education are governed in accordance with the Colleges of Education (Scotland) Regulations 1987.

departments of different fields of study. These cross-national variations in institutional differentiation by degree types and fields of study will be described in more detail below. In addition, the institutional analysis will be linked to the Casmin scheme, which is supposed to distinguish educational levels according to their decisive signals for utilisation on the labour market and their functional equivalence of its education categories across countries (Brauns et al. 1997b).

To begin with, undergraduate degrees did not exist in Germany prior to the sweeping Bologna reforms, and all degrees were conferred at the postgraduate level. The lack of a hierarchy among different degree levels signals a horizontally differentiated system. Moreover, all degrees conferred at German higher education institutions used to be organised and coordinated by the same regulatory framework. To ensure that the various institutions of higher education throughout the country provide a comparable standard of scientific and academic training and degrees, the *KMK* and the Association of Universities and other Higher Education Institutions (*Hochschulrektorenkonferenz HRK*) set up a Joint Commission for the Coordination of Study and Examination Regulations, which has drawn up a framework regulation, covering all subjects and degrees available in the German higher education system. The framework regulations contain the quantitative reference data for courses of study, in particular the *Regelstudienzeit* (standard period of study), the amount of hours of teaching on required and elective subjects, the number of certificates required for admission to examinations (*Leistungsnachweise*), examination details and the length of time allowed to complete the final dissertation.[24]

The only differentiation existing among German degrees in the period studied in this analysis is a horizontal one, associated with different fields of study and labour market segments. At university-type institutions, the most

---

24 These frameworks regulated all matters related to degree and field of study organisation until the end of 2002 when the changes proposed by the Bologna Declaration were introduced. Following from a KMK resolution in March 2002, a system of accreditation will replace the previous system of coordination of study and examination regulations in the future. For the accreditation of Bachelor's and Master's study courses, the KMK has set up an accreditation council (*Akkreditierungsrat*) acting on behalf of all *Länder*. In the long run, the system of accreditation will be extended to all courses of study. Furthermore, the KMK issued structural guidelines for Bachelor's and Master's degree courses that have already been incorporated into the Framework Act for Higher Education in October 2003. These rules, which are facultative for all *Länder*, regulate, amongst other issues, the structure and length of the study. The structural guidelines stipulate that Bachelor's study courses, as study courses which lead to a first degree qualifying for entry into a profession, must provide the academic foundation, methodological skills and qualifications related to the professional field. Furthermore, the structural guidelines distinguish between more research-oriented Master's study courses and more practice-oriented ones. Bachelor's and Master's study courses are provided with a credit point system which is based upon the European Credit Transfer System (ECTS).

important distinction is made between academic degrees (*Diplom* and *Magister*) and state examinations (*Staatsexamen*). The general *Regelstudienzeit* for most of these degrees is eight to ten semesters (with the exception of medicine). Academic and state examinations do not build upon each other; rather, professional qualifications are conferred on the basis of all of them. They provide for a horizontal differentiation because they vary in the degree of specialisation on specific subjects and the number of subjects studied. State examinations have to be taken in degree courses that prepare students for professions of particular importance to the public interest, such as medicine, pharmaceutics, law, or the teaching profession. Academic degrees, in contrast, are not considered to prepare for such a specific occupational field or profession, but are more generally related to specific research disciplines, such as mathematics or sociology. Thus, the difference between the two types of degrees essentially concerns their content and future occupational domain. Their curricular structure and type of examination are quite similar, with the main exception that in the case of *Staatsexamen*, where representatives of state examination bodies act as examiners in addition to university professors.

Within the academic degrees, a further differentiation exists. A degree is awarded on the basis of either the *Diplomprüfung*, which leads to the awarding of the *Diplomgrad*, or the *Magisterprüfung* leading to the awarding of the *Magistergrad*. The main difference between the two is again related to the fields of study, since *Diplom* programmes concentrate on a single subject, while those that lead to a *Magister* degree allow for a combination of several subjects, usually one major subject and two minor subjects, or two equally weighted major subjects. Both types of academic degrees are offered in a large range of subjects including the humanities, economics, social sciences, sciences, or engineering. However, the *Diplom* is more often awarded for subjects with a stronger focus on applicability such as engineering, while *Magister* degrees are generally conferred for subjects more general in nature, such as humanities or arts.

Even though all of these degrees are already conferred at a postgraduate level, further postgraduate degrees can be obtained in Germany following successful completion of a first degree. For instance, particularly well-qualified students, who have achieved a certain level of academic performance, may choose to complete a doctorate (*Promotion*). A doctorate is conferred on the strength of a doctoral thesis, which must be based on independent research, and an oral examination (*Rigorosum*) or alternatively the oral defence of the thesis (*Disputation*). In addition, postgraduate degrees of further, supplementary or follow-up courses (*postgraduale Studiengänge*) can be taken. Unlike further education taking place at the work place, postgraduate degrees are usually pursued immediately after or even parallel to first degree courses.[25]

The main distinction between academic and state degrees can be taken as an indicator for a horizontal institutional differentiation in the German university sector, since they are rather equal in terms of study organisation, duration of study, and degree level. Also, the various degrees conferred at German universities are generally classified as Casmin 3b level degrees – higher tertiary education. In this regard, the Casmin classification does not distinguish any further between state and academic examinations or between first and second stage postgraduate degrees. This can, on the one hand, be taken as another indicator that German university degrees differ more horizontally than vertically, but on the other that Casmin is not precise enough to capture the specificity of German degrees. As a consequence, labour market outcomes should be weakly stratified between academic and state degree holders. Fields of study are generally considered to differentiate the student population horizontally and should therefore support a low stratification of labour market returns.

In contrast to universities, German *Fachhochschulen* only award one kind of degree, the *Diplomgrad,* upon completion of a course, which normally lasts for four years. But just like university degrees, *Fachhochschule* degrees are only conferred at the postgraduate level, without any intermediary examination which would qualify for the labour market. Since the characteristic feature of this type of institution is an orientation towards the requirements of the labour markets, all fields of study taught at *Fachhochschulen* have to show a particular emphasis on applicability and practical knowledge, while aspects of basic research and theory advancement are of less importance. The subject canon in parts differs from the one taught at university institutions, comprising for example social work, social services, public administration, administration of justice, design, nursing, or public health management. Upon completion of a first *Fachhochschule* degree, further studies, supplementary and follow-up courses can be taken as well, which last two to four semesters and culminate in the award of a second *Diplom* degree or proof of academic achievement (certificate). It is not possible to obtain a doctoral degree from *Fachhochschulen,* given that only universities and equivalent institutions of higher education are entitled to award doctorates.

---

25 Unfortunately, information on degrees in the SOEP does not include such postgraduate degrees and therefore the main differentiation made in the individual analysis is between academic and state examinations. Bachelor's and Master's degrees, which are now available at German higher education institutions, are not included in the examinations of individual career trajectories either, since the implementation of the Bologna Process is still ongoing and since this study focuses on labour market entries prior to its beginnings.

The inclusion of *Fachhochschule* degrees in a system of institutional differentiation poses some difficulties. On the one hand, the organisation of studies and the associated fields of study differ strongly between both types of higher education institutions. Based on these differences, degrees awarded by *Fachhochschulen* have often been considered inferior to university degrees. In the Casmin scheme, they are classified as lower tertiary degrees in comparison to higher tertiary degrees awarded at universities (Brauns et al. 1997b), which signals a vertical differentiation between university and non-university degrees in Germany. However, the picture changes if the degree level and consecutiveness of degrees are taken into account. At the degree level, *Fachhochschule* degrees are rather similar to university degrees, since all are conferred as postgraduate degrees. In addition, *Fachhochschule* and university degrees do not constitute a two-tiered structure of degrees, with one degree building upon the other, as it is the case in Britain. They rather constitute different degree options at the same level, between which students have to choose at the beginning of their higher education studies. Studying for both types of degrees simultaneously or consecutively is uncommon. Based on these latter characteristics, it is also possible to classify the German degree system as being horizontally differentiated. As a consequence, labour market outcomes should not differ too strongly between university and *Fachhochschule* graduates. Rather than the mere differentiation by different types of degrees, field of study might matter in this regard, since all university and *Fachhochschule* degrees are also differentiated by the subjects associated with them.

In Britain, degrees can be divided into undergraduate and postgraduate level degrees at all types of higher education institutions, constituting a clearly vertically differentiated degree system. At the undergraduate level, two different kinds of degrees exist, so called intermediate level degrees and Bachelor degrees. Higher Education Diplomas and Certificates are intermediate level degrees and the shortest types of degrees available, lasting for a maximum of one to two years. However, they are recognized as higher education qualifications in their own right. Certificates of Higher Education normally take one year of full-time study and the holder is expected to have a sound knowledge of the basic concepts of a subject, and will have learned how to take different approaches to solving problems. Higher Education Diplomas usually take two years to complete by full-time study. Holders of these qualifications are expected to have developed a sound understanding of the principles in their field of study, and will have learned to apply those principles more widely than Certificate holders. Both types of degrees are often delivered through partnerships of further and higher education institutions, and are intended to help education providers to address the shortage of intermediate-level skills, to widen participation in higher education, and stimulate lifelong learning. They are usually offered for more vocationally oriented subjects with a more vocational orientation and in employment-related subject areas such as internet computing, learning support, or hospitality, leisure and tourism. According to the Casmin scheme, these intermediate level degrees are classified as lower tertiary degrees (3a), just as German *Fachhochschule* degrees (Brauns and Steinmann 1997).

The second undergraduate stage in Britain lasts for three or four years and leads to a Bachelor of Arts or Bachelor of Science Degree (B.A./B.Sc.), which can be taken as a first degree or build upon an intermediate degree.[26] Graduates with a Bachelor degree are supposed have developed an understanding of a complex body of knowledge, some of it at the current boundaries of an academic discipline. The Bachelor's Degree is conferred as a Pass Degree for more general studies or an Honours Degree where studies are more specialised. Honours degrees form the largest group of British higher education qualifications. Typically, courses last for three or four years (if taken full-time) and lead to a bachelor's degree with titles such as Bachelor of Arts (B.A.(Hons)) or Bachelor of Science (B.Sc.(Hons)). Longer courses include sandwich courses, which incorporate periods of practical work in organisations outside the university or college, and courses specialising in modern foreign languages, which normally include a year abroad in the target language country. Shorter courses include accelerated two-year degrees, which normally require students to study during the normal vacation periods.

The majority of Bachelor students are expected to have identified their field of study when they apply for admission. Most programmes specialise in a specific subject area, similar to the German subject canon, where that subject is set in its broader context. However, it is also possible to undertake a combined studies programme involving two or possibly three specialisations. Typically, there is a relatively fixed menu of course modules which are intended to cover the core knowledge of the subject, with an element of choice which increases in the later years of the course of study. Some programmes offer a wider range of subject areas providing a good advanced general education. In the Casmin scheme, Bachelor degrees are typically classified as higher tertiary degrees (3b). However, the more refined version of this scheme allows for taking into account their undergraduate status, categorising them as lower level 3b degrees (3b_low) (Brauns and Steinmann 1997).

---

26 The main difference between English and Scottish Bachelor degrees is related to their length, since Scottish honours degree courses generally last for four years in comparison to three years of study in England. This is mainly related to the younger leaving age of Scottish students from upper secondary education (see section 5.1.3. on 'Pathways into higher education', Footnote 28). Another Scottish specificity is related to the fact that the first degree in Arts in the four 'ancient' universities and Dundee University is the Master of Arts. MA degrees in all other faculties as well as in the other universities are conferred as post-graduate qualifications.

At the postgraduate level, a Master's Degree is conferred after one or two years of study in a specialised field following the Bachelor's Degree.[27] Much of the study undertaken at the Master's level will have been at or informed by the forefront of an academic or professional discipline. Master's degrees are awarded after completion of taught courses or programmes of research, or a combination of both. Common degrees obtained at this level include Master of Arts (MA), Master of Science (MSc), Master of Business Administration (MBA), Master of Education (MEd), Master of Social Work (MSW), Master of Musical Arts (AMusM), or Master of Medical Sciences (MMedSci). Some Master's Degrees – for example in science and engineering – are awarded after extended undergraduate programmes that last, typically, a year longer than honours degree programmes. Advanced short courses, also situated at this level, often form parts of continuing professional development programmes, leading to postgraduate certificates (PGCE) and postgraduate diplomas.

While a lot of Master's Degrees aim at teaching applicable knowledge for the professional life, the Master of Philosophy and the Doctor of Philosophy can be considered pure research degrees at the postgraduate level. Following an honours degree, the Master of Philosophy (MPhil) Degree is awarded after two years of additional study and the successful presentation of a thesis. After usually three years of further study beyond the Master's Degree, the candidate may present a thesis for the Doctorate of Philosophy (DPhil or PhD). Both of these titles are awarded for the creation and interpretation of knowledge, which extends the forefront of a discipline, usually through original research. In addition, there are doctoral programmes that have a substantial taught element and only include a minor research component, usually leading to awards which include the name of the discipline in their title (such as EdD for Doctor of Education).

Any type of postgraduate qualification awarded in the British higher education system is classified as upper tertiary degree (3a) by the Casmin scheme, often with the extension of higher level (3b_high). Thus, contrary to the differentiation between German university degrees, which cannot be captured by this cross-national classification, all British degrees have separate categories. Taking all different degree levels together, both Casmin and the explications above lead to the conclusion that the British degree system is strongly vertically differentiated into undergraduate and postgraduate degrees, with most of them building upon each other. Fields of study in Britain are less related to specific degree courses than in Germany.

---

27   At Oxford and Cambridge, the Master of Arts (MA) is conferred automatically after a certain period of time to all holders of Bachelor's Degrees. In other fields, it is awarded under the same conditions as in other universities. Some Master's Degrees are awarded as undergraduate degrees after four to five years of study (for example at the Imperial College, London), if the Bachelor's programme is included in the programme.

Therefore, labour market outcomes should be strongly stratified according to the type of degree in Britain, while fields of study should be less important in this regard.

5.1.3 Pathways into Higher Education

The previous discussion of stratification has considered the two dimensions relevant to this concept: the proportion of students achieving the highest degree available in an education system in combination with the number of tracks available at a particular level of education. The second one is strongly related to the structural set-up of higher education systems. In contrast, the first one not only depends on the level of higher education expansion, but also on the structure of secondary education and on the respective pathways into higher education available there. In addition, higher education and secondary education are often deemed complementary to each other. Allmendinger (1989a) has argued that highly stratified secondary education systems normally go hand in hand with weakly stratified higher education systems and vice versa. This has important consequences for the sorting function of education systems. Countries vary not only in their degree of stratification by educational level, but also in the relative stage in the degree to which age students are sorted into specific tracks relevant for labour market outcomes. A brief introduction to secondary schooling is given in order to understand how the different stratification regimes come about in both countries.

In contrast to its higher education system, secondary schooling in Germany is highly stratified (Allmendinger 1989a). It consists of three different tracks into which pupils are sorted very early at around the age of ten after completing four years of primary school. Lower secondary (*Hauptschule*) is the shortest track and consists of five years ending at age 15 with the termination of compulsory schooling. It provides a minimal level of academic curriculum and was originally installed to prepare students for craft apprenticeships. The German intermediate track (*Realschule*) lasts for six years. Its function is to obtain an intermediate general qualification (*Mittlere Reife*) and to prepare pupils predominantly for white collar apprenticeships. With a duration of nine years, upper secondary school (*Gymnasium*) is the longest track and it has a strict academic orientation leading to the award of the *Abitur*.

Regarding admission to higher education, there are several pathways in Germany. The main certificates for entry are the *Allgemeine Hochschulreife* (general entry certificate) or the *Fachgebundene Hochschulreife* (subject-specific entry certificate). The former is the *Abitur* and entitles school leavers to study at any institution of higher education in any degree and any field of study. In addition to upper secondary schools, it can also be acquired at

Abendgymnasien, i.e. evening schools for working people, and *Kollegs*, i.e. full-time schools for those who have completed vocational training. The *Fachgebundene Hochschulreife* or *Fachabitur* permits entry only into *Fachhochschulen* or specified courses of studies at university institutions and requires twelve years of schooling, with the last two years taking place at specialised upper secondary education institutions, so called *Fachober-schulen*. In certain subjects, the applicant's aptitude is not only based on the education qualification, but also determined via a subject-specific test procedure. This applies particularly to sports and the study of arts and used to be the norm for admission to medical school. All other certificates available in German secondary education do not qualify for higher education directly. However, in addition to admission based on these formal certificates, there is the option of taking a university-based entrance examination for employed persons with a particularly high level of intellectual ability (Eurydice 2006).

Due to the early sorting into different educational tracks, the German secondary school system is characterised as highly stratified (Allmendinger 1989b). Each track prepares for a specific place in the labour market – blue collar, white collar, academic – and the permeability between the tracks is relatively low, particularly if compared cross-nationally. In contrast to the higher education system, which apparently stratifies labour market outcomes more horizontally than vertically, the stratification of German secondary schooling is the decisive factor for sorting pupils into a vertically structured system of labour market outcomes. Thus, the low degree of stratification of German higher education is accompanied by a stratified secondary education system complementing the stratified structure of the labour market. But the tracking of secondary education also helps to ensure that the proportion of a given age cohort attaining higher education remains relatively low, since only about 34 percent of a given age cohort achieves upper secondary general education (OECD 2004a: Table A2.1). This ensures that higher education remains more elitist in character by being restricted to a lower percentage of students. The sorting taking place in German secondary education can be taken as important explanation of the more moderate higher education expansion taking place in Germany. This again leads to the conclusion that labour market outcomes for German higher education graduates should be in general unstratified and positive. Looking at the structural set-up of German education in total, one can derive the following hypotheses: Due to the high level of stratification in secondary schooling, labour market returns are generally rather high for higher education graduates. The expansion of higher education should weaken this relationship only moderately due to the sorting function of secondary education. In addition, the horizontally differentiated higher education system probably only weakly stratifies labour market outcomes among graduates from different types of institutions, degrees and fields of study.

In contrast, British secondary education nowadays is marked by a lower degree of stratification. Only until the middle of the 20th century, it also had a tripartite structure consisting of grammar, technical, and comprehensive modern schools, which provided different tracks of education. However, from 1964 onwards, the Labour government launched a series of legislative measures intending to establish a comprehensive secondary education system, since the inefficient and discriminating nature of the tripartite system had frequently been criticised. As a result, the early selection of pupils at age 11 into different educational tracks was replaced by a more comprehensive schooling approach up to age 16. Since the early 1980s, the majority of pupils follow a common curriculum until the end of compulsory schooling leading to the General Certificate of Secondary Education (GCSE). Afterwards, pupils may stay on at a school's sixth form for a further two years when they sit for the General Certificate of Education Advanced Level (GCE A Levels) or the General Certificate of Education Advanced Supplementary examinations (GCE AS Levels). Alternatively, they can also continue with vocational courses leading usually to General National Vocational Qualifications (GNVQs).

In Britain, the most common qualification requirements for entry into higher education are two or three GCE A-level passes, as well as a minimum number of GCSE passes at grade C or above.[28] These qualification requirements only stand for the most common pathways into higher education and do not necessarily apply for each higher education institution, since British universities have the right to determine their own admissions policies. In addition, many courses require some or all of the qualifications for entry to be in specific subjects or in a specific range of subjects. In practice, because admission is competitive, some institutions require levels of qualifications considerably above the minimum. These requirements may be expressed in the number of passes or in the grades to be obtained. For undergraduate medical and dental courses, a quota ensures that the intended number of medical and dental students required to meet national needs is

---

28 In Scotland, the range of upper secondary degrees has always differed substantially from those available in England, Wales and Northern Ireland. In addition, a new unified system of post-16 National Qualifications gradually introduced in schools, further education colleges and training centres since 1999, which makes comparisons even more complicated. However, some functional equivalents to the English ones exist. At age 16, Scottish pupils used to take the Standard Grade General degree, which corresponds to Intermediate 1 and 2 levels degrees in the new scheme. These are comparable to the English GCSE. After that, pupils may take Advanced Higher certificates, which have replaced the old Certificate of Sixth Year Studies (CSYS). Regarding entry into higher education, Scottish Advanced Higher certificates are equivalent to A-levels, since they both are valid entry certificates for both English and Scottish higher education institutions. The major difference is that Scottish Higher degrees only last for one year as compared to two years for A-levels. As a consequence, Scottish youth entering higher education at age 17 are even younger than their English counterparts and much younger compared to German ones (Eurydice 2006).

delivered. Entry requirements for such courses are therefore likely to be above average.

Besides the standard entry requirements, a wide range of other qualifications is acceptable for entry as well. These include, among others, Vocational Certificate of Education (VCE) qualifications or Business and Technology Education Council (BTEC) qualifications. Most institutions also welcome applications from mature candidates who have had appropriate experience but may lack formal qualifications. Increasing numbers of universities offer courses on a modular and part-time basis, and many institutions now also give credit for prior study and informal learning acquired through work or other experiences. The proportion of students admitted with non-traditional qualifications varies from one to over 70 percent, depending on the institution (Eurydice 2006).

Overall, a weakly stratified system became the dominant form of secondary schooling in Britain. The main type of stratification which continues to exist in Britain at this educational level today is the stratification between public and private schools. Private schools operate outside state policy intervention and in general offer an academically oriented curriculum for pupils from upper classes. They have been able to maintain their character as elite secondary education institutions, despite the changes in the education system. Pupils from private schools usually achieve A-levels more frequently than those from public ones and are over-represented in higher education, especially at highly renowned elite universities such as Oxford and Cambridge. However, since the majority of British pupils attend public schools, the overall stratification of secondary education can be considered low, with around 70 percent of British pupils receiving a general upper secondary certificate today (Babb et al. 2006). This again corresponds to Allmendinger's (1989) argument that weakly stratified education systems are complementary to a highly stratified higher education system. In Britain, therefore, the sorting of students into a hierarchically differentiated structure of the labour market takes place in the higher education system rather than beforehand. Labour market outcomes of different tracks should be more diverse than in Germany.

5.1.4 Stratification of German and British Higher Education: Diverse Trends

The stratification of higher education in Germany and Britain features interesting commonalities and differences. Both countries have experienced a remarkable increase of students participating in higher education since the 1970s; however, the degree of higher education expansion measured as age participation rate was much higher in Britain than in Germany, particularly during the 1990s. As a consequence, the British higher education system has become far less stratified over the past two decades than the German one, since the proportion of students acquiring higher education degrees is much higher nowadays. Competition among higher education graduates for favourable starting positions in the labour market should therefore become stronger among British graduates and resulting career outcomes accordingly should deteriorate more strongly in Britain than in Germany.

The analysis of the stratification by type of institution in Germany and Britain again shows a remarkable commonality between the two countries with regard to the existence of a binary structure, which has been established as a response to the increasing number of students – universities and technical colleges. However, the type of differentiation varies strongly between the two binary systems. Despite differences in institutional mission, the German system can be described as horizontally structured, with *Fachhochschulen* enjoying similar levels of institutional autonomy and standing as universities. In Britain, in contrast, the differentiation by type of institutions can be described as a vertical one, because organisation as well as social recognition and prestige of each track differ considerably. Even though the British system has moved to extinguish or diminish this hierarchical differentiation between the two types of institutions, the upgrading of the lower level polytechnics seems to remain a rather formal one. Therefore, labour market outcomes should be stratified more strongly between British higher education institutions than between German ones.

Table 4: Institutional differentiation and the stratification of labour market returns

Dimension of Stratification	Germany	Britain
Higher education expansion	Moderate (1990s) → moderate decline of labour market returns	High (1990s) → strong decline of labour market returns
Tracking by type of institution	Horizontal → low stratification of labour market returns	Vertical → high stratification of labour market returns
Tracking by type of degree	Horizontal → low stratification of labour market returns	Vertical → high stratification of labour market returns
Tracking of secondary schooling	High → high overall labour market returns	Low → low overall labour market returns

At the level of higher education degrees and fields of study, institutional differentiation becomes even more pronounced. German degrees are mainly horizontally differentiated, since they are conferred as postgraduate qualifications, without any intermediate level degrees, and their major differentiation is related to specific fields of study. British degrees, on the other hand, are clearly hierarchically structured between undergraduate and postgraduate and build upon each other. Horizontal differentiation by fields

124

of study is available more or less for any type of degree, even though some specialisations exist. Labour market outcomes in Britain are thus expected to be strongly stratified by different types of degrees, while fields of study should be less important. In Germany, a generally low level of stratification in labour returns should be related to different types of degrees, while the impact of various fields of study might be more pronounced.

The identified pattern of institutional differentiation pertaining to different higher education tracks is reinforced in both countries by secondary education systems and pathways into higher education. In Germany, a highly stratified school system complements a weakly stratified higher education system. The sorting of students into different tracks and accordingly the stratification of labour market outcomes takes place predominantly through secondary education. The British school system has become weakly stratified over the years and today complements a highly differentiated higher education system. Accordingly, the capacity to structure students' further career prospects is much higher in German secondary education and much lower in German higher education than in Britain. The highly stratified German school system sets an institutional barrier to the increasing intake of students. University participation remains strongly related to *Gymnasium* graduates, maintaining a more elitist character in higher education. Overall status returns to German higher education should therefore be high. The weakly stratified secondary school system in Britain, in contrast, lacks such a sorting function. This should lead to less favourable returns in general, but should also make the impact of higher education expansion more severe. The following table summarises these country-specific stratification patterns:

5.2 Occupational Specificity: Generalist and Specialist Curricular Orientations

The concept of stratification helps to explain why and how labour market outcomes are stratified vertically. But higher education systems vary also in the extent to which they offer curricula that are designed to prepare students for particular occupations or professions and award occupationally specific credentials. Originally designed for cross-national comparisons of vocational training, the concept of occupational specificity classifies systems as providing either fairly general training or more specific occupational training as a result of different linkages established between education and employment systems. In the field of VET, the German apprenticeship system has for a long time been the cross-national role model for effectively training young people for and integrating them into the labour market. Britain has lacked such an occupation-specific training system, which is why youth labour market entry has been more turbulent, marked by a higher prevalence of unemployment and sequences of stop-gap jobs.[29]

These country-specific differences of occupation-specific training might exist in the field of higher education as well. However, measurement of the concept at this education level requires some adaptation, since no clear-cut occupation-specific entity such as an apprenticeship exists. Arguably, the most important factor for determining the occupational specificity of a country's higher education system is the analysis of different fields of study, which can directly be examined in relation to the occupation-specific content taught and the applicability of knowledge for the labour market. Generally speaking, this is very much the case in Germany, where the respective field of study strongly determines the possible range of occupations to work in. In Britain, in contrast, enrolment in a certain field of study traditionally has not been perceived to be a clear decision for a certain occupational area (Teichler 1999: 32). Occupational specificity is also indicated by the incorporation of practical training phases in particular degree courses or by the extent to which particular degree types or fields of study are the necessary prerequisites for work in particular occupations. In addition, the general principles underpinning higher education are considered important empirical indicators of occupational specificity. In the following sections, all dimensions of institutional differentiation will be analysed as regards the importance of occupation-specific training. As a starting point, the general objectives associated with higher education in both countries are described, which already indicate how the link between higher education and labour market is perceived in Germany and Britain.

5.2.1 Historical Frames: Professional vs. Liberal Higher Education

German and British higher education systems have emerged from very different historical traditions as regards the applicability of knowledge for labour market purposes and the training of occupation-specific skills. The ideas associated with higher education in both countries can be traced back to the very beginnings of university establishment in Europe in the 12th and 13th centuries. At this time, the two first universities in Europe were founded in Bologna and Paris. These new types of education institutions offered certificates and credentials and thus provided the first form of organised higher education. However, the focus of both universities could not have been more diverse. While the University of Bologna specialised in the education of law and, to a lesser extent, in medicine, i.e. professional knowledge, the University of Paris had a focus on general education by specialising in courses of the *artes liberales*, such as philosophy, theology,

---

29   For a short description of German and British vocational training systems see Appendix D.

logic, or astronomy (see Moraw 2005; Verger 1993 for the following). These different directions of higher education can be explained by different historical circumstances that accompanied the foundation of universities in both cities.

The institutionalisation of higher education in Bologna was stimulated by the ongoing emancipation of Italian merchants from the overall dominance of the Catholic Church in educational matters. In order to gain more political power, independent of Christian sovereignty, and to improve the knowledge about successfully governing the flourishing merchant cities of Northern Italy, the focus of university education tended to be on applicable knowledge. The aim was to educate young men from the nobility for leading positions in public administration, and studying law was considered to be the best preparation to this end. In France, the Catholic Church still had a monopoly in educational matters. Higher education at the University of Paris was not aimed at professional training at all, but rather to develop the intellect and the personality of the young noblesse by educating them in the subjects of the *trivium* (grammar, rhetoric, logic) and to a lower extent of the *quadrivium* (arithmetic, geometry, astronomy, music) as a preparation for a clerical career (Leff 1993). In cooperation with the Catholic Church, the University of Paris provided this general and liberal education and soon became the intellectual centre of Europe. In this regard, it is important to note that in contrast to the legal education provided by the University of Bologna, the study of *artes liberales* was provided at an undergraduate level as preparation for the study of theology (Moraw 2005: 32).

After the foundation of these first two universities – the question which is the older one remains unsolved and disputed – other regions in Europe started to adopt this principle of formal higher education through universities. In England, the first universities, those of Oxford and Cambridge, were founded soon after Paris and Bologna. Both universities evolved as private bodies during the thirteenth century and followed the French tradition of liberal education specifically by focussing on philosophy and arts to prepare their students for careers in either the Church or, to a much lower extent, in public administration (Moraw 1993). Rather than preparing their students for particular professions, the "civil conversion of the gentleman" was the most prominent idea behind these early forms of higher education in Britain. The predominance of such a liberal education at the undergraduate level and the importance of personal development rather than professional education remains a distinct feature of higher education in Britain today. Professional training remained outside the British university system for a long time, even though a small minority of institutions, such as the Inns of Court (law) and Royal Colleges of Medicine and Surgery, became increasingly important as providers of professional training and regulation of competence starting in the Middle Ages. Over the centuries, governments promoted the teaching of science, technology and advanced vocational training at universities, and occasionally even offered financial aid for their development, but nevertheless professional training remained mainly a private enterprise. It was not until the 19th century that major public universities were founded in England, Wales and Northern Ireland, which included the more applied disciplines into their fields of study (Smith and Langslow 1999).[30]

The foundation of university institutions in Germany started later than in Britain, during the 14th century. Erfurt was the first university to be founded in 1379 on what is today German territory (Verger 1993). The principle adopted was quite different to the established traditions, because it combined both types of university existing so far, the more professionally oriented and the more liberal one in a single higher education institution (Moraw 2005). For the next centuries, until the development of disciplines in the modern sense, four faculties prevailed at German universities: theology, law, medicine and the liberal arts. Due to the incorporation of two traditions, the aim of higher education was twofold: to educate administrative personnel for government and society, and to promote students' personal development. Based on this dualism, the student population at German universities consisted of two separate groups, each of them with specific study preferences and labour market outcomes. Students born in nobility, on the one hand, predominantly focussed on the professionally-oriented subjects such as law or medicine and thereafter pursued careers in the upper levels of public administration or as doctors. Students from the lower or middle *Bürgertum*, in contrast, preferred to study liberal arts. After finishing university, they mainly returned to the region where they were born without having such explicit career prospects, many of them working in their fathers' craft, as clergy for the Church, or as writers in regional administrations (Moraw 1993). These origins are still in place at German universities nowadays, which should have major implications for the labour market entry of higher education graduates.

Comparing the university development in Britain and in Germany from its very beginning, history shows that both countries (or the regions that later became those countries) followed quite different paths regarding aims and objectives of higher education. While England adopted the ideal of a liberal education originating from the French tradition, Germany combined general

---

30 University education in Scotland also has a long, but very different history. Four universities – St Andrews, Glasgow, Aberdeen and Edinburgh, known collectively as the "four ancient Scottish universities" - were founded in the 15th and 16th centuries. From their beginnings, these higher education institutions concentrated from the beginning more on applied subjects than their English counterparts and stressed the importance of professional training, mainly to offer an alternative to the traditional universities of Oxford and Cambridge. Most of today's Scottish higher education institutions tend to specialise in particular areas, for example in teacher education, arts and architecture, or health care, and in addition offer a broad range of vocationally orientated subjects at all levels.

and professional education by establishing the four faculty university. For centuries, professional training in England was not at all connected to university education, since its major function was to form the personality of the predominantly noble student body attending Oxford and Cambridge. And even though English universities adopted some of the professional principles, their focus on the liberal arts still remains an important component of undergraduate education today, especially at traditional universities. In Germany, in contrast, a dual-type university in terms of content and student body existed from the very beginning. Professional training always had constituted an integral part of German university education, even though Wilhelm von Humboldt explicitly tried to overcome the focus on applicable skills by advocating for the importance of general knowledge conferred through universities (Ellwein 1985; Humboldt 1956). Both traditions of university education, the liberal education as well as the integration of general and applied professional disciplines into one single university, continue to exist are still existent today in Germany and Britain, strongly influencing the importance of occupation-specific training by higher education institutions.

5.2.2 General Objectives of Higher Education Institutions

These historical ideas associated with higher education are still in place today. German higher education places a much stronger emphasis on professional education and the applicability of knowledge, while British institutions still advocate the principle of a liberal education with a focus on more general skills, particular at the undergraduate level. In Germany, the importance of occupational specificity is indicated by the purpose of study at higher education institutions. According to the Framework Act for Higher Education, study at both universities and *Fachhochschulen* has to "prepare for occupational tasks that require the application of scientific and methodological knowledge or the ability of artistic expression" (BMBF 2002, §1, author's translation). In addition, the legislative framework requires "postsecondary education [to] prepare students for a particular field of occupation and to teach them the specific knowledge, skills and methods of the respective degree course, in order to enable them to perform scientific or artistic work and to act responsibly in a free, democratic and social state governed by the rule of law" (BMBF 2002, §1, author's translation).[31] Thus,

---

31 „Sie [Die Hochschulen] bereiten auf berufliche Tätigkeiten vor, die die Anwendung wissenschaftlicher Erkenntnisse und wissenschaftlicher Methoden oder die Fähigkeit zu künstlerischer Gestaltung erfordern" (BMBF 2002, § 1). „Lehre und Studium sollen die Studierenden auf ein berufliches Tätigkeitsfeld vorbereiten und ihnen die dafür erforderlichen fachlichen Kenntnisse, Fähigkeiten und Methoden dem jeweiligen Studiengang entsprechend so vermitteln, dass sie zu wissenschaftlicher oder künstlerischer Arbeit und zu

training for particular occupations or professions is an integral part of study at any German higher education institution, irrespective of types of degrees and fields of study.

While this basic principle applies to both universities and *Fachhochschulen*, the former differ from the latter in that their education has traditionally been closely linked to basic and theoretical research and accordingly considered to teach abstract and general knowledge rather than applicable skills. But despite this emphasis on theory, there are several measures offered at universities to ensure that their students receive an occupation-specific training. First of all, proof of work experience (from four to six months, in some cases even up to a year) acquired before or while studying is required in a large variety of fields, especially in the natural and engineering sciences. To improve the employment prospects of humanities graduates whose field of study, being more general in nature, tend not to prepare students for specific occupations other than a career in academia, a lot of university institutions have set up programmes in collaboration with employment offices to equip these students with key skills during their studies (for example a grounding in computing or elementary business skills) and to place them in industry thereafter. Additionally, many universities offer programmes designed to prepare students for self-employment and to encourage them to set up their own businesses. In this regard, it is also helpful that the universities' student counselling offices and the employment offices' career guidance services furnish information and guidance to help graduates move from higher education into the labour market (Eurydice 2006).

The importance of occupational specificity is even more pronounced at *Fachhochschulen*. Emphasis on the practical applicability of knowledge and specific reference to labour market requirements are characteristic features of the design of these degree courses and of the organisation of teaching and studying at this type of higher education institution. The purpose of occupation-specific training is served chiefly by incorporating one or two semesters of practical training within a business enterprise into every degree course offered (*Praxissemester*). Furthermore, it is quite common for students to derive their final thesis topic from problems they encountered during these training semesters. Some theses are even prepared in collaboration with industry and trade. All of these measures help students gain applied knowledge and insights into their field of specialisation and to establish contacts with prospective employers before graduating. The fact that teaching staff and course contents at *Fachhochschulen* are linked with applied research and development projects is also important for a high degree of occupation-specific training. Taken together, measures offered at

---

verantwortlichem Handeln in einem freiheitlichen, demokratischen und sozialen Rechtsstaat befähigt werden" (BMBF 2002, § 7).

universities and *Fachhochschulen* indicate a high importance of occupation-specific training provided at German higher education institutions. Though there are differences between universities and *Fachhochschulen* as to their extent and scope, their overall focus clearly points in the direction of the applicability of knowledge and close links to the labour market. As a consequence, German higher education can be characterised by a high degree of occupational specificity. Higher education students should face few problems in obtaining a job matching their qualification after graduation. Yet, intra-national variations in this regard might exist as well. On the one hand, *Fachhochschulen* degrees might lead to even closer matches between credentials and occupations as compared to university degrees. In contrast, more general fields of study such as the arts or the humanities should make it more difficult to find a matching job.

In Britain, in contrast, the concept of an education that provides training in abstract thought and that values knowledge for its own sake has always formed part of the rationale behind higher education. For example, the Robbins Report (1963) specified four aims for higher education: instruction in skills suitable to play a part in the general division of labour; promoting the general powers of the mind; the advancement of learning; and the transmission of a common culture and common standards of citizenship. Only the first aim is directly geared towards labour market requirements, while all other three emphasise the general benefits of higher education, both for personal development and for participation in society. Interestingly, most White Papers and higher education acts over the past decades rarely mention the need to train British students for particular occupations. Rather, they are responding to general problems of mass higher education in relation to study organisation, funding of students and universities, or quality control.

The most recent definition of British higher education was given by the 1988 Education Reform Act in Section 120, which describes higher education as 'education provided by means of a course of any description mentioned in Schedule 6 of the Act', that is, 'a course of a standard higher than the standard of courses leading to General Certificate of Education Advanced-level (GCE A-level) or Business and Technology Education Council National Diploma or Certificate'. The courses listed include the ones already introduced in the section on institutional differentiation by type of degree, such as first degree courses, postgraduate courses (including higher degree courses, courses for the Diploma of Higher Education, courses for the Higher National Diploma (HND) or Higher National Certificate (HNC), courses for the Certificate in Education granting Qualified Teacher Status in Britain, or courses in preparation for a professional examination at a higher-level. Only the last two explicitly refer to professional training, while the others are more general in nature.

The fact that liberal education and personal growth remain important principles in British higher education to this day can also be seen in the Dearing Report (1997) and in the Green Paper 'The Learning Age' (DfEE 1998), in which the British Government sets out its strategy for lifelong learning. The Dearing Report again stresses the intellectual and cultural purposes of higher education and states that higher education should aim to sustain a learning society through the intellectual development of individuals. Higher education should increase individuals' knowledge and understanding both for their own sake and for the sake of the economy and society. The Government's Green Paper (1998) argues in a similar manner, advocating for the major principle that anyone who has the capability for higher education should have the opportunity to benefit from it. Current objectives for higher education stress increasing and widening participation and improving standards and quality of teaching and learning (DfEE 1998).

But despite the persistent emphasis on general knowledge and personal development rather than occupation-specific skills, labour market requirements have nevertheless gained more importance for British higher education. A first step was, as already mentioned, the introduction of polytechnics to advance industrial skills on a part- or full-time basis and to link higher education with industry and businesses (DES 1966). But since the 1980s in particular, occupational requirements have become more relevant for higher education policy making. The Government's 1985 Green Paper on higher education stated that the design and content of courses should become more occupation-oriented by seeking advice from employers (DfE 1985). Most institutions responded to this advice by re-designing courses to take employers' needs into account. More occupational courses have been introduced and the curriculum for more general courses has been adapted to cover key skills such as information and communication technology. Statistics showed that in 1994, occupation-specific training was the fastest growing area of British higher education (DfE 1994). The Dearing Report also recognised the part played by higher education in preparing students for work and recommended that institutions should seek to increase work experience for students (Dearing Report 1997).

Today, sandwich courses are the main means for students to combine course work with work experience, but many higher education institutions now also offer opportunities for students to gain work experience as part of their degree. In addition, many employers regularly visit higher education institutions to give students the opportunity to discuss possibilities for employment. Much work is now on the way in this area, and funding has been provided by the Higher Education Quality and Employability Division of the DfEE for research and development projects to improve graduate employability. The latest reforms in particular, passed by the Labour Party elected in 1997, signalled a significant shift in the aims and functions of higher education. In the 2003 White Paper and the resulting Higher Education Bill (2004), the Blair Government repeatedly stressed the point that higher education is to improve national economics by tightening the connection between higher education, employment, productivity and trade, and furthermore, to enhance student outcomes in employment-related skills and competencies (DfES 2003). Thus, the British development is two-folded. Even though legislation on higher education continues to emphasise the importance of more general skills and personal development, the necessity to respond to labour market needs has become more apparent, particularly during the 1990s. Nevertheless, the long historical tradition of liberal higher education is still in place. This should strongly influence the types of jobs obtained after graduation, leading to a lower match between higher education credentials and occupational outcomes. But intra-national differences might be in place as well, resulting in better matches of graduates with occupation-specific postgraduate degrees and degrees in more applied fields of study. The more detailed discussion of training for particular occupational groups will give further information in this regard.

5.2.3 Occupation-specific Training of Different Types of Degrees and Fields of Study

The clear-cut differences between the importance of professional training in Germany and the focus on liberal education in Britain becomes even more apparent if particular types of degrees and fields of study are examined in more detail. The training of professionals, the training of engineers, and the training of managers serve as examples in this regard. This analysis again shows the tight connection between higher education and labour market requirements in Germany and the rather loose one in Britain.

The Training of Professionals

There is a longstanding sociological tradition to define a profession as an occupational group which, based on its claim to expert knowledge, enjoys a high degree of work autonomy, in return for professional self-regulation. But only recent years have seen a rising interest in the history of the professions in different countries. Cross-national research on professional development strikingly reveals that most of the established professions within a particular country developed in a similar way; however, national paths differ substantially. Especially Britain and Germany have had radically different historical trajectories of the evolution of professional systems (Abbott 1988). In Britain, the classical professions of law and medicine claimed their autonomy from the government as early as in the early 17th century and thereby defined and circumscribed the role of the liberal state. In Germany, in contrast, autocratic rulers, both before and after national unification in 1871, incorporated the equivalent occupations into the state and defined the professional service as public service (Lane et al. 2000; Neal and Morgan 2000). As a consequence, the professions in Britain developed independently from the state, being the result of voluntary association. In Germany, in contrast, the state has played – and continues to play – an active role in the establishment, structuring and administration of the professions.

The different historical trajectories have implications for the acquisition of professional qualifications. Since in Britain, the formation of independent professions preceded the secure establishment of higher education, professional autonomy has also meant control over education and training, accreditation, awarding of professional credentials, and admission to the professions (Lane et al. 2000). Even though academic routes were established in the course of development, only some of the professions, like those in medicine and teaching and recently, engineering, moved into the universities within the framework of a three to four year study programme (Lane 1989). Nowadays, universities in general provide a range of professionally accredited degree courses including engineering, accountancy, teacher training, librarianship and information science and medical studies. In particular some of the postgraduate degrees aim at teaching applicable knowledge for professional life (for example LLM for lawyers or MSc for engineers). However, qualifications specific to a profession and required for practice as a chartered member of the professional association still have to be obtained upon completion of a postgraduate degree, often through successfully completing further examination designed or accredited by professional bodies, such as the Chartered Institute of Public Finance and Accountancy and the Council of Legal Education. The 'new' universities, most of which were previously polytechnics, generally offer a wider range of courses leading to qualifications recognised by professional institutions. But despite these recent developments, it has been a characteristic of the British system of professions that professional associations remain to a large extent responsible for training future professionals. It is still true that no higher education qualification awards an automatic right to employment in a given profession.

In Germany, in contrast, independent professions only arose when the university system was well established. Hence, professional education has been firmly in the hands of the state-regulated higher education system (Lane et al. 2000). In the beginning, this was particularly true for potential state servants such as lawyers, but during the early nineteenth century universities gradually expanded the professional subjects, introducing new academic degrees for areas considered desirable for the state. Until today, the purpose of studying at German higher education institutions is to prepare students for a profession in a certain sphere of activity (BMBF 2002). Professional qualifications are conferred on the basis of examinations from universities and *Fachhochschulen*. At universities, professional training for the public sector is closely connected with a specific degree, the *Staatsexamen* as well as with particular fields of study. State examinations prepare students for professions of public importance, such as medicine, dentistry, veterinary medicine, pharmaceutics, food chemistry, law and the teaching profession (Eurydice 2006). An essential difference between state and other academic degrees taught at universities is the incorporation of practical training into courses with state examinations. The first state examination (*Erstes Staatsexamen*), which takes place after the theoretical part of studies, entitles students to work in the private sector only. Prospective public professionals, however, undergo an additional phase of practical training called preparatory service (*Vorbereitungsdienst*), which is concluded by a second state examination (*Zweites Staatsexamen*). Only this second examination grants them the right to practise their profession within the public service. Overall, the university in Germany and its close relationship to the state played a crucial role in the development of the German professions (MacDonald 1995). Professional associations, in contrast, neither have a direct influence on the content of training and accreditation nor on the number of new entrants into the profession.

Overall, the link between the professions and higher education in Britain and Germany has not only differed in terms of prevalence, power, and influence of professional associations, but also in terms of their level of integration within the state. In Britain, professional associations to a large extent rationalise and control professional education and training. Even though today, the state-controlled higher education system offers professional training in some postgraduate degree courses, the licence to practice is still bound to further examinations by professional bodies. Institutionally, the university system therefore cannot be considered to be complementary to the system of professions, since occupation-specific training predominantly takes place outside, previous examples notwithstanding. In Germany, it is the government that prescribes and sanctions the kind of training required for entry into established or new professions. Higher education is thus complementary to the systems of professions, since higher education degrees form the necessary prerequisite for entrance. A further interesting perspective in this regard is offered by Hage (2000) in his analysis of institutional path dependencies of elite education in Germany and Britain. By looking at the historical nature of elite education, he argues that country-specific features influence the professional division of labour by means of the relative emphasis on generalist vs. specialist education. In this respect German and British higher education are both specialised, but in quite different ways. While the Germans emphasise scientific and technical knowledge relevant to professions, British elite education is more disconnected from the British professions: most people who are trained in elite schools do not enter the professional system, but work in public administration or business. Thus British professionals are also specialised but much more frequently not trained in elite higher education. Instead they have moved up via the organisational chain of command and have started with various professional diplomas (Hage 2000).

The tight coupling between higher education and professions in Germany and the self-regulation and independence of the British professions can again be taken as an indicators of the fact that higher education is more occupation-specific in Germany than in Britain. At the same time, latest developments in Britain again point to strong intra-national differences as well. In both countries, particular degrees such as the German *Staatsexamen* or some British postgraduate degrees can be considered more occupation-specific than others. Furthermore, professional fields of study such as medicine or teacher training should lead to closer matches between higher education credentials and occupational outcomes.

The Training of Engineers

The historical development and present educational, occupational and social profile of the engineering profession also differs substantially between Germany and Britain. To begin with, in Germany the term 'engineer' has always been defined and protected by the government and referred to as a profession. In Britain, in contrast, it has remained a more ambiguous term, encompassing a range of occupational positions, from mechanics to university-trained engineers (Lane 1989). One major reason for the difference in legal status and association of engineers with the nation state is the historical institutionalisation of the training of engineers. Germany began to introduce formally organised technical education in the early decades of the 19th century, when technical universities were founded in Karlsruhe and Berlin (Ellwein 1985). Even though initially, such a technically oriented higher education was regarded as inferior to the emphasis on research at traditional universities, a technical university system, which could rival the rest of the German higher education sector both in terms of academic excellence and social status, began to emerge after these early beginnings.

In Britain, in contrast, the idea of a scientific education for those in technical occupations gained acceptance at a much later date. It was only after the 1851 Great Exhibition in London – which demonstrated the technical superiority of Britain's continental rivals – that the scientific education of engineers began to be organised formally (Lane 1989). The educational routes leading to the title 'engineer' had been very diverse well into the 1980s, and there has not been a clear distinction between graduates of vocational training schemes and higher education graduates with degrees in engineering. In general, the number of professional engineers in Britain, their level of expertise, and their social status has never been as high as in Germany.

Today, these different historical developments continue to have an impact on the training, level of competence and resulting status of the engineering profession in both countries. In Germany, engineering is considered a very prestigious occupation, and the salary of a senior engineer is higher than that of a civil servant or university professor (Briedis and Minks 2004; Kerst and Minks 2003). To qualify as an engineer, students can either graduate from universities after five or six years with a more theoretical orientation, or at the *Fachhochschulen*, which train the lower-level engineers during four years of study with a focus on applied knowledge. Engineering at higher education institutions in Germany is both independent from, and equal in status to science.

In Britain, until the mid 1980s, only a small number of engineers had been trained in universities, while the majority were former craft-workers and technicians who studied on a part-time basis at technical colleges and former polytechnics for Higher National Certificates and Higher National Diplomas (Mason 2000). This made them eligible for the title of Chartered Engineer, just as university graduates are today. Since then, British engineering education has been extensively reformed in an effort to raise standards and status and to make it more relevant to industry. A three to four year university degree has now become the normal entry route for aspiring engineers and is the precondition for the status of a Chartered Engineer. Despite these changes and although there has been an increase in engineering graduates their proportion remains small, both in comparison with German engineers and with graduates in arts and social sciences subjects.

In Germany, the education of engineers has traditionally shown a close link between higher education and labour market requirements in Germany–This linkage has for a long time been looser in Britain. The particular view on engineering as a profession and the introduction of an occupation-specific training during the 19th century indicates that higher education institutions have the important function of training students for particular occupational fields in Germany. This should yield a close match between higher education credentials in engineering and type of job acquired after graduation in Germany. In Britain, the rather unstandardised training options for engineers outside higher education shows that such an occupation-specific training was not considered to be important for a long time. Only recently has the training of engineers become part of the subject canon of higher education institutions, indicating the same shift in British education policy towards more applied knowledge, as pointed out above. Nevertheless, occupation-specific training has not been the major emphasis of British higher education, which should lead to lower matches between higher education and labour market outcomes.

The Training of Managers

More striking differences between Germany and Britain can be found when comparing the training of managers. Even though in everyday language the term 'manager' encompasses a lot of meanings, managers may be defined as individuals occupying positions of leadership within an organisation, required to carry out tasks such as policy formulation, work organisation and coordination, quality assurance or performance control. Since the word is of Anglo-American origin, it has entered German usage only in recent decades, where it still coexists, and competes with, the German title *Unternehmer* (entrepreneur) or *Geschäftsführer* (CEO). Both terms have different social and organisational implications, because the latter mainly refers to the top of the business hierarchy rather than to any leadership position, be it at lower or upper hierarchical level, as it is the case in Anglo-Saxon countries (Lane 1989).

In both countries, the larger companies today choose their future top and higher-level managers predominantly from among higher education graduates. However, there are substantial differences in degree level and subject of higher education, partly as a legacy of past practice, since German firms have chosen their managers from among graduates for a much longer time than British companies. Generally speaking, British managers at all levels are more likely to have professional management qualifications gained outside higher education at colleges of further education or from professional institutes. Furthermore, a sizeable proportion of British managers has come up from the ranks and possesses no management qualification at all. If managers possess a higher education degree, a more general field of study is the norm, and managers with a background in arts are still common. Only in recent years has there been a steady increase in the intake of graduates with management or business degrees and more people with engineering and science qualifications have moved into management, but they remain very often in non-managerial positions (Lane 1989).

In Germany, managers may come up from the ranks as well, but top and senior managers in large firms are now predominantly graduates from either universities or *Fachhochschulen*. Since the Anglo-Saxon concept of management as a unified profession has only started to become accepted, no general management education exists. Rather, executive staff members are specialists in a certain field who have taken on extra responsibility by executing some of the management functions. This is mirrored by the field of study held by German managers. The majority of them possess a degree in engineering or science which has a strong occupational component and

138

includes an internship in industry, particularly at the *Fachhochschulen*. To enable them to move into top management positions, engineers often receive in-house training in basic economics, accounting, and computing skills. A high proportion of top managers hold a doctorate as well, again usually in science or engineering. Many managers at all levels have also completed an apprenticeship and had a vocational qualification, which, unlike in Britain is highly valued by employers (Briedis and Minks 2004; Kerst and Minks 2003).

To sum up, scientific and technical knowledge, i.e. occupation-specific training obtained in higher education is a necessary prerequisite to acquire management positions in Germany. British management education is more general in content and on the whole more disconnected from higher education, because most managers have moved up the ranks, acquiring necessary qualifications part-time while already pursuing their careers. This again seems to be in line with the assumption that institutional links between higher education and management training in Germany are much more pronounced, since they strengthen the notion of occupation-specific education. In Britain, a rather generalist education still is the norm and British companies seem to put a stronger emphasis on personal qualities than occupation-specific knowledge.

5.2.4 Professional and Liberal Orientations in German and British Higher Education

The institutional analysis of occupational specificity has shown that in higher education systems, occupation-specific training is strongly associated with different types of institutions, certain types of degrees, and particular fields of study. German higher education can be characterised as placing a strong emphasis on occupational specificity, while in Britain general skills also play an important role.

On the whole, higher education in Germany shows a clear occupational orientation: this characteristic is prevalent not only at *Fachhochschulen* which set their aim explicitly on in the preparation for occupations, but also at universities, where the courses tend to be specific for future professions and the relationships between study fields and occupations are usually strong. The system of state examinations, through which the members of professions and public offices are recruited, connects university study with occupations rather directly. Professional subjects such as health or law, but also engineering exhibit a high degree of occupational specificity. Furthermore, the degrees *Staatsexamen* and *Fachhochschul-Diplom* are designed to prepare students for specific occupations. This should result in short transition phases to occupations matching the higher education credential.

But the German higher education system generally features a higher degree of occupational specificity than the British one, due to the historical development and the overall ideas associated with higher education. Thus, the level of matching credential and occupational outcome should generally be much higher than in Britain, even for rather unspecific subjects such as the humanities and the arts. However, the historical divide between occupation-specific and more general higher education at German institutions might remain prevalent today and is therefore likely to result in within-country differences.

Table 5: Occupational specificity and the matching of students to jobs

	Germany	Britain
Overall degree of occupational specificity	High → close match between higher education credentials and occupation	Low → weak match between higher education credentials and occupation
Occupation-specific degrees	*Staatsexamen, Fachhochschul-Diplom* → better match	Postgraduate degrees → better match
Occupation-specific subjects	Health, teaching, law, engineering → better match	Health, teaching, law, engineering → better match

The British higher education system historically lacks such a tight coupling between specific subjects and occupations, even though it has become much tighter in recent years. Therefore, the match between higher education and occupations should be lower than in Germany, and students with the same degrees are likely to work in a larger variety of jobs. But in Britain, too, the more professionally oriented fields of study, such as medicine, teaching, or engineering should be more closely associated with matching employment positions. In addition, some postgraduate MA degrees are designed to prepare for specific occupations. The overall degree of occupation specific training is nevertheless considered to be much lower due to the historically loose coupling between higher education and professions. Overall, obtaining a job in an occupation matching the higher education credential should be generally less common. The following table summarises the expectations related to varying degrees of occupational specificity.

5.3   Graduate Labour Market Segmentation: Between Professional and Public Spheres

The notion of labour market segmentation implies that the labour market is divided into several segments, all of which offer specific career prospects. It is assumed that a country's labour market is differentiated into distinct sectors or segments characterised by a high degree of social closure. This closure is based on specific certificates serving as a necessary precondition for entering a particular segment as well as specific allocation principles and career structures serving as a means for maintaining segmental closure and to prohibit mobility between the segments (Kalleberg and Sorensen 1979). In internal labour markets, employees are assumed to enter at specific entry positions and thereafter pursue their careers at least partly protected from market competition by following specific career ladders and opportunities for promotion. Recruitment from external labour market ideally takes place only once, when external applicants are employed for a restricted number of specific "entry-jobs".

The analysis of graduate labour markets focuses on the institutional organisation of different labour market segments, namely the professions and the public sector. Both have been identified as two types of internal labour markets, the former representing OLMs and the latter ILMs. If they are important segments for graduate careers, higher education credentials should form the prerequisite for entry, and career development should be strongly sheltered from the market. In this regard, the major focus will be placed on the degree of social closure inherent to these labour market segments in both countries. In systems with strong internal labour markets, shelter from market dynamics should be high, which, as a consequence, will lead to more stable and predictable career prospects of higher education graduates.

5.3.1 Higher Education and the Social Closure of Professional Labour Markets

The major distinction between occupations and professions lies in the different degree of social closure resulting from their specific knowledge base. Differences in power among occupational groups reflect differences in the ability of occupations to defend themselves against the incursions of others and to maintain or obtain advantages with respect to a variety of labour market outcomes. Professions can be considered as the most exclusive occupational group in this regard. Striving to achieve professional status has therefore always provided a motivation for members of occupational groups to gain a higher degree of independence and social closure. Research on the jurisdiction of professions suggests that professions have developed a set of boundaries which define the characteristics of potential entrants, allocate the tasks and activities of the profession vis á vis other occupations, and control the supply of professional labour through licensing and credentialing (Abbott 1988; Heidenreich 1999). The main source of professional power stems from their control of professional knowledge and skills particularly through certification requirements. The different linkages between higher education and professional labour markets in Germany and Britain are largely the result of different historical trajectories in the development of professions in both countries, which will be explored in the following. At the same time, these national forms of professional regulation have important consequences for the organisation of professional labour markets. The following sections will pay more attention to the relationship between professions and the state and the resulting degree of social closure for professional labour markets.

The Historical Relation between Professional Governance and the State

The major difference between German and British professions is related to the importance of state regulation. German professions are largely state-regulated, and the individual professional chambers are subject to statutory supervision. In contrast, British professions were for a long time largely self-regulated by professional bodies, with hardly any interference by the Government (Abbott 1988; Lane et al. 2000; Neal and Morgan 2000). Both trajectories are a legacy of history, according to which German professionalisation has been the result of state intervention, while development in Britain has been more spontaneous and driven by professional self-interest.

In Germany, the non-existence of an overarching civil service during the 19th century laid the foundation for the establishment of professions (Lane et al. 2000; Neal and Morgan 2000). Germany was not united until 1871 and even then consisted of 25 individual states, each having different political and cultural characteristics. German rulers of these states had wide-ranging authority and powers as compared to the federal government. They were at this time supported by a well trained but authoritarian civil service, which was largely the result of Napoleon's reform in Germany closely mirroring the French administrative structure. These involved reforms of many key institutions in the German states, such as the school system, the church, the legal system, and the establishment of expert ministries supported by a professional civil service. As a result, bureaucratic authorities and professions developed hand in hand in Germany. Autocratic rulers, both before and after 1871, incorporated professions such as law, medicine, or teaching, into the state and defined professional service as public service. At the same time, the lack of a central legislative authority was a serious deterrent to the development of fully independent associations, as were common in the Anglo-Saxon world at that time. National professional organisations could not evolve until the late 19th century, and even then, strong regional differences were maintained.

In Britain, the development of the British Empire and the beginning of the Industrial Revolution led to the rapid expansion of a wealthy middle class and early demand for all types of professional expertise in the 17th century

(Lane et al. 2000; Neal and Morgan 2000). Early professions such as legal advice in setting up commercial enterprises, accountancy, or auditing work, started to organise and professionalise at the national level without state interference. The laissez-faire policies of successive British governments in the 19th century further enabled and encouraged the emerging occupations to organise themselves in order to fend off competitors. For self-interested reasons, these groups were highly motivated to achieve social closure: to gain self-determination, and to establish barriers against to entry by related occupations. In direct contrast to Germany, social status did not come from state recognition, but from being a member of the relatively independent professional classes. Establishing professional associations was seen as way for members to follow an established route to success, sheltered from free competition, which would exert a downward pressure on prices and services (Neal and Morgan 2000).

This legacy of the past substantially influenced the development of professions in both countries and ensured their social closure. This was done by different means, however. Even today, the government regulates professional activity in Germany through laws, while in Britain regulation is rarely issued from parliament, and self-regulation through professional associations is more common. The most important difference in this regard is again related to professional training, since German legal regulation secured monopolies of occupational knowledge and practice at higher education institutions, while the British Parliament only protects the occupational title and usually has no control over occupational training. In this regard, the previous sections have already shown that in Germany the government continues to be largely responsible for professional education and admittance to the professions. Entry to high status professional positions is usually gained by means of higher education credentials. In Britain, in contrast, professional associations remain responsible for professional education, even though in the course of development some academic routes have been established. Thus, particular types of higher education credentials should be more important for German entry-ports to the respective profession than British ones. This should be strongly the case for the *Staatsexamen*, but also for specific fields of study such as health or education. At the same time, entry into the professions should occur much earlier after graduation in Germany than in Britain, since no additional entry certificates have to be obtained from professional associations.

The close link between higher education and the professions in Germany and the dominance of professional training outside higher education by professional associations in Britain can be considered a direct consequence of the different historical trajectories. However, the traditional British state-professional relationship has been radically transformed since the early 1980s. Margaret Thatcher introduced reforms that served to eliminate some of the self-regulatory advantage that British professions previously enjoyed, since the British Government has come to doubt that self-governing professions will act in the public interest. Hence, a succession of Acts from 1984 onwards have introduced the dual mechanisms of increasing market competition and more external supervision into the British system of professions, which strongly weakened the social closure of professional labour markets. The different boundaries established by professions in both countries to keep out competitors and the latest developments in Britain in this regard will be described in the following section.

The Social Closure of Professional Labour Markets

In both countries, markets for professional services have traditionally been highly protected, providing professions with either a market shelter or a cartel-like arrangement and more rarely with a genuine monopoly. As a result of recent reforms in Britain, however, the principle of uncontrolled professional self-governance has increasingly been questioned since the 1980s by the introduction of market elements such as increasing competition, more external quality assurance and cost containment (Lane et al. 2000). As a consequence, attitudes towards market regulation and what is deemed a legitimate suspension of competition have become more diverse between the British and German system.

Professional labour markets in Germany have always been sheltered almost completely from competition by various legal arrangements (Lane et al. 2000). By and large, suspension of competition has been much more prevalent, more effectively enforced and more legitimate in Germany than in Britain. The many regulations in restraint of competition regarding the activities of professions are still in place and not in danger of being revoked. For example, German lawyers still enjoy a legally enshrined virtual monopoly in all legal matters, laid down by the Law on Legal Advice and Legal Activity. At the same time, methods of calculating fees for professional services are still largely regulated by law. Only recently, external competition has started to emerge, when law practices opened up to related professions with similar constitutions, such as accountants. Furthermore, intra-professional competition has become more severe in the labour market of lawyers through steadily rising numbers of graduates moving in. But even in the course of higher education expansion in Germany, unemployment among new law graduates is not substantively higher than among professionals in general, and absolute figures are low (Lane et al. 2004). Overall, German professions still enjoy a high degree of market shelter closely representing occupational labour market characteristics. The only exception to this is the trend that fixed-term employment has risen considerably among German professionals, particularly in the law profession, but also in academia. But despite this development, career development of German professionals should closely follow an internal labour market pattern. Entry into this segment of the labour market should be strongly based on higher education credentials. Career mobility should largely proceed within the professional domain, and little mobility out of the segment should occur.

Although the British professions have been exempted from some aspects of the Competition Act (1998), they have nevertheless have become more and more exposed to a high degree of inter- and intra-professional competition. Governmental efforts to secure cost containment have also put limits on professionals' endeavour to determine their own levels of rewards. While these measures of increased external supervision and direct intervention began under the Thatcher government, Labour has continued this interventionist policy. These moves towards state-circumscribed self-government in combination with attempted marketisation and cost-cutting of publicly financed service in British professions have strongly reduced the social closure of the professional labour market traditionally secured by professional bodies. As a consequence, British professionals have experienced a dramatic increase in potential and actual competition from other professions and non-professionalised occupations. It is even argued that the traditional boundaries between various professional services are crumbling and will completely disappear (Lane 2000). Graduate career mobility in Britain should be less predetermined by the professional labour market segment. Due to the weak linkage between higher education and professions it should it be less common to directly enter the professions immediately after graduation. But even if entry has been successful, movements out of this segment should be more pronounced as a result of increasing marketisation.

In summary, the tight coupling between the state and the professions in Germany, and the self-regulation and increasing market competition in the British system of professions can be considered as empirical indicators of the fact that specific forms of labour market segmentation also prevail in both countries regarding the organisation of professions. Regarding entry into the professions, one can conclude that the link between the professions and higher education in Britain and Germany is different not only in terms of prevalence, power, and influence of professional associations, but also in terms of their level of integration with the state: While in Britain, professional associations rationalise and control professional education and training, in Germany it is the government that prescribes and sanctions the kind of training required for entry into established or new professions. Abbott (1988) refers in this regard to Britain as a country where a strong state was largely absent during the creation of modern professions. By contrast, the German government created the institutions that trained professionals in order to provide the loyal civil servants that are needed. The previous sections have shown how public service has historically played a different role in both countries in shaping the development of professions. The importance of further differences of public sector organisation for graduate career mobility will be discussed in the following section.

5.3.2 Public Services between Status Protection and New Public Management

Since the "golden age" of the welfare state, the public sector has developed into one of the largest sectors. In some countries, it has even become the largest employer throughout Europe. At the same time, the public sector has, to a large extent, been an important labour market for higher education graduates. However, the European public sector is characterised by a strong degree of diversity, since the definition of public service employment, its career structure and qualification requirements vary strongly across countries. The following section gives an overview of entry requirements in the public sector, examines career prospects in this labour market segment, and analyses the size and development of public sector employment in Germany and Britain. Special emphasis is given to reforms of the public sector during the 1980s and 1990s.

To start with, it is important to note that the definition of public employment varies strongly between the two countries, which makes comparisons rather complicated. Country-specific definitions of civil servants are especially diverse. In Germany, civil servants are called *Staatsbeamte* and civil service is regulated by the *Beamtenrecht*, the law of public service. The work of the British 'civil servant' is regulated not by law, but by the Civil Service Code. The size of these groups also varies strongly between the two countries: while German civil servants account for almost half of all public employees, their British counterparts constitute only a small minority (Rothenbacher 1999; 2001/2002). In order to overcome the obstacle of comparing societal groups that are not fully comparable, this study adopts a rather broad perspective by analysing the development of employment within the public sector in general and not of civil servants in particular, since comparative data are more often available. Only for a better understanding of employment opportunities in both countries the example of civil servants is employed in order to make cross-national diversity more explicit.

Qualification Requirements for Entry into the Public Service

In both countries, the rise of the nation state had profound consequences for the patterns of control and administration of public service and its relation to

146

the university system. In Germany, forging the nation state went hand in hand with incorporating academia into the ranks of public service, thereby placing upon it the implicit obligation of service to the national community. British public service institutions have historically been less integrated with universities; instead they have tended to formulate their own entry requirements for civil servants (Neave 2001).

As a consequence of this development, direct ties between German universities and public service emerged in form of the dual status of higher education qualifications – the split between academic qualifications (*Diplom, Magister*), which did not qualify for public appointments, and state qualifications (*Staatsexmanen*), which entitled the holder to apply for employment in public administration. In Britain, public service reforms and higher education reforms were kept in two separate spheres, and the status of the university as a self-governing institution remained intact. If the British civil service indorsed the principle of appointment on the basis of competitive public examinations, such examinations were not imposed on the universities.

In Germany, the dual employment structure of public service is part of this historical tradition. The core elements of public service are relatively uniform for public servants at all levels of government, with the term "public servant" being used as a generic term to include civil servants (*Beamte*) as well as public employees (*Angestellte*). Due to these traditions, posts for civil servants have been established for law and order functions and must be reserved for them – according to article 33, paragraph 4, Basic Law – while all other public service tasks are mainly fulfilled by public employees. Even though the dual employment structure made sense in the last century, it has become less and less appropriate and relevant, since the boundaries between the two categories of service law have become increasingly blurred in practice (Becker, R. 1993).

In keeping with the basic principles of a merit-based career system, entrance for civil servants into the civil service classes is strictly linked to certain formal qualification requirements (Becker, R. 1993; Kuhlmann and Röber 2004). The German civil servants' professional profile is largely shaped by the existing system of education and recruitment which combines professional training and career structure. For entering the upper level of German civil service, the so called "administrative class", a university degree is required which usually has to be completed by a two years preparatory service ("*Referendariat*") with practical stages in different public and private institutions and some courses on administrative topics. But there is no special education or training for the administrative class. A condition to enter the intermediate level of the civil service, the "executive class", is – after having passed the *Abitur*-examination – a degree at a college for public administration. Similar qualification requirements, however, apply to public employees as well, with higher hierarchical positions being reserved for higher education graduates. This again points to the fact that despite the continued dual employment structure, the two categories of public service employment have in practice been coming closer to each other.

An important aspect of training for the German public service is that no central elite schools for the education and training exist. In contrast to the still centralised French system of civil service training offered by the Ecole Nationale d'Administation (ENA), in Germany all higher education institutions are in principle equally responsible for education and training of public servants, even though the universities of Potsdam and Konstanz and the *German School for Administrative Sciences* in Speyer offer special courses in administrative sciences. Not surprisingly, a central unit responsible for recruiting civil servants or public employees does not exist. Each ministry at the federal level, each state, and each local authority has the right to recruit its staff members itself (Becker, R. 1993; Kuhlmann and Röber 2004).

In Britain, such a tight coupling between higher education credentials and the public service has traditionally not existed. The intake of higher education graduates into public employment only started to emerge with increasing higher education expansion. Higher education graduates comprised only five percent of recruits at the executive officer level in 1965, but around half the appointments at this level by the 1980s. However, particularly at the upper levels of the civil service hierarchy, charges of elitism have always been made. In this regard, Oxford and Cambridge have always been central institutions for the formation of an administrative elite. Whilst only 15 percent of those applying for high-ranked posts are from Oxbridge, they make up for over half of the total who enter (Dowding 1995). Apart from this, however, British higher education never established a separate curricular pathway for public service employees within the undergraduate syllabus. Rather, holding a university degree was deemed a prior condition for eligibility to sit for the public examination, results of which decided who should be called and who should be rejected. In this regard, competition continues to be an important feature of the public management bureaucracy. In particular, it emphasises competition in the form of a keen rivalry among the "best and the brightest" of university graduates for appointment to "fast stream" places in civil service (Hood, Christopher 2003).

National differences can also be found regarding the fields of study important for entry into public service in both countries. According to the "legalistic" administrative culture which has been generated by the prevalence of legal rule-application in Germany's administrative business, the personnel structure in public administration is very strongly moulded by a dominance of lawyers (Kuhlmann and Röber 2004). The proportion of lawyers in Federal ministries, amounting to 63%, has virtually remained unchanged for more than 30 years, succeeded by barely 15% of economists (Derlien 2003). In Britain, more general fields of study have been more important for entry into the public service. Far greater numbers of humanities and arts graduates apply to the civil service, with history being a traditionally highly valued subject based on its high degree of general education. There is also a strong bias towards arts degree holders amongst permanent secretaries, while specialist subjects have always offered fewer career opportunities than the generalist grades. The lower career opportunities for specialists in the British public service has always been justified on the grounds that specialists are too deeply involved in technical matters to take a detached view (Dowding 1995).

More similarities exist as regards subject requirements for professions in the public service which have traditionally been highly specialised in both countries. But national differences persist as well concerning the status of individual professional groups in the public sector. One of the biggest groups of public service employees in both countries are teachers. However, while German primary and secondary school teachers as well as higher education professors have the status of a civil servant, they do not belong to the civil service in Britain. Overall, higher education in Germany has always been much more tightly connected with entry into the public service than in Britain. Even though higher education there also constitutes a necessary precondition, further examinations to select candidates from the best graduates are still in place. Consequently, entry to the administrative class, be it civil servants of public employees, should be much easier for German higher education graduates immediately after graduation.

Career Structure in the Public Service

There are two basic models for employment in the core public service, a career-based and a position-based system . The choice of one system or the other has a profound effect on the career trajectories of public service employees. The first one closely represents the model of firm-internal labour markets, while the second exhibits more external labour market structures. In career-based systems, public servants are expected to stay in the public service more or less throughout their working life. Initial entry is based on academic credentials and/or a civil service entry examination. Once recruited, people are placed in positions by the organisation. This may include moving staff from one ministry to another or from one area of specialisation to another. Promotion is based on a system of grades attached to the individual rather than to a specific position. This sort of system is characterised by limited possibilities for entering the civil service mid-career and a strong emphasis on career development. Compared to the private sector public sector employees are rewarded for long-time employment with career stability. Position-based systems focus on selecting the best-suited candidate (OECD 2004c) for each position, whether by external recruitment or internal promotion. Thus, they are more similar to the private sector, allow for more open access, and lateral entry is relatively common. Traditionally, both Germany and Britain exhibited strong characteristics of a career-based system. However, while this is still the case in Germany nowadays, Britain has moved from a strongly career-based system to a strongly position-based system in the past two decades following the reforms of its public sector (OECD 2004c).

The essential feature of German civil service in its present form goes back to the end of the eighteenth century in the Prussian General Code of 1794. The prevailing philosophy had been confirmed in the "Reich Civil Service Act" (*Reichsbeamtengesetz*) enacted in 1873 (Siedentopf 1990: 236) and was enshrined after the Second World War in the German constitution especially by "reserving to civil servants the right to act on behalf of the state" (article 33, paragraph 4, Basic Law) and by emphasising the traditional principles of professional civil service (article 33, paragraph 5, Basic Law) (Siedentopf 1990: 237, cited in Kuhlmann and Röber 2004). Although there is no clearly defined enumeration of elements which constitute the traditional principles of the civil service, some features are widely seen as characteristic, e.g. lifetime occupation, an appropriate salary according to the maintenance principle (*Alimentationsprinzip*), loyalty, political neutrality and moderation, dedication to public service, no right to strike and subjection to special disciplinary regulations. However, traditional principles of professional civil service only apply to *Beamte* and are not aimed at regulating the legal status of *Angestellte*, who are subject to private sector law and public sector industrial relations. But despite these legal differences, career prospects are more similar, since the principle of seniority also applies to public employees, with pay-scales and promotion strongly prompting a continuous career development with the same employer.

German public service has been very resistant to reform. During the 1980s, the lack of new policy initiatives in West Germany, despite the triumph in 1983 of the Conservative Coalition government, was striking, especially compared to Britain. Yet, the new government did not change the basic policy approach to public sector organisation. Attempts at privatisation and de-regulation were almost non-existent before being implemented on a comparatively modest scale towards the end of the 1990s. Even the new challenges of the late 1980s, namely the impact of unification as well as the adaptive pressures that result from the ongoing process of European integration did not lead to far-reaching adaptations of the German public sector. Though the localities were successful in reducing some of their load of responsibilities by cut-back, retrenchment and contracting-out, privatisation and de-regulation initiatives of the public service have, until relatively recently, been rare occurrences despite a political rhetoric which suggested otherwise (Hesse 2003). Only recently, the reform overload following from these developments is documented by the growing awareness of the necessity to reduce the number of public servants and public employees significantly. German public service is not likely to escape scrutiny. However, the system of checks and balances – entrenched as much in German political culture as it is solidified in institutional relations – neither required nor encouraged dramatic structural changes as observed in Britain (Hesse 2003; Röber and Löffler 2000).

In Britain, the regulation of civil service employment dates back to the Northcote-Trevelyan Report of 1854. This Report established the British civil service in its modern form, with a division between superior and inferior posts corresponding to intellectual and mechanical tasks, merit-based entry upon competitive examinations, training-on-the-job, as broad a range of subjects as possible, and promotion based on merit (Dowding 1995). Until the late 1970s, competition for promotion on a closed career basis among an elite corps once appointed was a marked feature of the traditional British civil service, because it put the onus on providing information about loyalty and good service to the organisation on those best placed to provide it (i.e. employees) rather than review procedures or output-based pay systems (Hood, Christopher 2003). Until then, employment relations across the British public sector were distinct from those found in private firms in a number of key respects. Perhaps the most important difference was the high level of centralisation of employment relations policy. For most groups, pay determination was (and largely remains) linked to national structures of collective bargaining or, in the case of some professions (for example, the medical profession), pay review bodies. These structures offered little scope for local variation or interpretation of standardised grading structures and terms and conditions (Horton 2000). Also, the role of the state as employer served to standardise practice, demonstrated by the focus on continuity of employment, procedural fairness in collective bargaining, investment in training and equal opportunities. This status quo remained rather unchallenged until Margaret Thatcher came into power in 1979, which ultimately introduced market dynamics into public service.

Thatcher introduced market features into the so far shielded public sector. Much of the thrust of the reforms now dubbed as "New Public Management" (NPM) during the 1980s and 1990s was ostensibly designed to add new forms of competition to the traditional forms of public sector competition (in the form of individual rivalry for appointment, honours and promotion, and organisational competition for budgetary funds and policy responsibility), to release managerial energies within the public sector by relaxing rules that stifled managerial creativity, and put public sector professionals and bureaucrats under greater pressure to find ways of reducing resource inputs relative to measurable outputs and improve service quality (see Hood, Christohper 1995; Hood, Christopher 2003). The reforms were driven by the market-driven ideas of privatisation, quasi markets, public-private partnerships, contracting out, and performance-related pay. The intention of these public sector reforms was to cut costs by increasing their exposure to competition. This meant to strip away what were considered unwarranted "privileges" of the public service, which shielded public servants from the disciplines of the market and its attendant job insecurity. A related aim was to reduce collegial control[32] in many public service professions and to increase both the opportunities and obligations to those in management positions to exercise more discretion, for example over pay, personnel and contracts. The implication was that some measure of deregulation was needed inside public service by downgrading the force of producer-group mutuality and highlighting that of competition.

An important element of this new form of competition within the public sector was competition for "merit" or "performance-related" pay awards by public servants, in addition to competition for promotion (Horton 2000). In part, this development highlighted and extended previous arrangements for "special incrementation" that had always existed to some degree within the pay structure of the public service. What was different about the performance pay schemes of the 1980s and 1990s, however, was that instead of basing pay on objectively measurable aspects of performance (like delinquent tax recovered or exam grades achieved by students), they were based on subjective assessments of performance by superordinates in a style more familiar in the business world. Formal arrangements for performance pay in that sense began in the civil service in 1984 on a limited and experimental basis; by 1996 the old centralised grading structure had ostensibly been abolished for the "Senior Civil Service" introduced in those years (Grades 1-5), with all pay of those grades officially individualised in relation to performance, level of responsibility and marketability of skills and experience (Prime Minister 1995).

5.3.3 Trends in Public Sector Employment

Since the 1980s, almost all European countries have witnessed a decrease in public service employment. This reduction in employment is not only a result

---

32 The collegiality principle was particularly seen as a force that pushed up costs and maintained restrictive practices. The "philosophy" underlying this traditional style of public governance was never made very explicit, and that may explain the speed at which it buckled intellectually under the weight of "New Public Management" (Hood, Christohper 1995) challenges from the 1970s, which successfully portrayed the system as indefensibly "producerist" structure captured by public service trade unions.

of economic measures taken by the governments; it is also a reaction to important structural changes in public service itself, such as the strong staff expansion in the 1960s and 1970s or the increase in public employees in the highest career groups (Rothenbacher 2001/2002: 1). The exception to this trend, however, is Britain, where the public sector only recently started to decline. This is even more surprising when the reforms of the early 1980s are taken into account. Figure 5 shows the development of public sector employment in Britain and Germany since the early 1970s. It is striking that the British service sector was between 30 and 50 percent larger than the German one during the 1980s and early 1990s; since then a rapid decline in Britain has lead to equal levels of public service employment in both countries.[33]

Figure 5: Share of public employment over total employment in Germany and Britain

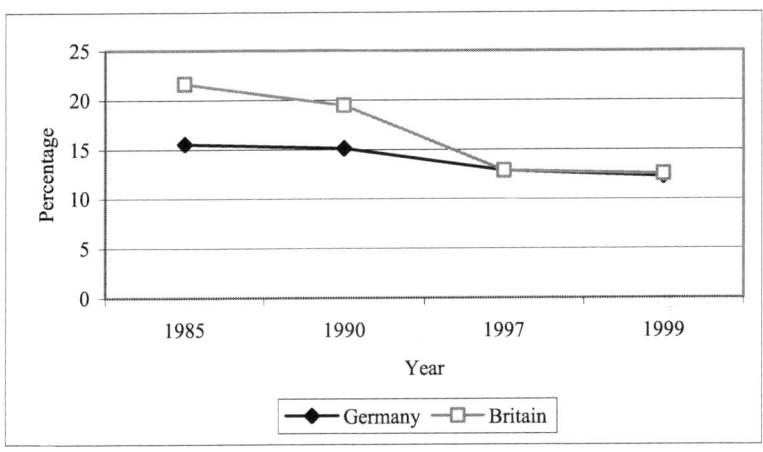

Source: OECD Public Management Service (OECD 2002)

British public sector reforms over the past twenty years have had the effect of substantially changing the way the public sector was organised as well as diminishing the rate of public sector employment (Hood 2003: 128). A mixture of dramatic downsizing in state bureaucracies combined with

---

33 Because of methodological difficulties, hardly any international comparative data on public employment exist so far that give a reliable account of the size and weight of employment in the public domain across OECD member countries. Across countries, and even within countries depending on the source of information, the definitions of "government organisations", "the public sector" and "the public domain" vary significantly. (http://www.oecd.org/document/11/0,2340,en_2825_495670_35849739_1_1_1_1,00.html, last access: 30/03/07)

outsourcing and privatisation of public services reduced direct government employment from nearly 20 percent of the total labour force in 1974 to 15 percent in 1994. As noted above, the state was rolled back noticeably in terms of direct public employment. Along with that went a programme of privatising public enterprises, a series of attempts to improve public sector management, packaged as measures designed to make such management more "businesslike" and create more "freedom to manage" within state bureaucracy. However, there has also been an expansion of public service employment, especially in education and health, which lead to a significant increase in the demand for well-qualified graduates.

The public sector share of the total workforce in Germany has been slightly decreasing over the past decades (but without any landslide changes) and has been fairly stable for more than 15 years. Even the decisive point of unification has not had a far reaching impact. Since fundamental changes in existing institutions could not be realised, as they partly concerned guaranteed legal claims, attempts were made to reduce the recruiting of staff. The main goal was to reduce the number of employees: this was to be achieved by reducing the hiring of new employees. The effects of staff reduction measures are demonstrated by the staff expenditures ratio. However, the present figure for public servants (13%) is nearly the same as that of the "old" Federal Republic at the end of the 1980s (with 15%).

5.3.4 The Social Closure of Graduate Labour Markets in Germany and Britain

These figures indicate that the public sector makes up for an important labour market segment in both countries. Together with the professional labour market, both segments might constitute important destinations for higher education graduates. However, strong differences between Germany and Britain exist. One difference is related to the immediate importance of higher education credentials for entry into these segments. In Germany, the state-organised higher education system has always been the main provider of entry certificates into professional occupations or a career in the higher-level public service. Both segments in Britain have traditionally been less connected to higher education. Instead, further training and additional entry examinations have been required. Even though academic routes are now established, especially for entry into the professions, entry nevertheless remains more disconnected from higher education. Therefore British higher education graduates should take longer obtaining a professional occupation or public sector job, while in Germany access to these segments should be open immediately after graduation.

Another important difference between professional and public sectors in both countries is related to their degree of social closure from competition and market dynamics. While the German professions could to a large extent maintain a high degree of social closure from competitors, the British system of professions was subject to a strong marketisation due to the reforms of the 1980s and 1990s. Furthermore, the introduction of a "new public management" in the British public sector much more strongly deregulated this segment of graduate employment, while German public service is still marked by strong internal labour markets. All of these processes lead to substantive differences in graduate labour market segmentation. Graduate careers in these segments in Germany should be much more stable and sheltered from market competition, following the principles of internal labour markets, while the British reforms during the past two decades should have substantially weakened the shelter provided by these segments for graduate career mobility. The following table summarises these expected relations between higher education credentials, entry port occupations and career development in internal labour market segments in both countries.

Table 6: Importance of internal labour market segments for graduate careers

	Germany	Britain
Importance of higher education for entry port occupations	High → immediate entry after graduation	Low → lagged entry after graduation
Social closure of labour market segments	High → stable career development within segments, little mobility between segments	Low → unstable career development within segments, high mobility between segments

5.4 Labour Market Regulation and the Protection of (Un-)Employment

A final institutional aspect to be analysed for graduate careers is the degree of labour market regulation in both countries. The regulation of a labour market can be broadly defined as the ability to adapt and respond to change. Strict labour market regulation normally goes hand in hand with a lower level of labour market flexibility and includes, among other features, employment protection and unemployment protection (Estévez-Abe et al. 2001). Employment protection refers to institutionalised employment security. The higher the degree of employment protection, the less likely a worker will be laid off even during economic downturns. Unemployment protection means protection from income reduction due to unemployment, and can thus reduce the uncertainty over wage levels throughout one's labour market career. High replacement ratios and longer benefit duration gives the unemployed enough time to find another job that matches their skills, especially if they are permitted to turn down jobs that are outside their core competencies. Overall, labour market regulation influences both the ease with which employees can be laid off as well as the ease with which unemployed workers are reabsorbed into employment. In the following sections, the degree of labour market regulation in Germany and Britain is examined by analysing employment protection legislation and unemployment legislation. Again, special attention is devoted to developments of the 1980s and 1990s.

5.4.1 Employment Protection Legislation and the Stability of Employment Relations

Germany and Britain vary considerably in the strictness of employment protection and the ways in which it affects the stability of employment relationships. The degree of dismissal protection in particular influences the ease with which an employee can be laid off and labour contracts can be adjusted to new economic circumstances. In Germany, legislation only defines minimum standards of employment protection, based on which the collective bargaining parties negotiate industry-specific or company-specific regulations (see Fuchs and Schettkat 2003: 231-235 for the following). Legislation guarantees the right to establish works councils, participation of workers at company board level, and legal protection against dismissals. The latter is highly restrictive for regular employment contracts, since after a contract is signed, the employment relationship is assumed to last for an indefinite period. According to the Dismissal Protection Act of 1969, unjustified dismissals are illegal. Any dismissal has to be justified, either by economic reasons such as changes in labour demand or production strategies, or by the performance of the employee concerned. In case of a justified dismissal, the period of notice for blue collar workers was two weeks, and for white collar workers six weeks before 1993. However, this distinction became blurred over time and nowadays, dismissed workers have to be given notice of at least four weeks. Collective bargaining arrangements, however, may lead to longer periods, usually increasing with seniority. In any case, employers are obliged to seek for alternatives to dismissal, be it reduction of working hours or a different job in the same firm. Additionally, the works council has to be consulted in advance. It is involved in negotiating severance payments, which normally have to be paid to the dismissed employee and which are usually quite high – equivalent to about five to ten months' wages.

Since the 1980s, several steps have been taken in Germany to deregulate dismissal protection based on the hope that relaxing constraints would reduce dismissal costs and thus increase employment (Clasen 2005: 72). A first major legislative change was introduced in 1985 with the *Beschäftigungs-förderungsgesetz* (Employment Promotion Act), which abolished the necessity for employers to give reasons for fixed-term contracts and provided them with an unconditional freedom to conclude fixed-term contracts lasting for up to 18 months. The scope of this law was even more enlarged in January 1996, when employers were allowed to offer fixed-term contracts for a period of up to two years without specifying reasons. In October of the same year, small firms with a maximum of ten employees – roughly 80 percent of all companies – were entirely exempted from dismissal protection legislation. However, this change was reversed by the Social-Democratic/ Green government in 1999. As a consequence of the generally high degree of dismissal protection, German standard employment relationships are strongly sheltered even in times of economic downturns and exhibit a high degree of continuity and stability. Higher education graduates should therefore experience considerable career stability even at the beginning of their work life.

In Britain, employment protection legislation has always been less strict than in Germany. The British system of labour legislation has traditionally played a relatively weak role in regulating employment as compared to collective bargaining arrangements negotiated between employers and employees (see Deakin and Reed 2003: 121-126). In general, employment legislation has made few restrictions on the principle that employer and employees are free to choose from a number of different forms of employment contract. In contrast to the German situation, British employers have never been required to present formal justification for the adoption of fixed-term contracts. "Standard" or "traditional" employment contracts, however, only enjoy a weak degree of legislative protection in the British system either.

General employment protection legislation was introduced comparatively late, with the principle of redundancy compensation coming into place only in 1965, and unfair dismissal legislation as late as 1971. However, the Conservative governments of the 1980s and 1990s introduced a number of measures to severely reduce labour market regulation (Clasen 2005). The general scope of their reforms was to limit the capacity of trade unions to organise industrial action in defence of terms and conditions of employment, leading to a decentralised system of workplace bargaining with a high amount of individualised employment contracts. Regarding dismissal protection, a new legislation in 1980 removed the burden of employers to prove fairness of dismissal. Provision was also made to allow fixed-term employees to give up their statutory rights to dismissal protection, while part-time workers working fewer than eight hours per week were excluded from many aspects of employment protection. The legislation on part-time employment, however, was abolished in 1995 after a court decision, which ruled that part-time work thresholds were indirectly discriminatory against women and hence contrary to the EC Directive on Equal Treatment in Employment of 1976. After the election of the Labour government, employment protection was slightly increased again. The Employment Relations Act of 1999 in particular aimed at broadening the scope of employment protection to previously excluded employees and restricted the possibility of waiver clauses in fixed-term contracts.

But despite these latest amendments, remedies for dismissal in Britain remain weak. The principal remedy against unfair dismissal in practice have been compensation payments, which are substantially lower than in Germany, amounting to a median award of roughly two months' wages in 1995/96 (Deakin and Reed 2003: 123). Average awards in general have been well below statutory limits, reflecting the low earnings expectations of successful unfair dismissal applicants, and the absence of an exemplary or punitive component within the compensation ordered by tribunals. Related legislation applies to fair dismissal and requires employers to pay redundancy compensations to employees dismissed on economic grounds, which are restrictively defined. However, these payments did not constitute much of a burden for employers, since redundancy payments above the statutory minimum qualify for corporation tax relief and in addition were subsidised by the state through the social security system until the late 1980s. Overall, the effect of redundancy compensation legislation was to encourage voluntary or agreed redundancies among British employees. The low level of employment protection in general and dismissal protection in particular makes the British labour market highly unregulated. Graduates may find employment after graduation relatively easily due to the low restrictions in contracting, but might be made redundant soon thereafter, depending on the economic situation. Unstable career trajectories following a sequence of stop gap jobs during the first years after graduation should be the consequence.

It is often argued that due to the different degrees strictness in employment protection legislation, the employment rates in both countries increasingly diverged. Figure 6 shows that the overall employment/population ratio in Germany declined markedly after 1990, to a level even lower than in the late 1970s.

The sustained improvement in the British labour market since 1993 has been achieved both by an increase in female employment and the reversal of the decline of male employment. However, labour market inactivity for prime-aged and low-skilled men continued to rise during this period (Deakin and Reed 2003). By contrast, male employment in Germany continued to decline to an extent which has not been compensated by rising female employment. In addition, in both countries the higher levels of female employment have involved higher rates of part-time employment (Clasen 2005, chapter 6). The development of employment in both countries suggests a strong degree of divergence, particularly since the early 1990s. Although remaining below the levels of the late 1980s for some years and despite a prevalence of women working part-time, the development in the British labour market has been favourable. By contrast, West German economic improvement in the late 1980s was achieved without much impact on the labour market. It remains to be seen whether the overall development of employment in both countries has had an impact on graduate career mobility.

Figure 6: Employment ratio of the population aged 16 – 64 years in Germany and Britain

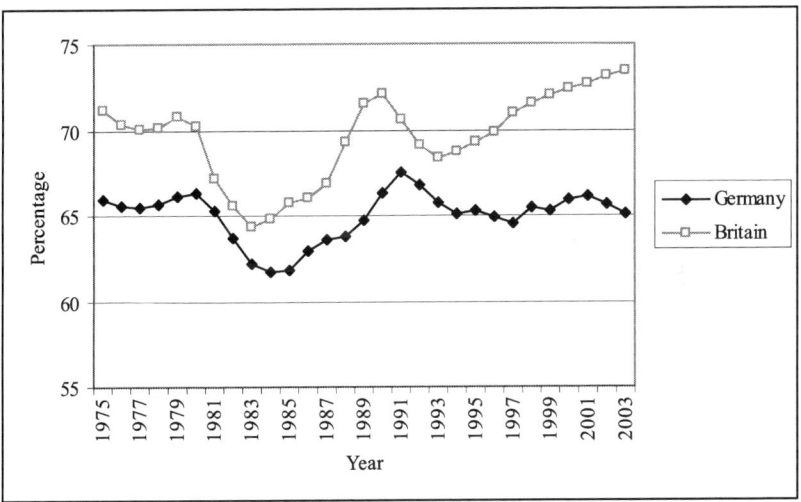

Source: Calculations based on data derived from the OECD Employment Statistics data base

In general, employees with higher education degrees are less affected by changing labour market environments than those holding lower level educational credentials.

5.4.2 Unemployment Protection and the Level of Skill Protection

Unemployment protection varies considerably between Germany and Britain, too. Despite rigorous entrenchments taking place in Germany particularly during the 1990s, German unemployment benefits have been generous compared to British standards. In the UK, the level of replacement and the duration of eligibility have always been lower than in Germany. However, cut-backs introduced by the Conservative government widened the gap between both countries even more.

Before the latest reforms coming into place in January 2005, protection against income loss during unemployment was based on a two-tier system in Germany (see Fuchs und Schettkat 2003: 230, Clasen 2005: 54-57, 64-76, Appendix A). Persons who were in insured employment or received vocational training in the dual system for at least twelve months during the three years preceding their unemployment were initially entitled to claim unemployment benefits for a specific period of time (*Arbeitslosengeld ALG*), and might have subsequently become eligible for the means-tested unemployment assistance (*Arbeitslosenhilfe ALH*). The former is closely guided by insurance principles and financed from compulsory contributions which, subject to ceiling, are proportional to gross earnings and equally split between employers and employees. Unemployment assistance was a safety net provision for those who did not find a new job during the period of receiving unemployment benefits or who were not entitled to claim them, but had previously been in insured employment for at least 70 days. Even though it was financed by general taxation rather than contributions, its level was earnings-related just as the *Arbeitslosengeld*, but at a lower rate of gross earnings. Contrary to the *ALG* system, however, eligibility for *Arbeitslosenhilfe* was means-tested and the benefit was payable indefinitely.

Even though unemployment benefits continue to be more generous in Germany than in Britain, the duration of payment and level of benefit entitlements changed during the course of the 1980s and 1990s, leading to a decline of replacement rates and a tightening of eligibility requirements. In Germany in 1980, unemployment benefit was equal to 68 percent of previous earnings, payable for a standard maximum duration of twelve months. Since then, reforms brought major improvements only for older contributors with longer contribution records, increasing their eligibility duration step by step to up to 36 months. In contrast, the level of income protection for claimants of unemployment benefits as well as assistance decreased continuously for employees, particularly those without children (60 percent of average net income since 1994). Cut-backs of unemployment assistance have also been also severe, since a gradual decrease in benefits rates of three points per year of claim was introduced in 1996. Unemployment assistance was abolished completely in 2000 for those without prior receipt of unemployment benefits.

In addition, stricter rules regarding the job search and more rigid matching criteria, defining jobs deemed acceptable for unemployed people, were introduced. Generally, unemployed persons who receive benefits are under obligation to accept the jobs offered to them by the employment agency as long as these jobs are "suitable". Throughout the 1980s and early 1990s, suitability was based on the qualifications of the recipient, the skill requirement of the job and the duration of the ongoing employment spell. It was the norm to aim for job offers which corresponded to individual skills and acquired status. By contrast, in 1998, the relevance of previous qualification and status was dropped, while the suitability of job offers was merely defined in monetary terms. After six months of unemployment, any job with net earnings higher than the benefit level was considered suitable.

But despite these restrictions, Germany is still considered a country with generous unemployment benefits, a high rate of replacement and long eligibility periods. The pattern of retrenchment during the 1980s and 1990s hardly changed the position of core workers, but mainly restricted benefit rights for groups more peripheral to the labour market, such as job starters or casual workers (Clasen 2005: 64). Overall, generous replacement rates and rather long eligibility durations should increase the chances of seeking matching employment after phases of unemployment in Germany. Unemployed graduates should have the option to maintain their occupational status to a large extent, particularly before the latest eligibility amendments in 1998. At the same time, status mobility should be rather low, be it downwards due to the high unemployment benefits or upwards due to shorter mobility chains following from the high degree of employment protection in Germany.

Compared to Germany, British unemployment protection has always been less generous. The major differences to the German system are the lack of a separate funding arrangement for unemployment support and, especially since 1981, the absence of earnings-related unemployment compensation (see Clasen 2005: 57/58, Appendix B). All British unemployment benefits are paid out of a national fund (NIF), which is also the source for other compensatory benefits, such as state pensions. Unlike the German system, the British system of unemployment compensation for a long time did not provide for earnings-related benefits; instead, means-tested flat-rate benefits are paid in exchange for flat-rate contributions. Earnings-related supplements for unemployment were only introduced during the 1960s and 1970. Due to the modest generosity and small margin between standard unemployment benefit and means-tested support, it was also very common for benefit recipients to claim additional means-tested benefits, such as housing benefits. In addition, eligibility rules were much stricter and the share of unemployed who did not meet the contribution conditions or who had exhausted their entitlement and were thus reliant on means-tested benefits has traditionally been higher than in Germany. The British system thus never focussed as much on wage replacement as the German system or those of other European countries.

In 1980 in Britain, the benefit level was set at 21 percent of average male earnings, contributory criteria were fairly moderate, and entitlements could be claimed for a period of up to twelve months. Since then, however, there has been a considerable decline in benefit generosity in relation to full-time adult earnings and the earnings-related supplement has disappeared. During the 1980s, the extent to which unemployment benefits compensated for lost earnings fell by 30 percent for single men on average earnings and even more for married men with children (Deaking and Reed 2003: 126). This was mainly due to the abolition of earnings-related and child dependency supplements, and the failure to upgrade short-term benefits in line with earnings. The introduction of taxation for unemployment benefits in the early 1980s also reduced their value.

The rules of eligibility for claiming benefits in Britain changed significantly as well, leading to an even further reduction in entitlements and stricter measures of job search tests. In 1988, the effective qualification period for contributory benefits was extended and abolished for those under 18. By the end of the decade, job search duties were increased, requiring claimants to show that they were "actively seeking work" and to accept jobs with lower wages or differing working hours. In addition, the maximum duration of entitlement to contributory support was reduced to six months in 1996. The previously separate insurance and means-tested support benefits became incorporated into a single system, the Jobseekers Allowance (JSA). Since then, the claimant has to enter into a "job seeker's agreement", which imposes a duty on the claimant to take positive steps towards employment and to accept any reasonable job offer. In sum, these measures are likely to prevent unemployed graduates from seeking jobs that correspond to their level of skills. Rather, they are forced to accept any kind of employment, be it in a similar or different occupation to the one held before unemployment. Downward mobility becomes more likely. At the same time, chances of upward mobility increase as well, since mobility chains are longer in a labour market where overall job turnover is high.

Overall, both countries already exhibited striking differences in unemployment protection at the beginning of the 1980s, which became even more pronounced over the next two decades. The British character of social protection for unemployed people has significantly shifted from a mixture of social insurance and means-tested support towards one which is mainly based on needs principles. In Germany, unemployment support has increasingly become more needs-based, too, but since the majority of unemployed is eligible for unemployment benefits, the principle of wage replacement remained an important pillar of German unemployment protection. The resulting figures of unemployment vary considerably between the two countries, where Britain has been labelled a "success story" (Pissarides 2003) due to its very low unemployment rates during the 1990s, while Germany still struggles with the consequences of unification. Even though it is problematic to directly compare absolute rates of German and British unemployment statistics due to different definitions, a comparison of within-country developments over time seems fruitful to exemplify cross-national variations.

Figure 7: Annual unemployment rates 1971-2004 in Germany and Britain

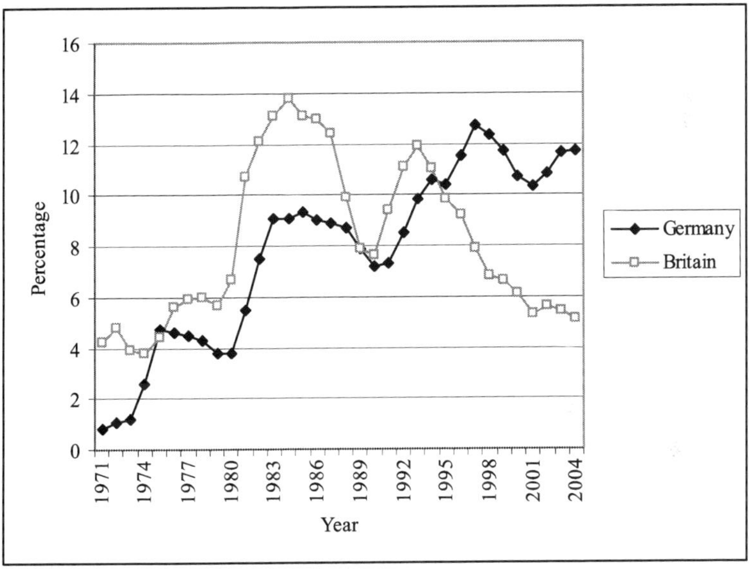

Unemployment in Germany is measured as percentage of dependent civilian employment in West Germany between 1966 and 1989 and since January 1990 as percentage of dependent and civil service employment in West and East Germany (Source: Statistisches Bundesamt). Unemployment in Britain deviates from official statistics, since the number of unemployed according to ILO standards is set in relation to the 16-59/64 year old working population instead of the population above age 16 as a whole to ensure slightly better comparability with the German data (Source: British National Statistics).

Figure 7 shows that Germany and Britain followed parallel paths in the 1970s and 1980s, but trajectories diverged dramatically in the 1990s. Especially after German reunification, the rate of unemployment increased in Germany, reaching 10.4 percent in 1995. Furthermore, in the new *Bundesländer* official unemployment was much higher. Average unemployment rates in the East are currently above 20 percent, more than twice the West German average. Economically, the political management of

163

unification had severe implications for the East German labour market in particular (Clasen 2005: 43). In sharp contrast, socio-economic conditions became more favourable in Britain during the 1990s. Unlike earlier patterns of "stop-and-go" macro-economic performance, characterised by strongly fluctuating rates of economic activity, British development has exhibited steady growth throughout the decade. Unemployment in Britain has continued to decline since 1993, and despite somewhat lower growth rates after 1999, the economy performed well with unemployment remaining relatively low. In short, labour market conditions since the early 1990s have become increasingly diverse between Germany and Britain.

In addition, there are different groups primarily affected by unemployment in both countries. In Germany, unemployment is mainly concentrated among low-skilled and older workers. These groups are less affected in Britain, where youth unemployment is a bigger problem (Ardy and Umbach 2004: 212). In addition, an increasing proportion of individuals are long-term unemployed in Germany, while the duration of employment decreased in Britain. In 1975, only ten percent of the German unemployed were without work for more than a year compared to almost one third in 1996 (Fuchs and Schettkat 2003: 212). In contrast to these precarious groups, unemployment among higher education graduates is rarely documented separately in official statistics. Therefore, German and British labour force surveys have been used to calculate unemployment among employees with a higher degree.

As Figure 8 shows, the unemployment quota of higher education-trained persons is substantially lower than the overall quota in both countries. However, the trends of unemployment among those with a higher education degree diverged substantially during the 1990s, following the overall pattern of national unemployment at a lower level.

In Germany, higher education degree holders experience higher levels of unemployment during this decade, though not to the same extent as qualifiers from lower educational levels, while their British counterparts profited from low overall rates of unemployment. Unemployment rates between the two countries are again more similar if the number of unemployed higher degree holders is compared to all unemployed. In Germany, higher education graduates show lower rates than British ones, particularly in 1995 and 2000. This leads to the conclusion that the pattern of unemployment in the labour force as a whole and among individuals with a higher education degree slightly converged in Britain over the years. In Germany, in contrast, the gap between the unemployment risk for weakly qualified and the unemployment risk for highly qualified individuals has widened since the mid 1980s. But despite these differences and despite the overall unemployment crisis in Germany, unemployment risks for higher education graduates remain fairly low in both countries.

Figure 8: Unemployment among higher education degree holders in Germany and Britain

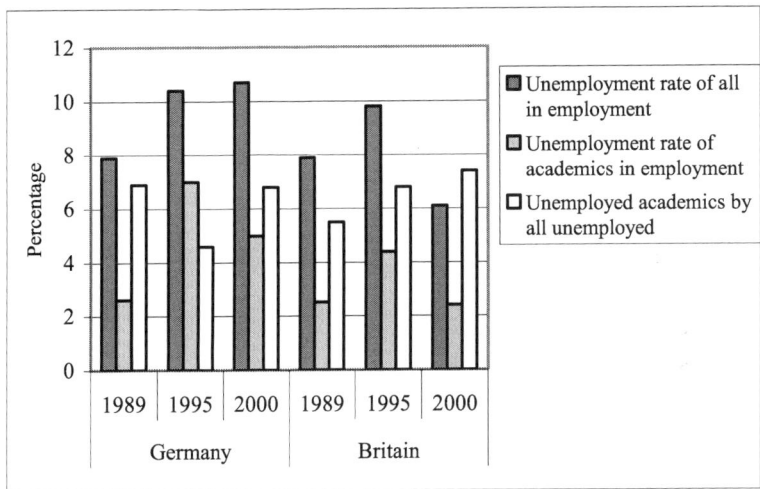

Unemployment rate of all in employment: ILO unemployed as percentage of all in employment.
Unemployment rate of academics in employment: ILO unemployed with a higher education degree as percentage of all in employment with a higher education degree.
Unemployed academics by all unemployed: ILO unemployed with a higher education degree as percentage of all ILO unemployed.

Source: Calculations based on weighted data from the German Mikrozensus (pooled waves of 1989, 1995, 2000) and the British Labour Force Survey (pooled waves of 1989, 1995, 2000)

5.4.3 Strictness and Flexibility of German and British Labour Markets

The previous sections have shown that labour market regulation differs substantially between Germany and Britain, even though Germany has recently moved in the direction of more flexibility by introducing elements of deregulation and retrenchment in German employment and unemployment legislation. Yet, despite these latest developments, Germany continues to be marked by a high degree of labour market regulation. As regards employment protection legislation, dissolving standard employment relationships remains particularly difficult, and compensatory payments are high. British employees lack such a high degree of protection, since labour contracting in general is more flexible and individualised, and employers have a much higher degree of freedom to hire and fire employees. The strictness of employment regulation is supposed to have important effects on graduate career development. In Germany, initial employment positions after graduation are assumed to be highly stable and job shifts are expected to remain low. British career trajectories are marked by shorter job durations and a higher incidence of job changes and are therefore expected to be more turbulent.

In addition, the generosity of unemployment benefits is likely to impact the career development of higher education graduates. High wage replacement rates, long durations of payments and generous rules that allow for seeking jobs corresponding to one's qualification level prevailed during most of the 1980s and 1990s in Germany. As a consequence, if phases of unemployment are experienced, higher education graduates will have the opportunity to remain unemployed until reemployment is found in a job similar to the one held before unemployment. In Britain, in contrast, low and means-tested benefit rates, short payment durations and strict rules regarding the job search set high incentives for the unemployed to seek reemployment as soon as possible, making them accept any kind of job, whether similar to the one held previously or not.

Overall, both aspects of labour market regulation should have important consequences for status mobility of higher education graduates in Germany and Britain. Generous unemployment benefits will shelter German graduates throughout their careers from severe downward mobility, allowing them to maintain a level of status matching their higher education qualifications. At the same time, the strictness of employment protection legislation has the indirect effect of lower overall vacancy levels, which as a consequence will restrict upward mobility among German graduates as well. The opposite effects are expected for Britain, where low levels of unemployment benefits provide no shelter from downward mobility. At the same time, higher levels of overall job turnover in the labour market following from the lower regulation of employment will imply increased opportunity levels for upward mobility. All expected impacts of labour market regulation on career mobility are summarised in the following table:

Table 7:   Impact of labour market regulation on career mobility

	Germany	Britain
Strictness of dismissal protection	High → stable employment positions, few job shifts	Low → unstable employment positions, many job shifts
Generosity of unemployment benefits	High → low occupational mobility after unemployment	Low → high occupational mobility after unemployment
Overall strictness of labour market regulation	High → low downward and upward status mobility	Low → high downward and upward status mobility

6. Graduate Employment between Elitist Ideals and the Realities of Mass Higher Education

The previous chapter has demonstrated strong cross-national variations in the institutional set-up of higher education systems and graduate labour markets in Germany and Britain. As a consequence of the identified institutional differences, labour market entry and career patterns of higher education graduates are expected to vary considerably in cross-national comparison. Although both countries have experienced some common developments, such as higher education expansion, growing flexibility of the labour market, or rising levels of unemployment among the labour force as a whole, the extent and rapidity of change has differed strongly. Moreover, education and labour market structures continue to be very diverse. In Germany, the lower level of stratification of higher education institutions in combination with the lower age participation rate following from a highly stratified secondary education system, a higher importance of occupation-specific training provided by higher education, particularly for professionals or engineers, stronger demarcations of labour market segments in the professional and public sector, and a higher degree of labour market regulation should facilitate the process of matching graduates to jobs. Higher education certificates should be of major importance for a smooth and more standardised transition process in Germany. These patterns are assumed to be rather stable over time due to the strong resistance to reforms both of the higher education system and the graduate labour market.

For Britain, a more turbulent transition from higher education to work is expected, consisting of a sequence of stop-gap jobs and higher mobility rates. The higher degree of stratification of higher education institutions going hand in hand with a higher age participation rate due to the weakly stratified school system, a lower relevance of occupation-specific training offered by higher education, more flexible labour market regulation and graduate labour markets less dominated by the professional and public sphere, make the matching of graduates and jobs more of an individual endeavour and less dependent on certificates. Placement in particular occupations or jobs should be structured less by higher education credentials. Rather, it should depend on additional factors such as economic circumstances or additional signals such as gender, ethnicity of parental socio-economic status. Entry patterns are expected to be more diverse and also to have undergone more changes over time, due to the strong reforms that have taken place both within the higher education system and the labour market.

6.1 Early Employment Patterns after Graduation

Before the impact of institutional environment on the transition from higher education to work is examined with multivariate methods, a description of the various spells during the first five years after leaving full-time higher education is provided. The analysis covers the whole range of employment and non-employment statuses available in both data sets, i.e. spells of full-time employment, part-time employment, unemployment, further education, parental leave or homemaker, and other activities such as military service, sickness, or early retirement, including a group with status not specified further. The overall aim is to provide a first impression of how the process of labour market entry in both countries evolves over time. The description is based on the monthly calendar information for each graduate. The two panels in Figure 9 indicate the cumulated frequencies of individuals in the various spell types during the first five years after graduation.

According to Figure 9, the largest proportion of people in both countries gains full-time employment immediately after finishing higher education, albeit at quite different scales. While 60 percent of British graduates start full-time work straight away, the respective proportion in Germany only accounts for roughly 45 percent. The initial relative disadvantage German graduates face in finding full-time employment is levelled out by a steeper increase of full-time employment rates. One year after finishing university, almost three quarters of graduates work full-time in both countries. In Germany, a plateau of about 80 percent working full-time is reached after about two years and from thereon remains rather constant. In Britain, the proportion of graduates in full-time employment continues to rise steadily during the first four years, but at a slower pace, until reaching 84 percent.

The percentage of students working in full-time and part-time positions is more similar immediately after graduation due to the high number of part-time employees in Germany. There, an additional amount of 16 percent enters the labour market straight away into part-time positions, while in Britain only 5 percent of all graduates work part-time immediately after graduation. Over the whole period, both countries exhibit a surprisingly constant rate of students working in part-time positions, but again at different levels: around 8 percent in Germany and around 4 percent in Britain.

A more detailed analysis of part-time employment patterns by gender (see Figure 27, Appendix E) indicated that in both countries, women are significantly more likely to work part-time than men.

Figure 9: Activities during the first five years after graduation in Germany and Britain

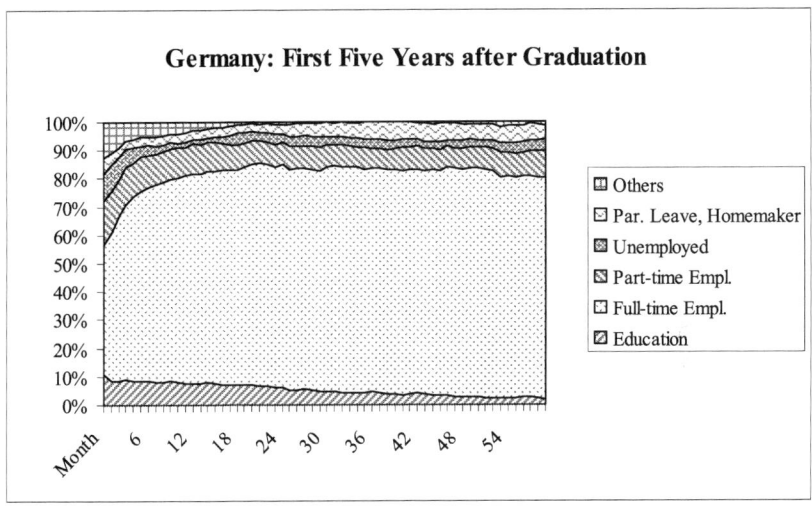

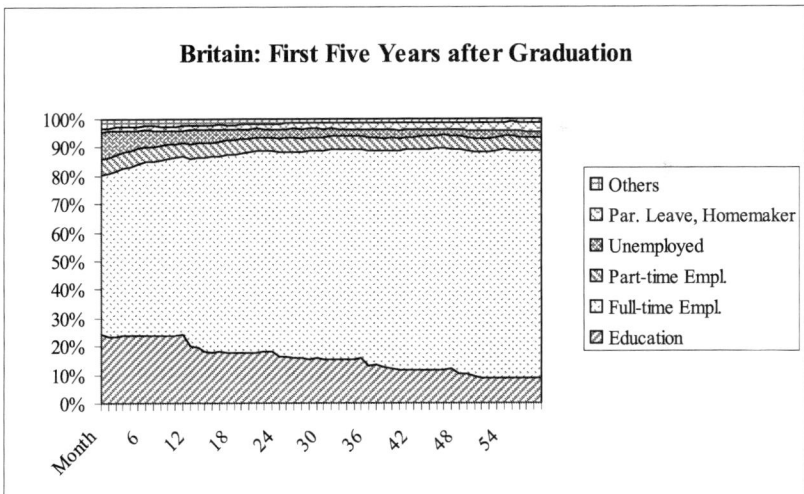

Data: Calculations based on data from the SOEP, NCDS/BCS70

But in general, part-time employment is more prevalent in Germany immediately after graduation, since German men are also more likely to be in part-time jobs than their British male counterparts.[34]

Taking full-time and part-time employment together, 61 percent of graduates in Germany and 65 percent in Britain find a job straight after leaving higher education and by the end of five years, 88 percent of all German and 86 percent of all British graduates are in employment. These figures correspond to the results of Teichler and his colleagues based on the CHEERS data (Schomburg and Teichler 2006; Teichler 2002b; 2007a), according to which 87 percent of graduates in both countries are employed four years after graduation. Overall, one can conclude that finding a job after graduation is rather unproblematic in both countries for the majority of students. Only in the first few months, British graduates seem to have a slight advantage in entering the labour market, but one year later, employment rates are roughly the same. Yet, this initial description does not take into account the quality of labour market outcomes, i.e. the type of occupation or the status of the positions obtained. Whether more significant differences between the two countries exist in this regard will be an important issue in the empirical analysis that follows.

The unemployment rate of higher education graduates lies at 9 percent during the first two months after graduation in both countries. Thereafter, it drops steadily. Initially, the decrease takes place at a higher pace in Germany, since one year after graduation, only 2 percent of German graduates and 4 percent of their British counterparts are unemployed. From then on, however, unemployment in Germany increases slightly again and remains rather constant at the 3 percent level. In Britain, in contrast, unemployment continues to decline and at the end of five years, the unemployment rate of the sample is less than 1 percent. But despite these small differences, unemployment stays at a very low level – below 5 percent – in both countries for most of the observation period, which indicates that the risk of unemployment cannot be considered problematic with a higher education degree in both countries. This again corresponds with the results from the CHEERS data, according to which 4 percent of German and 2

---

34 The fact that women in both countries are more likely to work part-time after graduation and, as will be seen in the following, that further gender differences of the transition process exist will be not be examined in more detail in this study. This is justified on the one hand by the study's broad focus on general transition patterns in both countries and on the other with the particular subject of gender inequalities and sex segregation in labour markets. A thorough analysis of gendered transition processes would require the application of a whole new set of theories and concepts to capture cross-national similarities and differences, since the theories introduced in this study as the main comparative framework can be considered "gender-blind" and hence do not allow for making a precise analysis in this regard. Therefore, gender is controlled in all models estimated, but a more profound examination of gender inequalities is left to further analysis, as, for example, already undertaken in Leuze (2007).

percent of British graduates are unemployed one year after graduation (Teichler 2002a). Nevertheless, issues of unemployment and its impact on further career development will be examined in more detail in the section on labour market regulation.

So far, the cumulative description of transition patterns from higher education to work exhibits only minor variations between Germany and Britain. This changes if spell types other than employment and unemployment are considered. The main difference is related to the extent of further education received in addition to a first higher education degree. In Britain, roughly one fifth of all graduates continue to study for a further degree, be it a second university degree, a professional certificate, or another type of postgraduate diploma. Even though the numbers of students remaining in further education drops continuously throughout the observation period, eight percent of British graduates are still in or have returned to some form of education and training five years after graduating for the first time. In Germany, in contrast, only about 10 percent continue to stay in education immediately after graduation, and by the end of five years the proportion has dropped to less than two percent. The main reason for these divergent findings should be the differentiation of undergraduate and postgraduate courses of study which are available at British higher education institutions but not at German ones. The multivariate analysis of the transition process will shed further light on how vertical and horizontal institutional differentiation by type of higher education institutions, type of degrees and fields of study shapes early labour market careers.

Additionally, strong differences exist in the amount of graduates doing other activities after graduation. In Britain, the ratio never exceeds five percent and even though it continues to decline, it never drops below two percent. A possible explanation for this pattern could be the so called gap year that many British graduates take immediately after graduation or a short period of employment. Even though their exact activities during a gap year are not coded in the data set, it is very common to take some time off for travelling or for doing voluntary work. In Germany, more than ten percent of all graduates are engaged in other activities, but the ratio drops dramatically during the first 12 months and is close to zero two years after graduation. Since a differentiation by sex (see Table 16 in Appendix E) indicates that men have roughly double the number of spells in this unspecified category compared to women, it is reasonable to assume that military or alternative civilian service are the main 'other' activities taken up by male German graduates after higher education.

Only a small proportion of graduates – fewer than five percent in both countries – takes parental leave or stays at home during the first five years after graduation. The ratio is lowest immediately after graduation and rises steadily thereafter; however, the vast majority of graduates seems to put greater emphasis on pursuing a career during the first five years as opposed to starting a family, an observation that is in line with current debates about the childlessness of highly qualified women. This issue will be controlled for in the multivariate analysis by including interaction effects for women with young dependent children.

In summary, the descriptive analysis of the cumulative spell distribution during the first five years after graduation in Germany and Britain so far exhibits more similarities than differences. Even though the ratio of graduates in full-time and part-time work differs substantially, the general employment rate is rather similar in both countries and points to the fact that obtaining a job with a higher education degree is quite easy. Overall, these descriptive findings are in line with results of large-scale country comparisons (Kivinen and Nurmi 2003; OECD 2004a; Schomburg and Teichler 2006; Teichler 2002b; 2007a), according to which the transition from higher education to work is still rather unproblematic across countries, especially when compared to qualifiers from other educational levels. Stronger differences, however, exist in the quality of employment positions, such as the type of occupation obtained, the status position of initial employment positions, the stability of early labour market careers, and further career development of higher education graduates. All of these issues will be dealt with in the multivariate analysis in order to examine the general influence of the institutional context on graduate career mobility.

6.2 Institutional Differentiation and the Stratification of Labour Market Returns

The first institutional factor that is taken into account for examining cross-national differences in the transition from higher education to work is the stratification of higher education systems. According to Allmendinger (1989b), the degree of stratification depends on the proportion of a cohort attaining the maximum number of school years and the number of different tracks provided by the education system. In countries with a high degree of stratification, education returns (such as occupational status or earnings) are higher, since the channelling of students into particular education tracks makes it easier for employers to select from fewer applicants with matching qualifications. This hypothesis has already been confirmed for secondary schooling and vocational training (Allmendinger 1989b; Bernardi et al. 2004; Kerckhoff 1996; Shavit and Müller 1998). In addition to status outcomes, Bernardi et al. (2004) have also compared the timing of transition processes of higher education graduates to those of qualifiers from other educational levels. They show that university leavers have much higher transition rates to a first job in highly stratified systems since there are fewer competitors for good jobs and the signal provided by educational credentials is more reliable.

In their comparison of 13 countries, Müller and Shavit (1998) demonstrate that higher education graduates generally have better chances of obtaining prestigious occupations when compared to qualifiers from lower educational levels. However, the scale of the comparative advantage differs substantially across countries. The effect of qualifications on EGP class of the first job is higher in systems with a high degree of stratification and a low percentage of students obtaining postsecondary qualifications. The highly stratified German secondary school system results in strong status differences between holders of the highest and lowest educational credentials, while in Britain, the differences are relatively small due to a low degree of stratification in secondary education. However, their results indicate as well that the effects of higher education are more similar across countries than those of lower level qualifications, such as vocational training.

While many studies already investigated the comparative advantage of higher education graduates following from different forms of institutional stratification (see for example Allmendinger and Hinz 1998; Gangl 2000a; b; Müller 2000; Scherer 2005), no empirical analysis has focussed exclusively on higher education graduates so far. How the stratification of higher education systems might stratify graduate labour market outcomes remains still an open question. Theoretical explanations pointed out that stratification is closely related to the degree of institutional differentiation in a country's higher education system along types of institutions, types of degrees, and fields of study. So far, comparative studies on the influence of institutional differentiation on labour market entry processes are rare. The few existing ones have mainly focused on differentiation by type of institution or by fields of study (see Brennan et al. 1996b; Kim and Kim 2003; Kivinen and Nurmi 2003; Müller et al. 2002; Teichler 2002b; van de Werfhorst and Kraaykamp 2001). The study by Müller, Brauns and Steinmann (2002), for example, reveals that different types of higher education institutions in Britain, France and Germany lead to country-specific stratification patterns of labour market returns. It indicates as well, however, that the gap between institution-related outcomes has decreased over time. According to these authors, stratification processes are more pronounced in Britain than in Germany. Furthermore, Kim and Kim (2003) point to the fact that different fields of study strongly stratify labour market returns of higher education graduates in Germany and Britain, but that the effects are much higher in Britain due to the lower level of stratification in secondary schooling.

Altogether, previous results indicate that institutional differentiation of higher education systems indeed stratifies graduate labour market outcomes. However, these studies have neither systematically linked their findings to the concept of stratification nor have they used longitudinal data to take into account the timing of transition processes. In the following, both the duration and the quality of the matching process will be examined in relation to the different dimensions of stratification. The institutional analysis of the previous chapter identified specific stratification patterns inherent to the higher education systems in Germany and Britain, but also demonstrated cross-national variations in the stratification of secondary schooling and corresponding age participation rates. At the level of higher education, differences are most pronounced as regards types of higher education degrees. While in Germany, degrees are stratified horizontally since only one degree level exists, the British degree system is stratified vertically through the differentiation into undergraduate and postgraduate degrees. Both forms of degree differentiation might matter for labour market entry; however, only the high degree of vertical differentiation in the British system is assumed to stratify labour market returns hierarchically and as such is associated with a high degree of stratification. Thus, stratification by degree is assumed to be stronger in Britain than in Germany. Stratification by type of institution is also rather different in both countries, following a similar stratification pattern. While German universities are more equal in terms of legal governance and institutional organisation and accordingly more horizontally differentiated, British types of higher education institutions differ more vertically in study organisation, financial endowments, or reputation, despite the reforms of the early 1990s. Therefore, stratification by type of institution should be more pronounced in Britain as well. On the other hand, different fields of study differentiate both systems horizontally and accordingly should lead to fewer differences in labour market returns in Germany and Britain.

The other dimension of the concept of stratification is related to the education system as a whole and refers to the proportion of students obtaining the highest possible degree. The lower this proportion, the higher the degree of stratification and accordingly, the better the comparative labour market advantage for higher education graduates. In the course of educational expansion and particularly since the late 1980s, the proportion of higher education graduates has risen much more strongly in Britain than in Germany. This is closely related to the stratification of secondary schooling, which sets institutional limits upon higher education expansion, but only if it is highly stratified as in Germany. As a consequence of the weakly stratified secondary education system and the steep increase of higher education participation, overall labour market returns of British graduates should generally be lower and in addition have decreased, since more qualifiers are competing for favourable labour market positions. Due to the highly selective secondary school system and the lower levels of higher education expansion, German graduates should on the whole have a higher likelihood of obtaining favourable starting positions in a shorter amount of time than their British counterparts.

6.2.1 Labour Market Returns of Initial Employment Positions

In order to examine the impact of institutional stratification on graduate careers, the overall labour market returns are estimated in a first step for German and British graduates. In this regard, both the duration and the quality of the transition process are expected to differ significantly due to different institutional environments in both countries. A rather straightforward representation of the time it takes to enter the labour market after graduation is provided by the survivor function, which indicates the share of persons that have not yet made the transition to a first job at any given point of time (Allison 1984; Blossfeld and Rohwer 1995; Jenkins 2004). The so-called failure function is the inverse of the survivor function, referring the share of individuals that already have made a particular transition (or failure) at any time of observation. Since the analysis of the transition from higher education to work is more interested in the latter group, the failure function for various labour market outcomes is presented in the next sections. A graphic comparison of survivor and failure functions in Germany and Britain has to take into account the 95 percent confidence intervals (95% CI) of the curves as well, since only a non-overlap of these intervals indicates significantly different transition rates in both countries (Blossfeld and Rohwer 1995). To measure the quality of labour market returns, several measures will be employed in the following, consecutively raising the quality level of outcomes. A first, rather basic differentiation is made between full-time and part-time jobs. Figure 10 displays the Kaplan-Meier failure functions for the transition to any first job, be it full-time or part-time, and to a first full-time job.

All four panels indicate that labour market entry takes place at a fast pace in both countries, as expected from the descriptive results of the previous section. Around 70 percent of all graduates in both countries have found a job, full-time or part-time, in the first month after graduation, and 50 percent have obtained full-time employment in the second month after graduation. By the end of five years almost a hundred percent of all graduates have made the transition to a first employment position. This does, however, not necessarily mean that there is full employment by the end of the observation period, since some graduates might already have lost their jobs again. For those obtaining a full-time or part-time job, hardly any country differences exist at the beginning and at the end of the five year period. Between month 6 and month 36, however, British graduates take significantly longer to enter employment, which might be the result of further training periods. German graduates, in contrast, initially have more difficulties in finding a full-time job, probably due to military service and the higher prevalence of part-time positions.

Figure 10: Transition to first employment in Germany and Britain

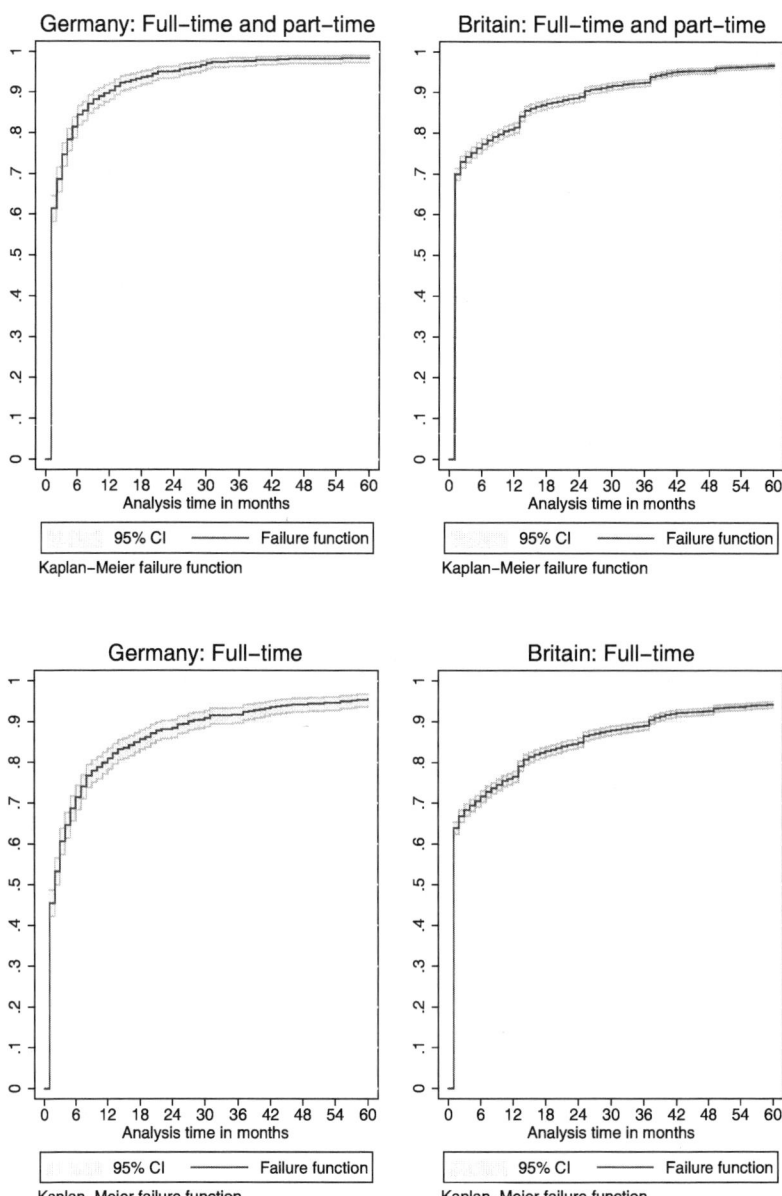

Data: Estimations based on data from the SOEP and NCDS/BCS70

Overall, if one applies the criterion of duration dependence as an indicator of a smooth transition from higher education to work, entry into part-time and full-time employment takes place at a very high speed in both countries. Other research has shown that the phenomenon of a quick transition process to a first job is very common for higher education graduates not only in Germany and Britain, but in other European and OECD countries as well (OECD 2004a; Schomburg and Teichler 2006; Teichler 2002b; 2007a).

Thus, overall returns do not seem to differ much by institutional environment in Germany and Britain. Neither does a stratified secondary school system nor the lower levels of higher education expansion, as it is the case in Germany, increase transition rates to employment as compared to Britain. This indicates that the differentiation between employment and non-employment cannot be considered a good measure of stratified labour market returns for the level of higher education. This is different if employment opportunities of higher education graduates are compared to those of individuals holding different education credentials. Studies investigating labour market outcomes of the education system as a whole have shown that such a basic indicator already captures cross-nationally stratification differences between various educational levels quite successfully (Bernardi et al. 2004; Hillmert 2001; Scherer 2005).

The picture of stratified labour market outcomes changes considerably if the EGP class of first employment is taken into account in both countries. Class outcomes can be considered a more adequate measurement of status differences in labour market returns as compared to full-time or part-time employment, since they clearly indicate a hierarchy in terms of high status and low status positions. Figure 11 shows the failure functions for obtaining a job in either EGP class I or II or in EGP class I only. Again, all four panels indicate evidence of negative duration dependence for the transition rates in both countries. The longer the search duration for a job in the service class in both countries, the more difficult it becomes for graduates to actually obtain one. In addition, it is much easier for the majority of graduates to obtain a job in EGP class I or II than to enter the more exclusive high service class.

When approached this way, however, country differences become very pronounced from the beginning and seem to increase as more time passes by. Comparing the two panels suggests that labour market entry into the service class is less common and takes longer in Britain than in Germany. Entry into the high service class (EGP I) in particular is much more difficult for British graduates.

For example, the Kaplan-Meyer failure functions of the transition to employment in EGP class I demonstrates that more than 25 percent of all German graduates manage to obtain a high service class job within three months of graduation, while it takes one and a half years for the same proportion of British graduates to be successful.

Figure 11: Transition to first employment in the service class in Germany and Britain

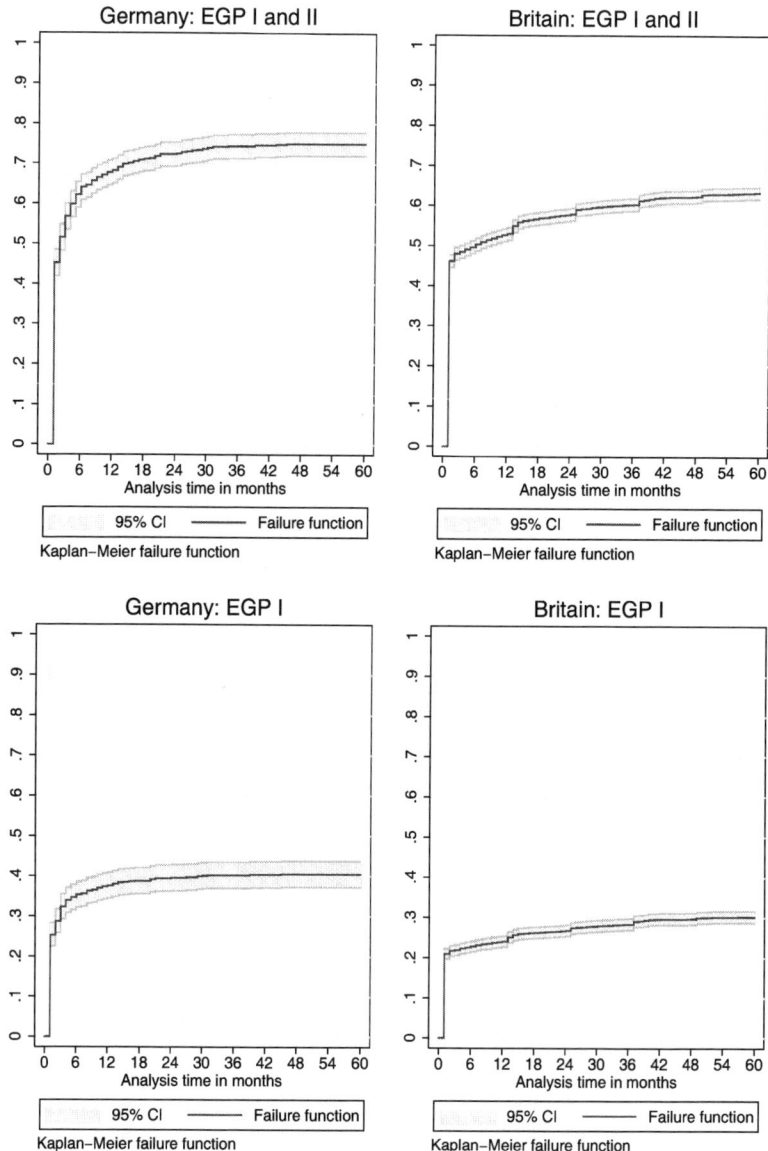

Data: Estimations based on data from the SOEP and NCDS/BCS70

By the end of five years, roughly 45 percent of German graduates have entered the high service class, but just over 30 percent of their British counterparts have managed to do so. It is important to note, however, that more than 50 percent of all graduates in both countries do not succeed in entering these upper status positions at all during the first five years following graduation.

In summary, market entrants in both countries find initial employment after graduation very soon, be it full-time or part-time, but only Germans are much more likely to obtain occupations in the upper sector of the job hierarchy. This observed pattern is consistent with the stratification hypothesis that German graduates generally have higher chances of obtaining favourable labour market positions immediately after graduation. The transition to EGP class I employment can be taken as an especially clear first indicator that the highly stratified secondary education system in Germany complements a stratified labour market. Sorting according to educational credentials already occurs at this educational level, which leads to high overall labour market returns of those with higher education degrees. Weakly stratified secondary school systems, such as the British, lower overall status outcomes of higher education graduates, since sorting has not yet taken place, but competition takes place at the level of higher education. Even though the direct comparison of labour market returns for different educational levels cannot be captured by this type of analysis, these findings stay in line with the results of Müller and Shavit (1998), who found that highly stratified secondary education systems yield generally higher EGP returns for higher education graduates.

It might of course be argued that the more favourable starting positions of German graduates are less a result of a stratified education system, but rather a consequence of different class distributions. Evidence against the validity of this argument is provided by Figure 12, which displays the EGP distribution of initial employment positions obtained after graduation and compares it to a country's class distribution of all persons in employment and of those with a higher education degree.

The most substantial country differences can be found between German and British graduates employed in lower and upper class positions immediately after graduation. In Germany, more than 40 percent of all graduates find an occupation in EGP class I, but only 22 percent work in lower class occupations. In Britain, in contrast, a higher percentage of graduates start their employment careers in lower class jobs (32 percent) than in high service class occupations (29 percent).

This again implies that German higher education is more closely linked with high service class occupations due to the highly stratified secondary school system, while in Britain class outcomes of higher education graduates are more diverse.

Figure 12: EGP class distribution in Germany and Britain

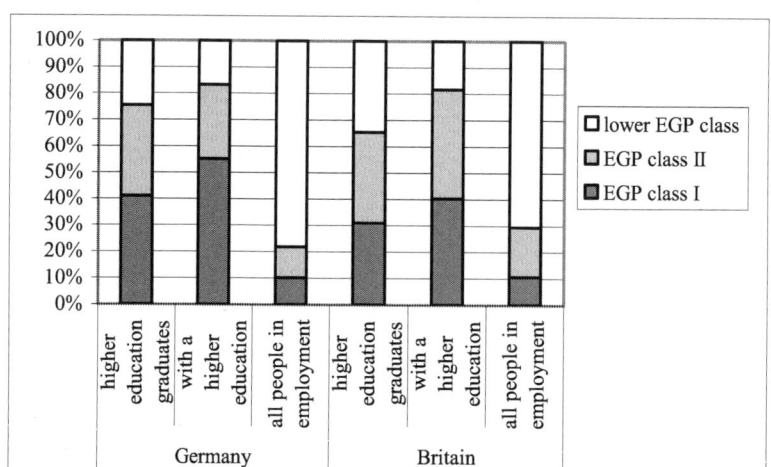

Higher education graduates: EGP class distribution of graduates in the SOEP and the NCDS/BCS70;

With a higher education degree: EGP class distribution of all in employment with a higher education degree in the Mikrozensus 1995 and the British Labour Force Survey 1995, both weighted;

All people in employment: EGP class distribution of all people in employment irrespective of educational qualification in the Mikrozensus 1995 and the British Labour Force Survey 1995, both weighted.

Data: SOEP, German Mikrozensus 1995, NCDS/BCS70, British Labour Force Survey 1995

Class distribution, however, changes if all persons with a higher education degree in employment are considered. Again, a larger proportion of Germans hold occupations in EGP class I; yet, the proportion of people in lower EGP classes is similar in both countries. This indicates that in Britain, labour market entry after higher education is in particular associated with lower status employment positions, while upward mobility in later work life seems to occur more often from lower EGP classes. Country differences become even more pronounced, but turned upside down when the distribution of occupational classes among all people in employment is compared. The amount of EGP class I positions is roughly the same in both countries, but the number of people employed in EGP class II is almost twice as high in Britain than in Germany. This again points to the fact that higher education credentials and service class positions are strongly connected in Germany. In Britain, in contrast, this link seems to be less pronounced and higher EGP classes are obviously open to individuals without a higher education degree as well.

In summary, the descriptive empirical results confirm the expected country differences with regard to obtaining more favourable starting positions after graduation. Apparently, in Britain the transition from higher education to employment in the service class takes longer and is less common for the majority of graduates. In Germany, starting a career in the upper segment of the labour market after graduation is much more likely. This can be taken as an indicator that the sorting through the highly stratified German secondary education system is an important institutional stage for channelling higher education graduates into high service class jobs, while degree holders from lower educational levels are generally more prone to hold lower status positions. The low degree of stratification in British secondary schooling and the high degree of higher education expansion makes labour market entry more competitive and thus prohibits a quick entry into the most favourite labour market positions for the majority of graduates. Turning from the stratification of secondary education to the stratification of higher education systems, a more detailed multivariate analysis will shed further light on the question of which role higher education credentials have for a more or less smooth transition from higher education to work in both countries.

6.2.2 Mechanisms of Stratification and the Transition to Employment

So far, the results have highlighted pronounced differences in the distribution of class outcomes and the time it takes to enter upper class positions after graduation. If these differences originate from the institutional differentiation of higher education systems in both countries, they will remain so after controlling for socio-structural characteristics. And in fact, they do remain. In order to examine the impact of institutional stratification on labour market entry processes, a single event hazard rate model for the transition from higher education to first employment, be it full-time or part-time, was estimated (see Table 8). Following from the Kaplan-Mayer failure functions, transition rates to any type of employment differ most strongly during the first year after graduation, while later on they level off. Therefore, the chosen bands of piecewise constant time intervals are narrow during the first year and are wide thereafter. In total, six different time intervals are differentiated: entry in the first month after graduation, entry in the second or third month after graduation, entry between month four and month six, entry in the second half of the first year, entry in the second year, and entry thereafter. As will be seen in the following discussion, these bands proved to be highly valuable for grasping the time dependent variation of hazard rates. To evaluate the quality of the chosen model, a likelihood ratio test was performed after each estimation which compares the parameter model to the one with piecewise constant time intervals only.

Table 8: Transition to first employment and first employment in EGP class I (both full-time and part-time)

Transition to a first job	full-time or part-time		in EGP class I	
	Germany	Britain	Germany	Britain
Piecewise duration dependence				
Base line (Ref.: Entry during 1. month after graduation)				
Entry 2.-3. month	0.155 (0.020)**	0.038 (0.004)**	0.153 (0.024)**	0.023 (0.004)**
Entry 4.-6. month	0.119 (0.017)**	0.020 (0.002)**	0.048 (0.010)**	0.016 (0.003)**
Entry 7.-12. month	0.060 (0.010)**	0.014 (0.001)**	0.019 (0.005)**	0.011 (0.002)**
Entry 13.-24. month	0.048 (0.010)**	0.021 (0.002)**	0.008 (0.002)**	0.013 (0.001)**
Entry 24.-60 month	0.038 (0.011)**	0.013 (0.001)**	0.002 (0.001)**	0.006 (0.001)**
Institutional differentiation				
Type of higher education institution (Ref.: *Fachhochschule*, polytechnic)				
University institution	0.632 (0.074)**#	1.104 (0.069)	1.107 (0.161) #	1.322 (0.101)**
Type of degree (Ref.: Casmin 3a = *Fachhochschul*-degree (D), diploma/certificate (GB))				
Diplom, Magister (3b)	0.652 (0.079)**		1.112 (0.167)	
Staatsexamen (3b)	0.580 (0.083)**		1.091 (0.218)	
Casmin3b low		1.146 (0.113)		1.752 (0.249)**
Casmin3b high		2.087 (0.315)**		2.156 (0.352)**
Field of study (Ref.: Humanities, Arts)				
Engineering, Construction	0.917 (0.159)	1.065 (0.095)	6.358 (2.422)**	2.119 (0.252)**
Science, Agriculture	1.002 (0.209)	1.033 (0.115)	3.365 (1.425)**	2.614 (0.322)**
Social Sciences, Business, Law	1.216 (0.213)	1.144 (0.154)	3.515 (1.366)**	3.402 (0.461)**
Health, Welfare	1.345 (0.321)	1.323 (0.165)*	9.791 (4.044)**	2.699 (0.401)**
Education	1.012 (0.223)	1.500 (0.190)**	1.098 (0.661)	1.086 (0.209)
Control variables				
Female	0.924 (0.101)	1.148 (0.073)*	0.626 (0.096)**	0.508 (0.038)**
Female with child < 6	0.476 (0.115)**	0.478 (0.065)**	0.854 (0.329)	0.567 (0.136)*
Non-German / Non-White	0.737 (0.114)	0.842 (0.133)	0.513 (0.128)*	0.854 (0.137)
Father: higher degree (D)/ upper class (GB)	0.934 (0.099)	1.025 (0.060)	1.154 (0.167)	1.184 (0.080)*
Vocational education	1.108 (0.162)	0.827 (0.064)*	0.956 (0.159)	0.798 (0.069)*
Graduation age (Ref: 24-29 years old at graduation)				
younger than 24 years	0.610 (0.139)*	2.511 (0.207)**	1.007 (0.302)	0.778 (0.077)*
older than 29 years	1.060 (0.152)	0.194 (0.029)**	0.718 (0.121)	0.843 (0.109)
Degree of East Germany	1.013 (0.137)		1.009 (0.178)	
Yearly unemployment rate (%)	0.996 (0.044)	1.052 (0.018)**	0.903 (0.053)	0.989 (0.018)
Yearly GDP (in 1.000)	1.047 (0.110)	1.009 (0.001)**	1.000 (0.001)	0.999 (0.001)
Age participation rate (%)	1.000 (0.000)	0.916 (0.013)**	1.000 (0.000)	1.006 (0.007)
Size birth cohort (in 1.000)	1.000 (0.000)	0.953 (0.006)**	0.963 (0.120)	1.014 (0.016)

Transition to a first job	full-time or part-time		in EGP class I	
No. of observations (person months)	3895	26861	26838	154626
No. of failures	847	3655	348	1134
Log-likelihood null model	-1528.9405	-6384.3064	-1156.3817	-4307.2022
Log-likelihood end model	-1486.9763	-6016.4278	-1092.0460	-4083.5067
Likelihood Ratio Test Chi^2	83.93**	735.76**	128.67**	447.39**

Discrete time PCE models based on logistic regression, odds ratios reported, standard errors in parentheses
* significant at 5%; ** significant at 1%
# Coefficient stems from a separate model without types of degrees, since *Fachhochschul*-institution and *Fachhochschul*-degree both measure the same empirical fact.

Data: SOEP, NCDS/BCS70

Estimates for the transition from higher education to first employment, be it full-time or part-time, indicate that both duration, dependence, and the effects of institutional differentiation of higher education systems matter; however, not precisely in the direction expected. Since model coefficients are reported as odds ratios, they can be interpreted as relative transition rates to employment, being higher for values above 1 and lower for values between 0 and 1. In terms of key variables of interest, the estimates show clear evidence of negative duration dependence in both countries. In Germany, transition rates are already around 85 percent lower in the second month after graduation as compared to the first month, and this relationship is even higher in Britain. Clearly, the more time it takes to search for a first job, the more difficult it becomes for graduates to actually obtain one.

With respect to the role of higher education[35] in finding a first job, the statistical evidence in Table 8 lends only weak support to the hypothesised association between institutional differentiation and stratification of labour market returns.

---

35 As regards coding of higher education degrees for the British case, the more refined Casmin levels of general lower level tertiary degrees (3a_gen = Diploma, Certificate of Higher Education), first degree qualifications (3b_low = BA, BSc) and post-graduate degree qualifications (3b_high = MA, MSc, MBA, PhD, Postgraduate Certificate) are used. Since the German higher education system was less differentiated during the period of observation, the basic Casmin levels of lower tertiary education (3a = *Fachhochschule* degree) and upper tertiary education (3b = *Diplom, Magister, Staatsexamen*) are taken into account. A further differentiation between different types of university degrees, which cannot be captured by the Casmin scheme, was implemented as well: the difference between academic (*Diplom, Magister*) and state (*Staatsexamen*) examinations. In all models, the coefficient of German university institutions is always given in italics, since its estimation stems from a model different from the presented one. The effect of types of degrees and types of institutions had to be estimated separately, because both variables are highly correlated, particularly in the case of *Fachhochschulen*, where both *Fachhochschule* institution and *Fachhochschule* degree measure the same empirical fact.

While in Britain, differences between university and non-university institutions do not exist, there is evidence that transition rates of students with postgraduate degree (Casmin 3b_high) are twice as high as for those holding diplomas or certificates (Casmin 3a). Thus, at least as regards type of degrees vertical institutional differentiation has an impact on labour market outcomes according to the predicted pattern. However, in Germany, the importance of institutional differentiation is turned upside down: seemingly horizontally differentiated dimensions of higher education systems stratify labour market returns. Transition rates of university graduates are on average about 40 percent higher than those of *Fachhochschule* graduates, and the differentiation by type of degrees also shows that Casmin 3a qualification holders (*Fachhochschule* degrees) find a first job much quicker than those with Casmin 3b qualifications, be it a university *Diplom, Magister,* or *Staatsexamen.* The stratification of labour market returns by horizontal institutional differentiation can also be observed for particular fields of study in Britain, namely education and health/welfare, where students have much shorter transition periods than those of other disciplines. These findings point to the fact that not only vertically differentiated higher education systems have important implications for labour market stratification, but that additional factors that cannot be grasped by the concept of horizontal differentiation might play a role.

Estimates so far only weakly support the expected relationship between higher education differentiation and labour market stratification. However, the control of macro variables, especially of those associated with higher education expansion, exhibits interesting country differences. The age participation rate in particular can be taken as a good indicator of how rising numbers of students influence the employment opportunities of higher education graduates. By and large, British transition processes are very sensitive to changing structural environments, be it rising unemployment, a rise of the GDP, a higher number of students enrolled, or higher birth rates. Larger birth cohorts and in particular higher age participation rates in higher education make it generally more difficult for graduates to find employment. Apparently, increased competition among higher education graduates lowers the chances of finding employment in Britain. This is in line with the hypothesis that labour market returns of graduates decrease if more students obtain a higher education degree. Contrary to findings on the transition from vocational education to work, however, which have shown that high levels of unemployment tend to lower young people's chances of finding a first job (Gangl 2000a), both higher unemployment rates and increases of GDP influence transition rates positively. On the whole, the transition from higher education to work in Britain is obviously strongly influenced by an abundance of labour supply rather than by a shortage in labour demand. Interestingly, German higher education graduates are not at all affected by changing macroeconomic environments and neither supply nor demand factors matter, despite having experienced an increase in the number of students as well. This might be explained with the lower scale of higher education expansion, but might also be taken as an indicator that higher education in Germany is generally closely linked with upper status positions due to the highly selective secondary school system, irrespective of any macro-structural changes.

The analysis of control variables shows that individual characteristics are more important in Britain for finding employment after graduation than in Germany. There is no evidence that gender, nationality, fathers' education, or additional vocational training influence the transition rates of German graduates. Only mothers with young dependent children have significantly longer transition periods, indicating that starting immediately after graduation, motherhood creates an obstacle to successful labour market integration. The same is true for Britain, where females with children younger than six years take much longer in their job search, just as holders of vocational qualifications. Interestingly, though, women without children have better chances to find employment than men. Interesting country differences can also be found concerning the importance of graduation age. While young graduates in Germany have substantially lower transition rates, British graduates under 24 find a job much faster than their older counterparts. Thus, age norms play a different role in the transition from higher education to work in both countries.

Overall, these results only partially support the stratification hypotheses, since vertical differentiation of the higher education system does not necessarily stratify labour market returns. And interestingly, horizontal differentiation also matters. But again, differentiation between employment and non-employment is not necessarily a good indicator of how labour market returns of higher education graduates are stratified, since it does not capture hierarchical differences of job outcomes. A more convincing explanation of some of the observed patterns in both countries might be the higher degree of occupational specificity associated with particular types of institutions such as *Fachhochschulen,* types of degrees such as postgraduate degrees, or fields of study like health or education. The higher relevance of practical knowledge for the labour market is likely to increase transition rates to employment, an issue to be examined further in the section on occupational specificity.

Turning back to the stratification of labour market returns, differentiation between different EGP classes of first employment can be considered a more adequate measure for identifying the association between institutional differentiation and stratified labour market returns. Table 8 displays the logistic regression transition rates of entering EGP class I as first employment. Again, three types of explanatory factors related to institutional differentiation are of interest: type of higher education institution, type of higher education degree, and field of study. As expected, types of higher education institutions and degrees have no influence on the chance of making a successful transition in Germany, since they only establish a horizontal differentiation of institutional features and therefore are not likely to stratify labour market returns. Interestingly, though, field of study, which was also assumed to produce horizontal differences between students, becomes the major predictor of entering EGP class I, with health professionals having the highest transition rates and humanities and arts graduates the lowest. Apparently, a horizontal differentiation along subjects more strongly stratifies labour market returns than any other form of institutional differentiation in Germany. This indicates that, in the context of a stratified labour market, different fields of study signal status differences rather than merely signalling the specific form of knowledge studied.

In Britain, the association between fields of study and type of first job can be found as well, but at a much lower level. There, type of institution and the higher education degree attained are of equally high importance for stratifying labour market outcomes. Consistent with the hypothesis of vertical differentiation of higher education, these results demonstrate that the higher the degree, the shorter the duration of obtaining a high service class position. Also, there is a clear advantage for graduates from university institutions independent of the degree obtained. Even though the majority of British graduates do not obtain a job in EGP class I during the first five years after graduation in Britain, some institutional features, such as postgraduate degrees, degrees from universities and in particular subjects are closely linked with such favourable starting positions. The stratification of upper and lower labour market returns in Britain is, accordingly, based on a strong stratification by the higher education system, which channels only students with higher degrees or particular fields of study into high service class positions.

The association between institutional differentiation and labour market returns remains surprisingly stable over time in both countries. None of the macro-economic control variables show any significant impact on the transition rates. Obviously, neither higher education expansion nor changing economic circumstances have had an effect on the class positions of higher education graduates. This finding can be taken as a first indicator of the fact that the linkage between an institutionally differentiated education system and a stratified labour market is very stable in both countries. In Germany, this linkage is based on the stratification of secondary schooling, where sorting of students into particular career paths takes place very early and consequently higher education yields more favourable labour market returns. In Britain, the weakly stratified secondary school system has a lower capacity to structure labour market returns; instead a high stratification of the higher education system sorts students into a hierarchically structured labour market. The rising number of students does not seem to worsen labour market chances of German graduates at all, and in Britain it only influences the general chances of finding employment, while the occupational class obtained remains untouched.

Strong differences between both countries are also revealed by the control variables, which, again, are more decisive in Britain. In Germany, socio-structural factors have only a weak influence on the transition process. In Britain, in contrast, a strong negative selection of women with dependent children, graduates from lower class backgrounds, or graduates with vocational education takes place. This indicates that in Britain, institutionalised forms of human capital interact with socio-structural attributes when shaping early labour market opportunities. In particular, the importance of parental socio-economic status supports the theoretical assumption that stratification of labour market returns does not follow from different productivity levels associated with different credentials, but rather that stratification serves chiefly to maintain the status of upper class children and thus to reproduce existing patterns of social inequality (Collins 1979). In Germany, no such relationship seems to exist. These differences might simply result from from the different coding of parental background in both data sets, which is based on qualifications instead of EGP classes in Germany. But it might also be that the reproduction of German class inequalities already takes place in secondary schooling. Students with a lower class background who succeeded to enter higher education might experience chances similar to those of upper class students. Further research is needed in this regard to fully disentangle the interrelation between the reproduction of class inequalities in the labour market and the structure of education systems.

One remarkable similarity between both countries exists, though. Women in general have significantly lower transition rates to upper status positions than men. Even though no gender differences were found for the transition to any form of employment, the gender inequalities found for the transition to EGP class I clearly point in the direction of vertical sex segregation occurring in both labour markets immediately after graduation. Moreover, interaction effects calculated between gender and fields of study indicate that, most importantly, the range of subjects studied by a female majority yield significantly lower class outcomes (see Leuze 2007). This work shows that the prevalence of cultural gender stereotypes, such as gender essentialism and male primacy, can be considered an important cause of these status differences among male and female higher education graduates in both countries. Further research in this regard is needed to fully disentangle the relationship between higher education institutions and gendered labour market careers.

Overall, the analysis of institutional differentiation and its capacity to structure graduate careers mainly supports the hypothesis that a vertically differentiated higher education system is more likely to stratify labour market returns. However, the result that horizontal differentiation along different fields of study also has a strong impact on class outcomes, particularly for Germany, is not in line with the expectations. Regarding the effect of higher education expansion, results only weakly support the hypothesis that higher age participation rates significantly lower status returns. In Britain, the strong degree of educational expansion matters, but only as regards general employment opportunities after graduation. Despite these limitations, the cross-national variations of the institutional impact on graduate careers imply that different *stratification regimes* operate in both countries. In Germany, horizontal differentiation by field of study stratifies the labour market returns of higher education graduates most strongly, while the differentiation by type of higher education degree and type of institution matters less.

In Britain, both, types of degrees and fields of study matter for the stratification of labour market return. Compared to Germany, however, stratification by field of study is much less influential in Britain; on the other hand, labour market returns differ more strongly according to vertically stratified degrees and types of institution in Britain than in Germany. Figure 13 shows the predicted probabilities of entering EGP class I by field of study and type of degree derived from the above model to highlight these findings.

Interestingly, these country-specific stratification regimes follow a logic similar to that related to the stratification of vocational education to work transitions. There, the differentiation between occupational and organisational spaces (Maurice et al. 1986) also demonstrates that the German system is horizontally stratified along different occupations, while the British system is vertically stratified between different hierarchical levels within organisations. Even though the current analysis only takes into account labour market entry and not further career mobility, it is remarkable to note the institutional congruence. Thus, even though the institutional lines along which stratification occurs vary between different educational levels, the underlying logic follows a similar pattern. In addition, these national stratification regimes are obviously prepared by a high or low level of stratification of secondary education, which seems to be the decisive factor for explaining both the overall class distribution among higher education graduates and the degree and nature of sorting taking place through the higher education system. These findings stay in line with research examining the stratification of the education system as a whole, which shows that highly stratified secondary education systems complement weakly stratified higher education systems and vice versa (Allmendinger 1989, Müller and Shavit 1998). However, the stratification of labour market returns in Germany needs further empirical investigation, since this relationship cannot be completely captured by the concept of stratification. The analysis of how occupational specificity impacts graduate careers will shed further light on a political economy of the process of transition.

Figure 13: Predicted probabilities of entering EGP class I
by field of study and type of degree

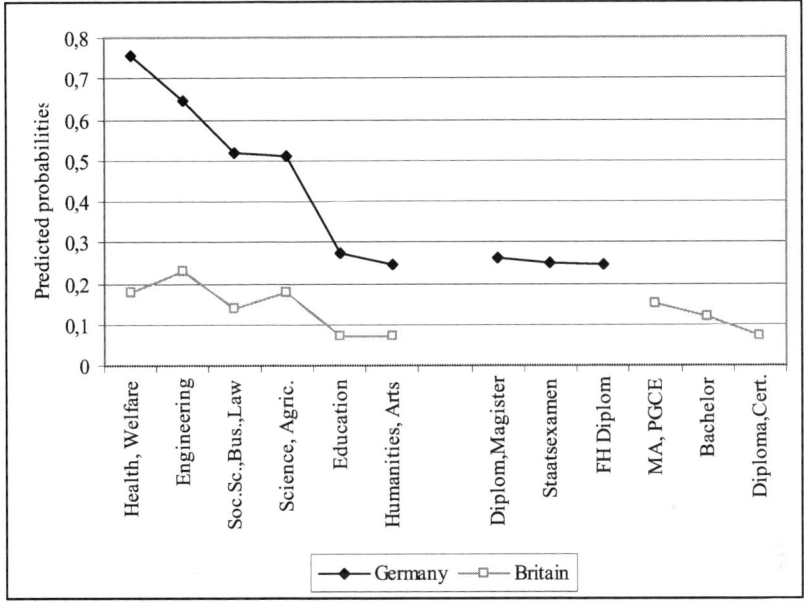

Data: SOEP, NCDS/BCS70

6.3   Occupational Specificity and the Match between Field of Study and Occupation

Higher education systems vary in the extent to which they offer curricula designed to prepare students for particular occupations or professions and award credentials that are occupationally specific. The degree of occupational specificity of an education system influences the relative reliance of market matching processes on formal education credentials as opposed to labour market experience. In countries with a high emphasis on occupationally relevant training, the education system performs an effective pre-sorting of students and allows selecting among applicants based on certified skills. In the absence of an occupation-specific education system, matching processes have to rely to a relatively greater extent on previous work experience or on other signals in addition to educational credentials.

Research on vocational education and training has widely acknowledged the fact that the transition process from education to work is strongly influenced by the existence of occupation-specific training systems. In particular, it influences the extent to which young people entering the labour market are subject to spells of unemployment, employment in specific entry-level occupations and industries, or prolonged periods of precarious employment situations (Gangl 2000a; b; 2002a; Hillmert 2001; Kogan and Müller 2003; Müller and Gangl 2003; Shavit and Müller 1998). In countries with low levels of occupation-specific training, such as Britain or Ireland, young people are allocated to lower-level initial employment positions and undergo excessive job hopping in early years after finishing education. In countries with a higher degree of occupational specificity, in contrast, such as Germany, Austria, or Denmark, young people experience a rather smooth transition process and concerns about allocation of labour market entrants to matching entry positions are relatively weak due to the existence of a highly standardised apprenticeship system. In addition to these general findings, Müller and Shavit (1998) highlight how, in countries with low occupational specificity, the overall educational level matters more for labour market returns, since higher qualifications improve career prospects considerably. In occupation-specific systems, it is more important to obtain specific credentials for successful labour market entry, while the overall level of education has a lower effect.

For the field of higher education, the theoretical discussion on occupational specificity has shown that cross-national differences of occupational specificity should exist along the lines of institutional differentiation by type of institutions, type of degrees and fields of study. Empirical evidence which includes all of these dimensions and evaluates their importance for occupation-specific matching processes is rare. So far, most studies focus on the impact of different fields of study on labour market outcomes, but none of them systematically link their findings to differences in the institutional set-up of countries. In a large-scale comparison of higher education in nine European countries, Kivinen and Nurmi (2003) illustrate the finding that the professional orientation of different fields of study exhibits both cross-national similarities and differences. In most countries, fields of study are rank-ordered in more or less the same way, with education and health care showing the strongest professional orientation and science and humanities showing the weakest. In addition, graduates in more professionally oriented disciplines such as health and particularly engineering usually gain more relevant work experience during their studies than others. These similarities are outshone, however, by the differences between countries. In some countries, various subjects do not differ very much from each other in terms of their professional orientation, while in others the level of professionalism is clearly dependent on the field of study. In a study on Dutch graduates, van de Werfhorst and Kraaykamp (2001) show that each field of study is strongly related to certain types of resources and that this relationship influences graduates to take corresponding occupations in which their achieved resources can be applied best.

Regarding labour market returns of different subjects, Davies and Guppy (1997) show that students from fields directly related to prestigious professions or higher economic demands such as medicine, law, engineering, or business generally attain higher incomes than those from fields such as education, the humanities, or home economics (Davies and Guppy 1997). Kim and Kim (2003) also show that the field of study to a large extent influences the status position obtained in the labour market. Their comparative assessment of labour market outcomes of different subjects in Britain and Germany reveals that German graduates from all fields are more likely to be employed in the service classes than their British counterparts. In particular, British graduates from education and arts/humanities show a quite low probability of obtaining high class positions when compared to graduates of medicine in both countries, who are much more likely to obtain high service class positions.

More explicit hypotheses on the impact of occupational specificity on graduate career mobility were obtained by institutional analysis. These hypotheses will be tested in the following sections. It has been shown that the German system of higher education can be considered more occupation-specific than the British. One reason is the different historical trajectories and ideas associated with university education, which has led Germany to place greater emphasis on professional knowledge and applicable skills as a means to educate future public administrators. These ideas are still inherent in current legislation and lead to a strong emphasis on applied knowledge and the integration of practical training into many degree courses. In Britain, the historical ideal of "liberal education for gentlemen" as established by Oxbridge is still effective, particular at the undergraduate level. Personal growth and participation in society beyond mere training for the labour market are still important goals in British higher education today. The tight connection between the systems of professions and higher education further underlines the importance of occupational specialisation in the German system, while British professionals were for a long time been trained outside higher education, while professional training has only recently become available at universities as well. The analysis of the training of engineers highlights the different perceptions of occupation-specific training in both countries. While engineering in Germany has always been highly valued and is even an important prerequisite for acquiring management positions, engineering in Britain was for a long time held in low esteem and taught mainly as a vocational qualification outside higher education. And even today, where engineering is part of almost every university's subject canon, it still fails to offer career prospects in upper management positions.

As a consequence of the different importance given to occupational specificity in higher education, only German graduates should generally obtain occupations matching their higher education credentials immediately after graduation. Moreover, career development should proceed much more along occupational lines with fewer shifts between different occupations and with more stable career development. British graduates should face more difficulties finding a job matching their qualification after leaving higher education. This should increase the likelihood that they end up in initial employment positions not suiting their skills and/or interests. Consequently, occupational mobility should be much higher during the first years after graduation until a better match is obtained. In addition to these general patterns, strong within-country differences are expected as well, since some degrees and fields of study provide training with a stronger focus on labour market requirements than others in both countries. The following empirical analysis will shed light on how these different institutional environments impact the matching of students to jobs.

6.3.1 Transition to a Job in an Occupation Matching the Field of Study

In order to examine the influence of occupation-specific higher education on graduate career development, a single event model for the transition to a first occupation matching the field of study was estimated. A job match is defined as the congruence between the first occupation a graduate is working in and his or her field of study. Individuals working outside their field of study are treated as graduates with a non-matching job. Figure 14 displays the Kaplan-Meier failure functions for obtaining a matching job in both countries.

As expected, transition rates are much higher in Germany than in Britain, particularly during the first year after graduation, since almost 50 percent of German graduates make the transition, while only 30 percent of their British counterparts are successful. Thereafter transition rates level off in both countries. By the end of five years, almost 60 percent of German graduates are working in matching occupations, while only about one third of graduates in Britain have found matching employment. These results confirm on the one hand that German higher education is more occupational-specific than the British system, and on the other that strong intra-national variations exist. This might be due to the fact that in Germany, too, a considerable amount of graduates study subjects such as humanities or arts, which are generally regarded to prepare less for specific occupations. In Britain, in contrast, some of the subjects have become more occupation-specific than others over the last decades. Thus, it should be easier for students enrolled in professional fields of study including engineering to find a job matching their credentials. It remains to be seen whether the ranking of fields of study follows a similar pattern in both countries, which might point to the fact that within-country differences are more pronounced than between-country variations.

Figure 14: Transition to a first job matching the field of study

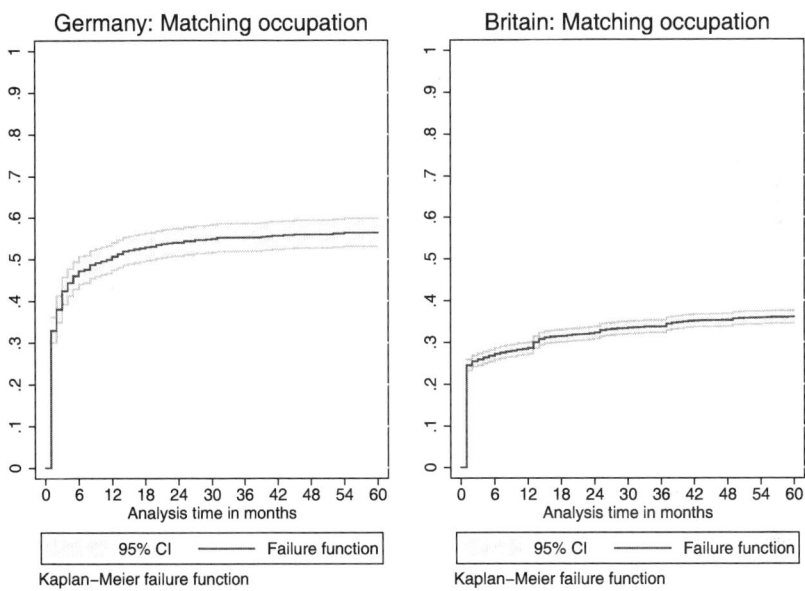

Data: SOEP and NCDS/BCS70

A first explanation of these different matching processes could be, of course, that British graduates simply study different subjects compared to their German counterparts. Before carrying out the multivariate analysis, it makes sense, therefore, to review the descriptive distributions of fields of study at graduation and association between fields of study and matching / non-matching occupations in both countries in order to evaluate how each graduate population is composed (see Figure 15). The subject distribution indicates that graduates in Britain are indeed more likely to attend subject courses that are less occupation-specific than in Germany.

More specifically, the largest country differences are found between the proportion of students studying engineering and humanities/arts: while the former is studied by 26 percent of German graduates, only 11 percent of British students graduate in engineering.

Figure 15: Field of study distribution at graduation and after finding a matching job

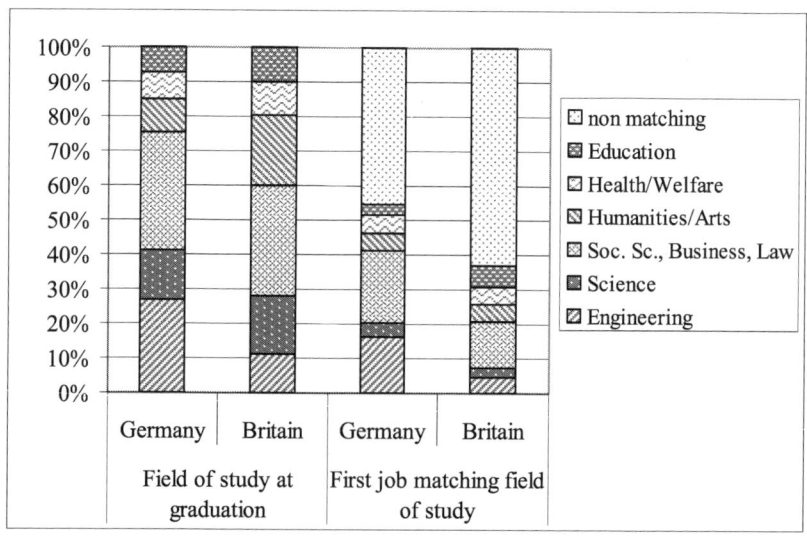

Data: SOEP, NCDS/BCS70

British graduates are much more likely to have studied humanities and arts, where the proportion of 20 percent is more than double the German one. Social sciences, including business and law, are studied by roughly one third of graduates in both countries. The proportion of graduates from education, health/welfare and sciences are also comparable.[36]

In general, these results indicate that the field of study distribution exhibits both similarities and differences between Germany and Britain. However, the variation of occupation-specific subjects such as engineering is substantial. The country-specific variations are confirmed when the percentage of graduates finding a matching job are compared by field of study. More than 50 percent of German graduates start their work-life in an occupation matching their subject, with the largest proportions having graduated in social science, business, law, or engineering. In Britain, only slightly more than one third of the graduate population obtains a matching job; only social scientists seem to be highly successful in this regard.

---

36   The field of study distribution in both countries is similar to the one calculated by Kim and Kim (2003) with the nationally representative cross-sectional samples of the 1996 Mikrozensus and the 1996 UK Labour Force Survey. Therefore, subject distribution among graduates in the SOEP and the two British cohort studies can be considered to represent national patterns of subject distributions.

The multivariate analysis applying piecewise-constant exponential models for the transition to a first employment matching the field of study confirms these descriptive results. For this analysis, different types of higher education institutions and degrees were taken into account in order to evaluate their importance for the matching process; however, the major focus is laid on the influence of fields of study. Before turning to these variables of interest, it is worth noticing that control variables do not play a major role for finding a matching occupation in both countries. Most interestingly, no gender differences exist, as Table 9 demonstrates.

This finding points to the fact that the matching of credentials to jobs is a more gender-neutral process when compared, for example, to obtaining high status positions. Similarly, graduates from ethnic minorities have significantly lower transition rates in both countries. In Britain, females with young children and mature graduates are particularly disadvantaged. But apart from these findings, the transition to matching employment seems to depend mainly on variables related to the higher education system.

Regarding the variables of major interest, i.e. fields of study, the results of Table 9 show the predicted pattern, but also yield surprising outcomes. As expected, graduates from health/welfare have much higher transition rates to a matching occupation, but fields such as engineering, business or law also prove to be advantageous in this regard. This is not surprising since these fields of study place a stronger emphasis on professional training, include practical training more often into their degree courses, and, as it is the case for German professions, are closely linked with particular occupations. In Britain, professional subjects or engineering are also predominantly taught at higher education institutions nowadays, which obviously results in close matches between credential and job outcome. This is supported by the positive coefficient of the age participation rate, which signals that in the course of higher education expansion over the last two decades, closer links with the labour market have been established in Britain. In addition, the larger variation between subject odds ratios in Britain indicates that transition rates vary more strongly between fields of study. German graduates in general have better chances of finding employment matching their higher education credentials, whilst within-country differences are more strongly stratified by fields of study in Britain.

The only exceptions are students graduating in education as a field of study. Here, British graduates have considerably better chances than the German graduates. The reason for this might be that the British subject 'education' generally refers to a specific training for the teaching profession, either as an undergraduate degree course for primary school teachers or as a postgraduate degree course for secondary school teachers. In Germany, teacher education is just as specific, but it means studying for a *Staatsexamen* degree. The corresponding field of study is normally not education, but rather the subject that will later be taught at school. Thus, training for German teachers is occupation-specific, but the empirical indicator is their type of degree rather than their field of study. In Germany, students enrolled in the subject 'education' normally cannot become school teachers, but have a large variety of occupational outcomes, more comparable to students in humanities or arts.

Table 9: Obtaining an occupation matching the field of study after graduation

Transition to a job in a matching occupation		
	Germany	Britain
Piecewise duration dependence		
Base line (Ref.: Entry during 1. month after graduation)		
Entry 2.-3. month	0.164 (0.023)**	0.030 (0.004)**
Entry 4.-6. month	0.074 (0.013)**	0.018 (0.003)**
Entry 7.-12. month	0.026 (0.005)**	0.011 (0.002)**
Entry 13.-24. month	0.015 (0.003)**	0.014 (0.001)**
Entry 24.-60 month	0.004 (0.001)**	0.005 (0.001)**
Occupational specialisation of higher education		
Type of higher education institution (Ref.: *Fachhochschule*, polytechnic)		
University institution	*1.197 (0.148)***[#]	1.024 (0.070)
Type of degree (Ref.: Casmin 3a = *Fachhochschul*-degree (D), diploma/certificate (GB))		
Diplom, Magister (3b)	1.114 (0.143)	
Staatsexamen (3b)	1.479 (0.241)*	
Casmin 3b low		1.737 (0.206)**
Casmin 3b high		3.218 (0.453)**
Field of study (Ref.: Science, Agriculture)		
Humanities, Arts	2.214 (0.563)**	1.632 (0.216)**
Engineering, Construction	3.169 (0.664)**	2.978 (0.410)**
Social Sciences, Business, Law	3.047 (0.613)**	3.275 (0.389)**
Health, Welfare	4.072 (1.033)**	5.159 (0.741)**
Education	1.857 (0.502)*	7.006 (1.001)**
Control variables		
Female	0.859 (0.102)	0.941 (0.063)
Female with child < 6 years old	1.570 (0.421)	0.500 (0.094)**
Non-German / Non-White	0.394 (0.094)**	0.670 (0.115)*
Father with higher degree / upper class	0.942 (0.114)	1.071 (0.068)
Vocational education	0.918 (0.135)	0.861 (0.073)
Graduation age (Ref: 24-29 years old at graduation)		
younger than 24 years	0.899 (0.206)	1.198 (0.111)
older than 29 years	0.809 (0.111)	0.528 (0.086)**

Transition to a job in a matching occupation

	Germany	Britain
Graduation in East Germany	1.054 (0.151)	
Yearly unemployment rate (%)	1.031 (0.052)	1.040 (0.017)*
Yearly GDP (in 1.000)	1.000 (0.000)	1.000 (0.001)
Age participation rate (%)	0.989 (0.095)	1.058 (0.016)**
Size of birth cohort (in 1.000)	1.000 (0.000)	0.979 (0.007)**
No. of observations (person months)	20614	141944
No. of failures	455	1380
Log-likelihood null model	-1468.5101	-4851.3008
Log-likelihood end model	-1421.0827	-4704.6207
Likelihood Ratio Test Chi^2	94.85**	293.36**

Discrete time PCE models based on logistic regression, odds ratios reported, standard errors in parentheses
* significant at 5%; ** significant at 1%
[#] Coefficient stems from a separate model without types of degrees, since *Fachhochschul*-institution and *Fachhochschul*-degree both measure the same empirical fact.

Data: SOEP, NCDS/BCS70

Another surprising result is the outcome of graduates of the sciences, depicted in Table 9 is also the outcome of graduates from science subjects, who in both countries have far inferior chances of obtaining occupations matching the field of study. Their transition rates are substantially lower than those of all other graduates. Even students with a degree in humanities or arts find a matching occupation more quickly than scientists. There are several possible explanations for this finding. First of all, scientists are known to stay at universities to complete a doctorate and only later start their careers in a matching occupation. Therefore, their transition phases will be much longer immediately after graduation than those of other graduates starting employment straight away. What is more, the lower chances of success for scientists do not indicate that they tend to find low status jobs. Estimates of the transition to employment in EGP class I have shown that scientists in both countries have a relatively good chance of obtaining high status jobs. In combination with the results of the institutional analysis according to which managers are likely to have studied sciences or engineering, the reason for a non-matching employment of scientists may be that they are more likely to obtain administrative jobs only loosely connected to their field of study.

Looking at the impact of different degrees, results of Table 9 again follow the predicted pattern. As expected, German students with a *Staatsexamen* have better chances of finding matching employment, since their education involves a large amount of training for specific professions in the public service. In Britain, postgraduate degrees in particular increase the hazard rates substantially, a finding which is in line with the institutional analysis, since it demonstrates that most MA degrees and postgraduate certificates are strongly specialised for particular occupations. Interestingly, technical colleges in both countries do not improve the chances of finding matching employment as compared to university institutions, even though in the course of higher education expansion, they have been established in response to requirements of the labour market. In Germany, it is obvious that the differentiation by fields of study and degree courses is much more important for obtaining specific training than the type of institution in general.

The descriptive and multivariate results together demonstrate that German graduates are more successful in finding a matching job after graduation than their British counterparts. The comparison of the predicted failure functions based on the above models, which is a straightforward way of directly examining the relative advantage in both countries, supports this conclusion graphically.

Figure 16 reveals that in almost any field of study, German graduates have higher transition rates to matching employment than British students.

Figure 16: Predicted failure functions by field of study in Germany and Britain

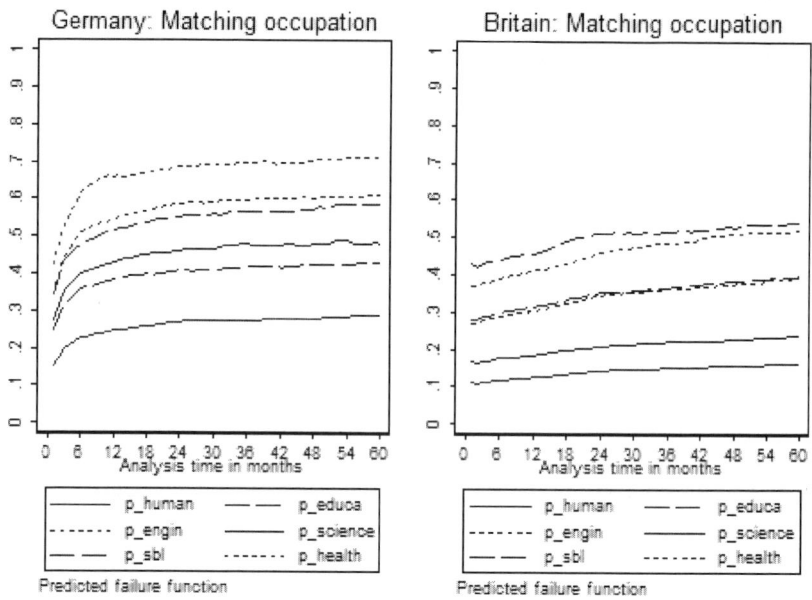

Data: SOEP, NCDS/BCS70, derived from estimates in Table 9

The difference is particularly pronounced for German graduates from humanities and arts, who have relatively good chances to succeed as compared to the majority of British graduates, despite their lower degree of occupation-specific training. But despite these variations in scale, within-country differences follow a similar pattern, with graduates from health/welfare, engineering or social science subjects having much higher transition rates than those with a degree in science.

Figure 16 again confirms that obtaining an occupation matching the field of study is much more likely in Germany than in Britain. German higher education institutions seem to prepare their students much better for particular occupations and professions, indicating a smoother labour market entry in Germany. This indicates that the overall idea of German higher education, namely to "prepare for occupational tasks that require the application of scientific and methodological knowledge or the ability of artistic expression" (BMBF 2002, §1, author's translation) is effective for students of all different kinds of subjects. In Britain, the legacy of the ideal of higher education providing training in abstract thought and valuing knowledge for its own sake still appears to make it more difficult for British graduates to obtain occupations matching their field of study. Within-country variations between different subjects are substantial in both countries, but more important in the British case, where only some occupation-specific routes into employment have been established recently.

Thus, the degree of occupational specificity related to higher education institutions follows a pattern similar to that shown for the field of vocational training. For both levels of education, the German education system trains qualifiers more effectively for particular occupations than the British one. This contradicts the general claim made by Estévez-Abe and her colleagues (2001, 2005, 2006), who argue that higher education confers general rather than specific skills and that this holds true for all countries, irrespective of differences in VET systems. Even though it can be argued convincingly that higher education is on the whole more general than vocational training, the previous analysis has shown that the degree of occupational specificity of higher education systems does vary considerably between different political economies.

Furthermore, one has to keep in mind that obtaining a matching job after graduation does not necessarily mean that the job is of upper status. As the previous analysis of class outcomes has shown, transition rates to the high services class are much more stratified in Germany by fields of study than in Britain. Subject differences in Germany are not so much related to variations in occupational specificity; rather, a horizontally stratified subject structure corresponds to a vertically stratified occupational hierarchy. In Britain, this relationship is the other way around, since different fields of study much more differentiate occupation-specific labour market returns as compared to status outcomes. Consequently, status differences are not necessarily produced by productivity differences, which result from better or worse matches between credentials and jobs, as job matching theory predicts. Rather, further social mechanisms, such as the reproduction of either cultural gender stereotypes or of existing class inequalities might become manifest in a particular choice of fields of study. For the field of vocational training, Estévez-Abe et al. (2001) have argued that in coordinated market economies like Germany, gender inequalities are more pronounced while in liberal market economies like Britain, class inequalities are more evident. All of these considerations imply that the institutional dimension "fields of study" might transport different meanings for labour market outcomes, depending on the theoretical concept applied and statistical measure employed. Since results so far have been based on rather broad subject clusters, further research on the basis of less aggregated field of study categories is needed.

6.3.2 Occupational Mobility after First Placement

To investigate the consequences of occupation-specific higher education for further career development, occupational mobility after first employment was analysed to see whether it occurs within or between occupational groups. To this end, occupations were grouped into eight broad occupational groups (see methods chapter). This classification distinguishes between (1) management occupations, (2) professional occupations, (3) technicians and associate professional occupations, (4) clerks, (5) service and market sales personnel, (6) craft and related trades workers, (7) plant and machine operators, and (8) elementary occupations including skilled agricultural workers. A competing risk model was estimated with no job shifts as baseline category and job shifts within or between these eight occupational groups as dependent variables. Before turning to the estimation results from these models, Kaplan-Maier survivor functions for the two possibilities of making a job shift were calculated separately (see Figure 17).

Overall and as expected, occupational mobility rates between occupations among German students are well below those found for their British counterparts. When measuring mobility across the eight broad occupational fields, it becomes clear that more than 40 percent of the British graduates but only about 15 percent of their German counterparts change their occupation during the first five years after graduation. The curves also give evidence of a stronger mobility pattern within occupations in Germany after initial job placement and a weaker one in Britain. It is particularly striking that transition rates do not differ between British graduates who stay in the same occupation and those who change occupation. In Germany, in contrast, job shifts mainly take place within the same occupational group, while occupational changes rarely occur.

Figure 17: Survivor functions for making a job shift within or between occupations

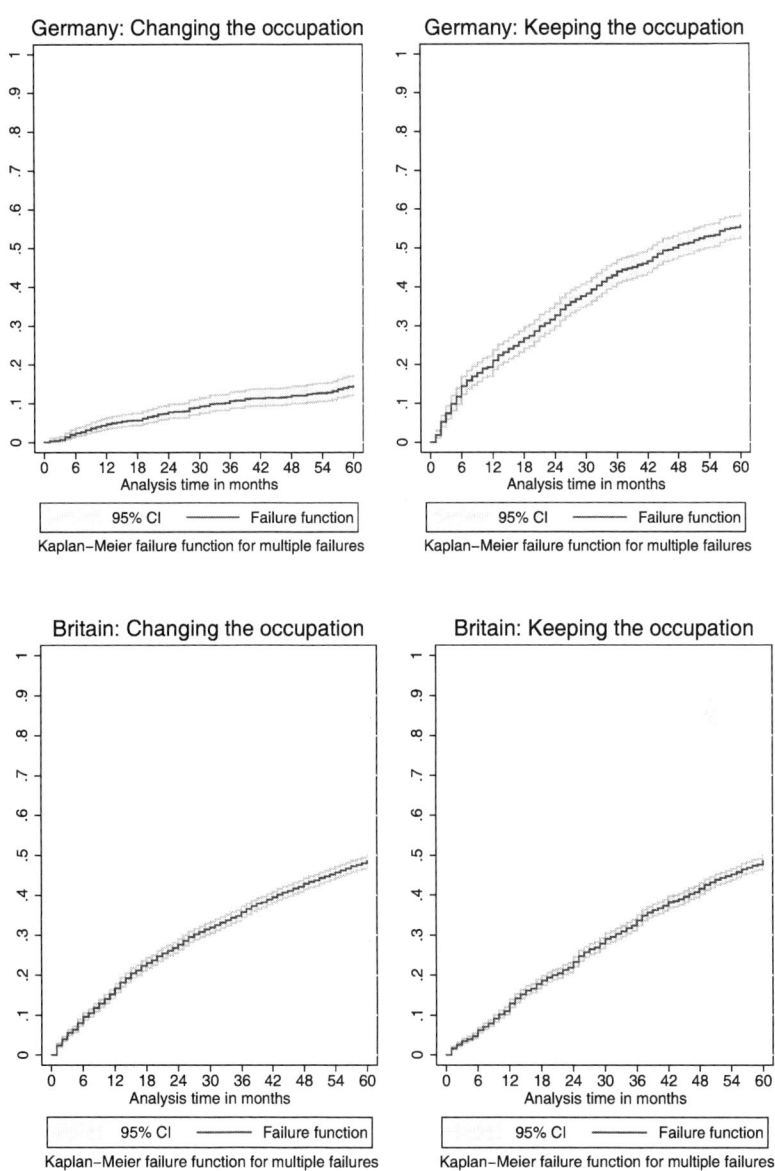

Data: SOEP, NCDS/BCS70

German graduates are clearly less occupationally mobile than British ones, which should be the result of occupation-specific skills obtained during higher education, but also of a labour market strongly segmented along occupations.

The result of a more strongly skill-based allocation in the German labour market is also robust when a competing-risk model for occupational mobility within and between occupations was estimated. Table 10 reports odds ratios for a model with a multinomial logit specification, where graduates not experiencing any job shift during the first five years are the baseline category, and those experiencing job shifts within and between the eight occupational groups the possible outcomes. The major focus will be put on the occurrence of occupational shifts and how they are determined by the type of occupation held previously as well as to variables indicating the duration dependence, such as labour market experience, spells of unemployment, or further education.

In the first place, the models for Germany and Britain generate some standard results regarding the determinants of job mobility behaviour among graduates entering the labour market. For any kind of job shift in Germany and for occupational shifts in Britain, job mobility rates are consistently lower for those with more labour market experience and with shorter times of unemployment. This finding is in line with other research, indicating that the transition period is most turbulent immediately after leaving the education system, while it becomes more stable with more work experience acquired (Gangl 2000a). At the same time, periods of unemployment are likely to disrupt any career development, leading to a higher occurrence of job shifts thereafter, be they within or between occupations (Brauns et al. 2000). The non-significance of work or unemployment experience for job shifts within the same occupational group in Britain, however, indicates that an unstable career development is the norm rather than the exception, a finding which can be attributed the lower degree of labour market regulation in this country.

Interestingly, while periods of further education positively influence a switch in occupations in Germany, they are important for shifts within occupations in Britain. It might be that further education in Germany is associated with new forms of skills that make it possible to work in a different occupational field. In Britain, in contrast, postgraduate certificates often build on the subject of the previous degree with a stronger specialisation, thus preparing for possibly higher status positions within the same field of activity as before. In order to control for the occupational specificity of the higher education credential, a dummy variable indicating whether the first occupation obtained matched the field of study was included in the models. Surprisingly, this variable shows no significant effect in Germany, even though is has been shown beforehand that the higher education system as a whole is more occupation-specific than the British one.

Table 10: Making a job shift within or between occupations

Making a job shift	Germany		Britain	
	within occ.	between occ.	within occ.	between occ.
Previous labour market experience				
Work experience (months)	0.959 (0.004)**	0.955 (0.008)**	1.001 (0.001)	0.996 (0.002)**
Unemployment (months)	1.127 (0.013)**	1.090 (0.019)**	1.006 (0.006)	1.014 (0.005)**
Further education (months)	1.014 (0.009)	1.028 (0.015)*	1.008 (0.003)**	0.998 (0.003)
Other Activities (months)	1.006 (0.007)	1.032 (0.013)*	0.996 (0.006)*	1.004 (0.006)
Occupational group 1st job (Ref.: Manager)				
Professionals	2.913 (1.010)**	1.037 (0.573)	3.059 (0.312)**	1.091 (0.104)
Associate Professionals	1.839 (0.671)	2.199 (1.249)	2.923 (0.324)**	2.536 (0.252)**
Clerks	2.577 (1.004)*	1.437 (0.917)	3.249 (0.368)**	4.184 (0.398)**
Service/Market Sales Personnel	0.876 (0.428)	5.116 (2.981)**	2.383 (0.35)6**	5.839 (0.613)**
Craft/Related Trades Workers	1.427 (0.948)	5.087 (3.593)*	2.155 (0.559)**	4.002 (0.548)**
Plant/Machine Operators	2.762 (1.828)	5.510 (5.040)	1.276 (0.378)	6.865 (0.889)**
Elementary Occupations	2.647 (1.536)	3.681 (2.950)	1.980 (0.394)**	7.586 (0.884)**
Subject matching first job	1.124 (0.124)	1.064 (0.259)	1.130 (0.067)*	0.923 (0.061)
Control variables				
Female	1.377 (0.145)**	1.235 (0.262)	1.060 (0.059)	0.831 (0.046)**
Female with child < 6 years	1.482 (0.226)**	0.584 (0.284)	0.540 (0.084)**	0.461 (0.078)**
Non-German / Non-White	0.810 (0.142)	0.798 (0.284)	1.134 (0.143)	0.890 (0.113)
Father: higher degree (D)/ upper class (GB)	0.952 (0.105)	1.003 (0.248)	1.147 (0.063)*	1.075 (0.057)
Vocational training	0.563 (0.089)**	0.976 (0.230)	1.022 (0.061)	0.976 (0.060)
Yearly unemployment rate	1.035 (0.035)	1.096 (0.069)	0.970 (0.014)*	1.017 (0.015)
No. of observations (person months)	42260		206299	
No. of failures	348	101	1319	1279
Log-likelihood null model	-3840.4951		-21478.651	
Log-likelihood end model	-3632.4535		-20814.571	
Likelihood Ratio Test Chi^2	416.08**		1328.16**	

Models based on multinomial logistic regression, odds ratios reported, standard errors in parentheses
Baseline category: making no job shift after first employment
* significant at 5%, ** significant at 1%

Data: SOEP, NCDS/BCS70

Thus, an assumed correction of initial mismatches does not necessarily seem to take place. British students, who obtained a first job matching the field of study, are much more likely to stay within the same occupation rather than change the occupation after job shifts. This finding points towards a stabilising effect of initial matches between field of study and jobs in Britain.

203

Turning to the variables of interest, namely the occupation held before job shifts, the estimates in Table 10 indicate that in Britain, occupational mobility might be compensating for initial occupational mismatches. This compensatory effect is expressed by a more or less constantly increasing chance of changing the occupation, especially for those initially employed in a low-status position. Obviously, graduates that had to take on lower status jobs immediately after graduation, e.g. as plant and machine operators – probably simply to earn money – are much more likely to change the occupation rather than keeping their current job when compared to managers or professionals. Generally, leavers with relatively favourable occupational outcomes in their previous jobs tend to be less likely to change occupations than graduates who ended up in initial employment positions clearly less adequate to their levels of training.

This compensatory effect is substantially weaker among German graduates. Even though graduates working as service personnel or craft workers also have a much higher likelihood of changing the occupation than those starting as managers, other lower status occupations are less prone to permit exit. This implies that even though the proportion of graduates working in non-matching jobs after graduation is much smaller in Germany than in Britain, the type of initial job placement more strongly determines future mobility opportunities. Once placed in non-matching occupations, the likelihood of changing is rather low. Obviously, the occupational structure of the German labour market is much less permeable and therefore prohibits later corrections of initial job mismatches, even in cases of apparent over-qualification. British graduates have a lower chance of occupation-specific matches straight after graduation. However, the more flexible British labour market allows for compensating for an initial misallocation by permitting occupational shifts.

Overall, it seems that in systems with a high degree of occupational specificity, the critical step takes place immediately after higher education with the choice and/or availability of a first occupation. Although the analysis of Germany has shown that there is some movement between occupations, it tends to occur only at the lower level of the job hierarchy and job shifts mainly take place within the same occupational group. Thus, the initial employment positions serves as a kind of "lock-in" of further career development within particular occupations. In systems with a lower focus on specific skills such as Britain, entry occupations determine further career mobility to a lesser degree and provide more opportunities for moving out of lower employment positions gained immediately after graduation.

Taken together, the effects of occupational specificity on graduate labour market entry and career mobility demonstrate that the German graduate labour market is strongly segmented along occupational lines. Entry to particular occupations is based on specific higher education credentials for the majority of graduates, and career mobility thereafter proceeds within the same occupational group. This again indicates a strong institutional congruence between different educational levels in Germany. Just as the labour market for qualifiers with vocational training likewise follows an OLM pattern, the labour market for higher education graduates also follows an OLM pattern, with clear-cut occupational segmentation and little occupational mobility. In Britain, similar patterns can also be found in the career development of graduates from vocational training and higher education. Both transition phases are less determined by the occupational specificity of education credentials, but are rather characterised by a phase of strong occupational mobility. While these country-specific logics refer to general patterns of occupational specificity, the theoretical section has identified OLM and ILM segments that might be particularly important for shaping graduate careers, namely professions and the public sector. In the following section, career mobility in these segments will be examined in more detail.

6.4 The Importance of Occupational and Internal Labour Markets for Graduate Employment

The concept of labour market segmentation suggests that the labour market is differentiated into several segments with little or no mobility between them. In contrast to external labour markets, where allocation and pricing of labour is assumed to function in line with the principle of demand and supply, internal labour markets are sheltered from market mechanisms. Selection based on qualifications ideally occurs only once for particular entry-port jobs, while later career mobility is governed by firm-internal (ILM) or occupation-specific (OLM) rules. For graduate labour markets, the public sector and the professional labour market segment have been identified as important segments for graduate career development. Both feature principles associated with the traditional internal labour market. They are characterised by specific ports of entry with particular qualification requirements and offer a combination of permanent employment contracts with the same public employers or professional career ladders guaranteeing steady career progression. A graduate labour market is differentiated into public and professional segments, if particular forms of higher education credentials – either specific degrees or fields of study – are the necessary precondition for entering such an internal labour market segment. If this is the case, early career mobility should be strongly determined by initial employment positions, leading to little mobility between different segments.

The institutional analysis of professional and public sectors has shown that both countries had radically different historical trajectories in the importance of higher education for providing entry credentials. In Germany, higher education has always been important for entry into both segments, since German professionals and civil servants traditionally were required to obtain specific university degrees such as the *Staatsexamen* or specialist qualifications. Coupling in Britain has historically been loose, since professional training for a long time took place outside higher education and entry into the public service was based on examinations separate from higher education. Career structures of public and professional labour markets were more similar in both countries, particularly until the 1980s, when both countries applied the principle of strong social closure from competition and external markets to public and professional labour market segments. However, since then, the British government has introduced more market-based elements in recruitment practices and career structure for public and professional employees, with the aim of at eliminating the traditional market shelter in both segments. For the transition from higher education to work, the institutional analysis suggested that the German graduate labour market should be stronger segmented along public and professional lines than the British one. This should make entry more dependent on particular higher education credentials and result in higher transition rates and short transition periods into these labour market segments. Later career mobility of graduates is likely to occur within rather than between different segments, strongly sheltered from the (private) external labour market. Their British counterparts are expected to have lower transition rates, since entry is less based on higher education credentials. Rather, they are more likely to obtain private sector jobs as initial employment, while entry into the more sheltered segments only occurs later in their careers after further training. But even if entry into the professional or public sector was successful, career mobility is less likely to proceed along sheltered lines of progression. More between-sector mobility is expected due to the strong deregulation of these labour market segments during the last two decades.

There is plenty of empirical evidence for cross-national variations between OLM- and ILM-type labour markets and the respective importance of vocational training credentials for labour market entry and career mobility (see Gangl 2000a; b; Kogan and Müller 2003; Marsden 1990; 1999; Scherer 2005). For example, Gangl's (2000b) analysis of labour market entry in Europe finds strong differences in the relative importance of educational credentials or work experience for allocation processes between an ILM system group formed by Britain, France, Ireland and Belgium, and a set of OLM systems operating in Austria, Denmark, Germany, and the Netherlands.

Studies that apply the concept of internal labour markets to the transition from higher education to work do not yet exist. However, research on professional and public service career development in general points to similarities and differences between Germany and Britain. For Germany, Blossfeld and Mayer (1988) found a high degree of labour market segmentation between occupation-specific and non-specific segments in large and small firms (Blossfeld and Mayer 1988). According to these authors, the majority of higher education graduates are employed in OLM segments of the labour market, which confirms the general assumption that educational credentials are important for segmenting the labour market along occupational lines. At the same time, the strong German labour market segmentation restricts mobility between segments, particularly among high-skilled employees. For Britain, Li (2002) finds that professionals show a higher degree of career stability during their work-life trajectories than other occupational groups. However, their propensity to leave the professional sector seems to be higher than in Germany, particularly among men. Interestingly, British male professionals are increasingly likely to move into managerial positions outside the system of professions. His results also indicate that higher education credentials are a necessary prerequisite for stable career development in a professional occupation.

Regarding career development in the public service, Becker (1993) finds that a higher education degree is an important prerequisite for public sector recruitment in Germany. He explains this finding by pointing to the educational requirements and the strong formalisation of recruitment processes in this sector. According to Becker (1993), within-sector mobility is strongly determined by the length of service and the overall amount of work experience, findings that support the assumptions of internal labour market mobility. Between-sector mobility is relatively low in Germany and depends on the continuity of the previous work biography, since spells of unemployment and a high number of previous jobs make shifts more likely. All of these relationships prove to be rather stable across different cohorts. In Britain, employees in the public sector more often possess a higher education degree than workers in the private sector. This is based on the fact that the occupational mix of employees in the public sector is very different from the one in the private sector. Public sector employment tends to be concentrated among professional and clerical jobs and therefore tends to require a higher level of education. Despite the ongoing deregulation of the public sector in Britain, it still has the characteristics of an internal labour market providing an opportunity for skill development and offering long-term security (Dolton and McIntosh 2003; Grimshaw et al. 2001). However, findings of Grimshaw et al. (2001) also point to an erosion of the traditional ILM in public service companies since open ended contracts become increasingly rare, promotion more temporary, internal job ladders shorter, and contracts in general more flexible.

These studies were neither comparative in nature, nor did they focus exclusively on higher education graduates. In the following analysis, the transition from higher education to different segments of the labour market will be examined in more detail. The major question is whether the identified OLM and ILM segments are distinctive for the labour market entry of higher education graduates and how they impact further career mobility. The stronger the labour market is segmented along these axes, the more explicit should be the link between higher education credential and entry into particular segments, and the lower should be the mobility out of particular segments after initial placement. Country differences can occur either in the predominance of a specific pattern of labour market segmentation or in the absence of distinct segments at all. In order to assess the importance of labour market segmentation for graduate careers in Germany and Britain empirically, the transition to all four identified segments as well as the mobility between them is analysed.

6.4.1 Labour Market Segments and Entry Ports after Graduation

In order to assess the extent to which graduate labour markets are segmented along the axes of ILMs and OLMs, the distribution of entry jobs and transition rates for the four identified labour market segments – private sector only, public sector only, private sector profession, public sector profession – will be analysed. Generally speaking, both forms of internal labour markets are much more important for graduate employment in Germany than in Britain. Figure 18 shows the descriptive distribution of initial employment positions in the four sectors.

This figure reveals striking differences between the two countries. In Britain, a much higher proportion of graduates enter the private sector than the public sector immediately after graduation. Almost 50 percent of British students in the sample obtain a job in the non-professional private labour market sector. But also among those obtaining professional jobs, larger numbers begin their working life in a private company. In Germany, the distribution between public and private sector employment is more equalised. Also, only a quarter of German graduates enter the labour market without any reference to internal labour market structures, while the majority obtains a professional position straight after graduation. The proportion of graduates entering the public non-professional sector is comparatively low in both countries.

Apparently, the tight coupling between German higher education and professional and public sectors already influences the first placement. Entry port jobs in internal labour market segments are much more common immediately after graduation in comparison to jobs in the private non-professional sector, while it is the other way around in Britain.

Figure 18: Labour market segment of first job in Germany and Britain

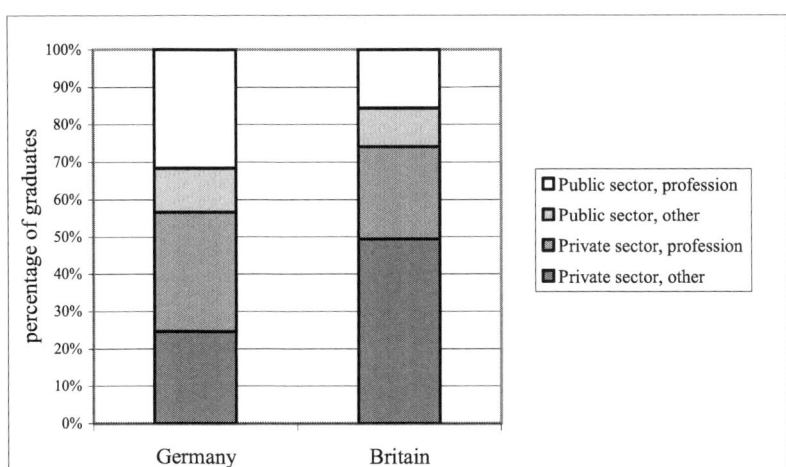

Data: SOEP, NCDS/BCS70

This can be taken as a first indicator of the fact that the German graduate labour market is more strongly segmented along occupational and public lines than the British one. Such differences in entry port allocation should also be reflected in the transition rates to different labour market segments. Figure 19 presents the Kaplan Meier failure functions estimated separately for each labour market segment. Again, strong cross-national differences become apparent: the broad majority of British graduates enter the private sector very soon after graduation and substantially faster than their German counterparts.

Germany, in contrast, exhibits an OLM pattern of labour market entry, since graduates generally exhibit higher transition rates to professional positions as compared to non-professional jobs, be they in the public or the private sector. Even though the professional labour market also seems to be important in Britain, its accessibility for higher education graduates is much more restricted. Lower rates of transition into the non-professional public sector are again rather similar in both countries, indicating that this segment attracts the lowest number of German and British graduates. At the same time, this segment exhibits the strongest ILM pattern, since entry either occurs immediately after graduation or not at all, as demonstrated by the transition rates being close to zero after the first year.

Institutionally, lower rates of transition into professional occupations can be explained with the lower degree of professional training provided by the British higher education system.

Figure 19: Transition to public and professional labour market segments in Germany and Britain

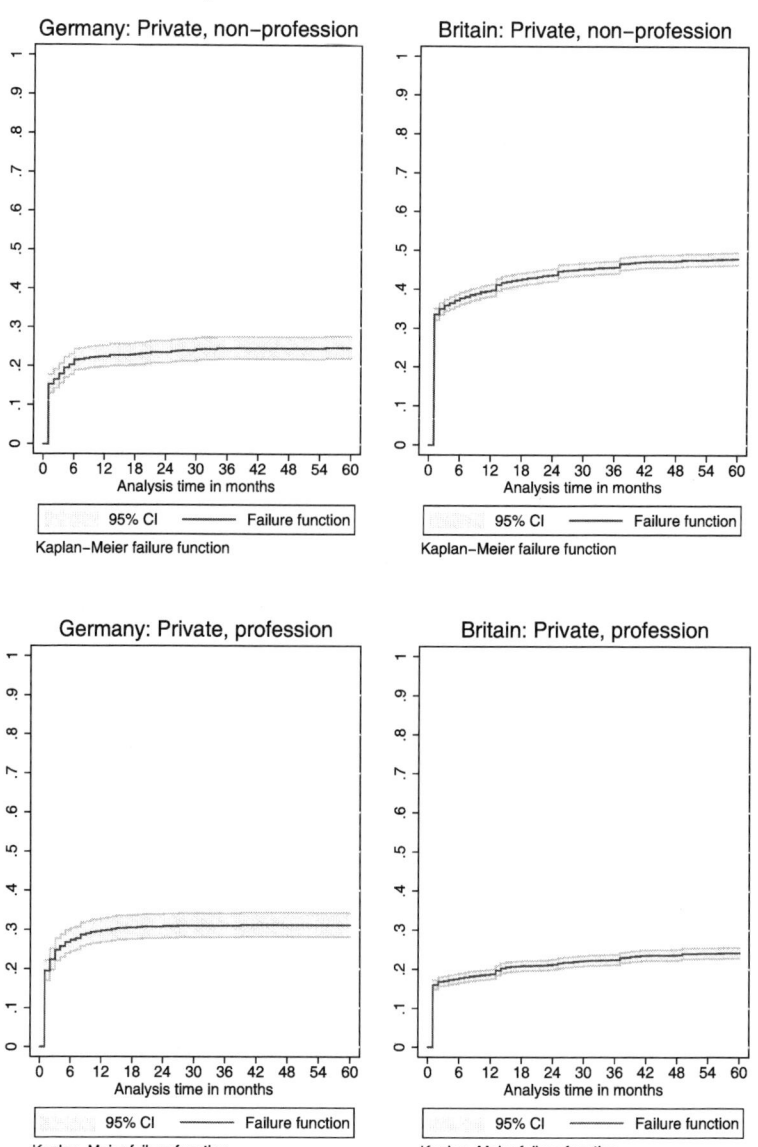

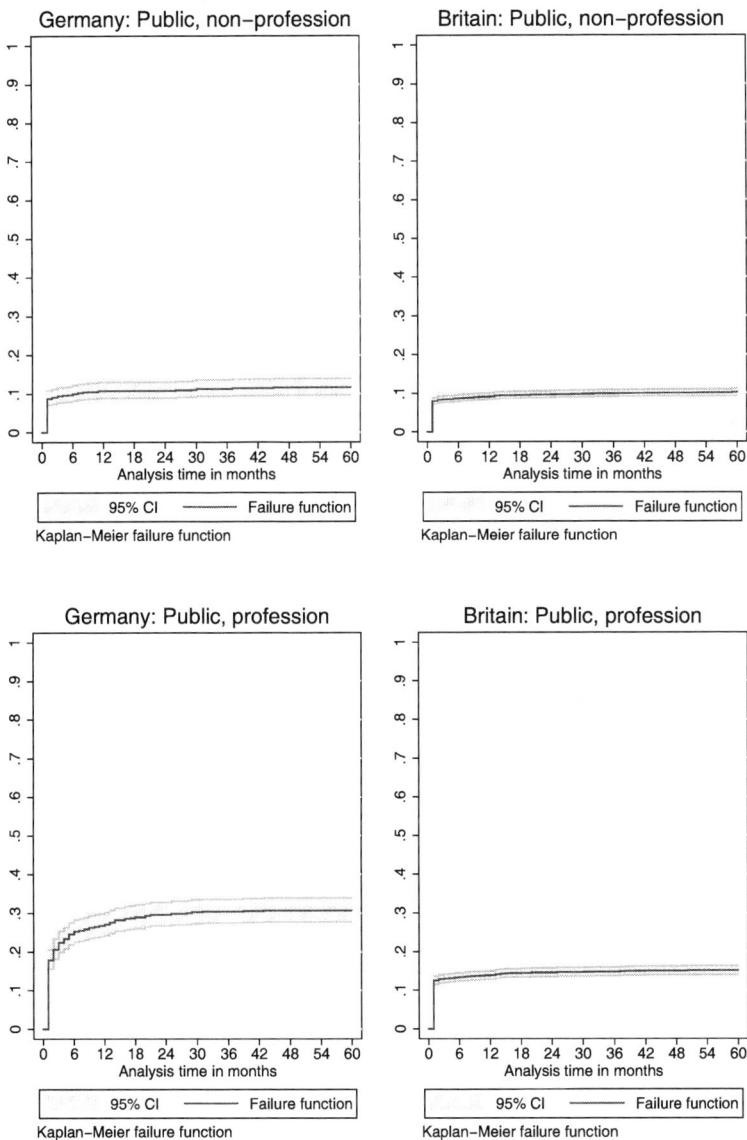

Data: SOEP, NCDS/BCS70

As shown in previous sections, only some professions have established academic routes of training, while for the majority, training occurs outside higher education at training institutions organised by professional bodies.

Therefore and as expected, British graduates more often and more quickly seek employment in occupations of the private non-professional sector, which do not require profession-specific skills. The analysis of career mobility between the various labour market segments will show whether acquiring additional education improves transition rates into the system of professions in Britain. In Germany, entry into professional occupations is straightforward after graduation, which again indicates a stronger segmentation of the German graduate labour market along professional lines. Contrary to the expectations, though, similarities in the transition rates to non-professional public sector employment seem to indicate that entry into this labour market segment follows more analogous rules in both countries.

A general criticism of the applied classification of OLMs and ILMs in graduate labour markets might be that segments do not necessarily vary in the quality of job outcomes, even if entry is restricted to particular credentials. Indeed, the classification does not take hierarchical differences into account, for example between high-level and low-level occupational positions, or between high-skill and low-skill jobs. In order to assess the quality of entry port occupations, it is therefore worth looking at the EGP class of first employment in the various segments. Figure 20 reveals that the largest number of low status jobs is obtained within the private sector in both countries, accounting for almost 60 percent. Professional occupations are, by definition, higher class jobs, either in the high or in the low service class, but non-professional jobs in the public sector also exhibit a higher proportion of graduates in EGP class I or II than the private sector. This confirms the finding that entry positions in the internal labour markets segments of both countries are more favourable than in the private sector.

At the same time, this figure indicates that German higher education graduates enter the labour market at much better class positions than their British counterparts. The strongest cross-national differences in this regard can be found among graduates working as professionals in the public sector. Here, almost 50 percent of German graduates enter the labour market in EGP class I, while only one third of British graduates do so. Overall, the mixed form of OLM and ILM segments, namely the public sector profession, seems to be most attractive in Germany, where high status employment is obtained relatively easily after finishing university.

The brief discussion of job distributions among different labour market segments and the respective transition rates provided some initial evidence of the fact that labour market segmentation works differently in Germany and Britain. Even though all four types of OLM/ILM type segments exist in both countries, obtaining a professional and/or public sector job immediately after graduation is much more common in Germany and achieved by the majority of graduates. In Britain, the "normal" labour market entry seems to take place via the private sector, where lower status jobs are the norm. The multivariate

212

analysis of the transition process will show the role of higher education credentials for being successfully chosen at such ports of entry.

Figure 20: Labour market segments and class of first job in Germany and Britain

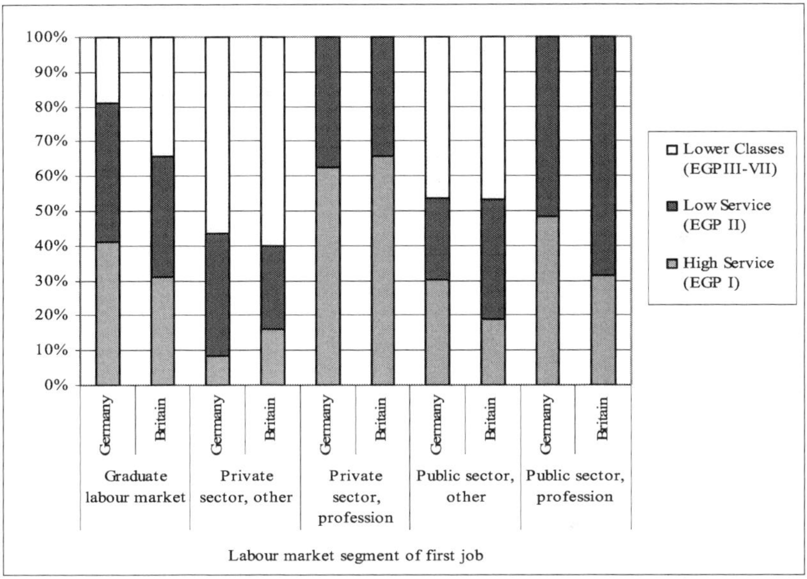

Data: SOEP, NCDS/BCS70

6.4.2 The Educational Determinants of Employment in Entry Port Occupations

The theory of labour market segmentation predicts that in internal labour markets, the strongest competition occurs at specific ports of entry, where applicants are not only employed for the particular entry position, but for a whole line of career following thereafter. Selection at entry port positions therefore seeks to appoint the best suited candidates who are likely to need the least amount of further training. In this regard, education credentials are a particularly valid tool for employers to judge the likely employability of candidates. If the two identified internal labour market segments – professional and public sectors – are important destinations for higher education graduates, employment should require specific higher education credentials in order to enter and to proceed. The multivariate assessment of this assumption shows that this assumption can be confirmed for both countries. The application of a single-event logistic hazard model to each of the four segments points to a strong linkage between credential and transition rate in Germany and Britain; however, the type of higher education credential that is important for entry port occupations varies between the two countries (see Table 11).

In Germany, the strongest linkage exists between the *Staatsexamen* and entry into a profession in the public sector, which is no surprise given that this type of credential is specifically designed to prepare for public sector professional services. Teachers or health care professionals such as medical doctors or pharmacists are especially bound to this type of degree.

However, it is not only graduates holding a *Staatsexamen* who experience a smooth transition to the respective labour market segment thereafter. Holding an academic university degree such as a *Diplom* or *Magister* is also helpful at entry port positions for public sector professions when compared to degrees from *Fachhochschulen*. No differentiation according to type of subject seems to matter in this regard, indicating that the stratification by degree is more relevant for specific labour market segments than the stratification by field of study.

In Britain, it is the other way around. Here, entry into a profession in the public sector is also strongly determined by various higher education degrees, but the subject seems to be even more important. Even though graduates holding a postgraduate credential exhibit higher transition rates than those with *diplomas* or *certificates*, the strongest differentiation is between those studying subjects important for professions in the public service such as health or education and those studying professional subjects for jobs outside the public sector, such as engineering or social sciences. Thus, in both countries, selection is strongest for professions in the public sector, but with different emphasis on differentiation by subject or degree.

This pattern is valid for all other labour market segments as well. Even though field of study matters in Germany, too, the type of degree is much more important for sorting students into the various internal labour market segments. Table 12 gives an overview of various credentials which guarantee a higher degree of success at entry port occupations of the various labour market segments in Germany and Britain. Entry into a non-professional job within the public sector is most likely for graduates with a *Fachhochschule* degree, mainly in social sciences or business, while in Britain, non-professional health subjects such as nursing or midwifery predominate. The importance of different fields of study and degrees in both countries also indicates that even though labour market segments are constructed by similar means, namely professional occupations and the public sector, the particular type of occupations dominant in each sector varies substantially between the two countries.

214

Table 11: Transition to ILM and OLM labour market segments after graduation

Transition to first job in	Private sector, non-profession		Private sector, profession		Public sector, non-profession		Public sector, profession	
	Germany	Britain	Germany	Britain	Germany	Britain	Germany	Britain
Piecewise duration dependence								
Base line (entry 1st month)								
Entry > 1 month	0.072 (0.017)**	0.022 (0.003)**	0.107 (0.020)**	0.025 (0.004)**	0.034 (0.015)**	0.025 (0.006)**	0.095 (0.019)**	0.014 (0.003)**
Entry > 3 months	0.066 (0.014)**	0.011 (0.001)**	0.032 (0.008)**	0.012 (0.002)**	0.019 (0.009)**	0.011 (0.003)**	0.039 (0.009)**	0.007 (0.002)**
Entry > 6 months	0.007 (0.003)**	0.007 (0.001)**	0.017 (0.004)**	0.009 (0.002)**	0.006 (0.003)**	0.008 (0.002)**	0.012 (0.003)**	0.004 (0.001)**
Entry > 12 months	0.005 (0.002)**	0.006 (0.001)**	0.004 (0.001)**	0.011 (0.001)**	0.004 (0.002)**	0.004 (0.001)**	0.008 (0.002)**	0.003 (0.001)**
Entry > 24 months	0.002 (0.001)**	0.002 (0.000)**	0.000 (0.000)**	0.004 (0.000)**	0.001 (0.001)**	0.001 (0.000)**	0.001 (0.000)**	0.001 (0.000)**
Importance of higher education at entry ports								
Type of higher education institution (Ref.: university)								
Polytechnic		1.137 (0.055)*		0.967 (0.071)		0.939 (0.105)		0.732 (0.079)**
Type of degree (Ref.: Casmin 3a = Fachhochschul-degree (D), diploma/certificate (GB))								
Magister/Diplom (3b)	0.991 (0.151)		0.861 (0.111)		0.406 (0.089)**		2.292 (0.437)**	
Staatsexamen (3b)	0.468 (0.128)**		0.427 (0.099)**		0.364 (0.120)**		4.348 (0.889)**	
Casmin3b low		1.034 (0.073)		1.034 (0.124)		0.864 (0.154)		0.936 (0.160)
Casmin3b high		0.513 (0.055)**		1.450 (0.198)*		0.703 (0.163)		3.145 (0.608)**
Field of study (Ref.: Humanities, Arts)								
Engineering, Construction	0.420 (0.110)**	0.892 (0.080)	1.840 (0.462)*	1.972 (0.251)**	4.037 (2.929)	1.052 (0.248)	0.796 (0.174)	0.318 (0.083)**
Science, Agriculture	0.900 (0.220)	0.763 (0.062)**	1.093 (0.308)	1.959 (0.232)**	3.041 (2.412)	0.980 (0.195)	0.874 (0.195)	0.710 (0.110)0*
Soc. Sc., Business, Law	0.857 (0.188)	1.134 (0.072)	0.896	1.281 (0.146)*	7.063 (4.996)**	0.969 (0.160)	0.811 (0.160)	0.495 (0.075)**
Health, Welfare	0.281 (0.126)**	0.599 (0.068)**	1.092 (0.367)	0.730 (0.143)	2.521 (2.282)	1.910 (0.344)**	1.482 (0.301)*	2.531 (0.386)**
Education	0.523 (0.194)	0.375 (0.051)**	0.819 (0.298)	1.640 (0.231)**	4.303 (3.385)	0.635 (0.144)	1.602 (0.367)*	4.435 (0.648)**

Table 11: Transition to ILM and OLM labour market segments after graduation (cont.)

Transition to first job in	Private sector, non-profession		Private sector, profession		Public sector, non-profession		Public sector, profession	
	Germany	Britain	Germany	Britain	Germany	Britain	Germany	Britain
Control variables								
Female	0.775 (0.120)	0.981 (0.047)	0.895 (0.125)	0.659 (0.048)**	1.703 (0.342)**	1.925 (0.232)**	1.080 (0.131)	1.383 (0.139)**
Female with child < 6	0.983 (0.499)	1.034 (0.125)	0.581 (0.352)	0.712 (0.155)	0.379 (0.248)	0.779 (0.207)	1.746 (0.518)	0.940 (0.229)
Non-German/Non-White	1.859 (0.341)**	1.022 (0.104)	0.770 (0.170)	0.982 (0.155)	0.876 (0.341)	1.391 (0.360)	0.643 (0.162)	0.602 (0.155)
Father Upper SES	1.093 (0.171)	0.978 (0.044)	0.791 (0.113)	1.102 (0.073)	0.716 (0.171)	0.996 (0.107)	1.191 (0.139)	0.988 (0.089)
Vocational education	1.559 (0.265)**	1.220 (0.065)**	1.094 (0.144)	0.869 (0.079)	0.639 (0.176)	1.001 (0.164)	0.604 (0.122)*	0.666 (0.076)**
Graduation age (Ref: 24-29 years old at graduation)								
younger than 24 years	1.327 (0.345)	1.273 (0.066)**	0.459 (0.151)*	0.889 (0.066)	1.241 (0.334)	1.133 (0.144)	0.762 (0.243)	0.880 (0.090)
older than 29 years	1.044 (0.157)	1.319 (0.136)*	0.869 (0.120)	1.418 (0.178)*	1.056 (0.210)	0.784 (0.202)	1.034 (0.131)	0.047 (0.023)**
Degree East Germany	0.759 (0.150)		1.125 (0.177)		1.140 (0.252)		1.034 (0.157)	
Unemployment rate (% year)	1.021 (0.056)	1.025 (0.015)	0.953 (0.041)	0.984 (0.017)	0.896 (0.079)	1.093 (0.031)**	1.008 (0.047)	1.034 (0.029)
Graduation before 1989	0.977 (0.188)	1.275 (0.073)**	1.143 (0.181)	0.761** (0.057)	2.097 (0.726)*	0.287 (0.038)**	0.762 (0.115)	2.526 (0.319)**
No. of observations	43572	209515	43572	209515	43572	209515	43572	209515
No. of transitions	209	1803	271	904	99	386	268	575
Log-likelihood null model	-851.79437	-5942.514	-1004.7025	-3852.9929	-627.99672	-1694.4227	-1065.3899	-2218.3772
Log-likelihood end model	-823.12193	-5794.098	-970.18556	-3760.6979	-594.27784	-1598.5015	-999.30113	-1922.2016
Likelihood Ratio Test Chi2	57.34**	296.83**	69.03**	184.59**	67.44**	191.84**	132.18**	592.35**

Discrete time PCE models based on logistic regression, odds ratios reported, standard errors in parentheses
* significant at 5%, ** significant at 1%

Data: SOEP, NCDS/BCS70

Overall, the type of degree seems to be most important in Germany, while the field of study is generally more decisive in Britain for obtaining entry port occupations in internal labour market segments. In addition, there are some further distinctive characteristics of credential requirements in both countries. In Germany, the strongest difference exists between *Fachhochschule*-degrees and *Staatsexamen*, both of which are linked to specific labour market segments and are mutually exclusive. An academic university degree is apparently more flexible and therefore functions as an entry certificate to several segments. In Britain, the strongest division is between professional and non-professional occupations, where the former require some form of postgraduate higher education, while the latter ones are also available for graduates with undergraduate degrees.

Table 12: Credentials important for entering different labour market segments

	Germany		Britain	
	Non-Profession	Profession	Non-Profession	Profession
Private sector	*Fachhochschule* degree, academic university degree, no subject specificities	*Fachhochschule* degree, academic university degree, engineering	Undergraduate degree, humanities, engineering, social sciences	Postgraduate degree, engineering, science, education
Public sector	*Fachhochschule* degree, social sciences or business	*Staatsexamen,* academic university degree, health, education	Any degree in health/welfare	Postgraduate degree, health, education, and to a lower extent humanities

In Britain, these general patterns have undergone important changes in the course of historical development, as is evident from the coefficient of the older graduation cohort (before 1989). Obviously, British reforms of public and professional sector organisation in combination with higher education expansion strongly changed entry patterns into different labour market segments. Regarding non-professional occupations, graduates leaving higher education during the 1980s exhibit higher transition rates to the private sector and lower rates to the public sector. The relationship is the other way around for professional occupations, which were more easily obtained in the public sector during the 1980s, while during the 1990s, more graduates moved to professions in the private sector. The identified marketisation of professional services seems to strongly impact private sector employment patterns, while reforms of the public sector apparently have mattered less. In Germany, only non-professional occupations in the public sector lost their relevance for higher education graduates over the years; transition rates to this segment were more than double during the 1980s than they are now.

217

In addition to specific higher education credentials, further socio-structural factors have an impact on the transition rates in both countries. First of all, women are much more likely than men to enter the public sector, particularly in Britain, where they obtain both professional and non-professional public sector occupations. At the same time, British women are less likely to work in private sector professions, which can be taken as an indicator of a gendered horizontal segregation between public and private sector professionals. Interestingly, transition rates of mothers with young dependent children do not differ from those of women without children, indicating that sex segregation along professional and public lines does not increase the labour market disadvantages that mothers tend to face. Vocational training enhances transition rates to non-professional private sector employment and decreases the chances of finding employment in public sector professions in both countries.

Overall, the analysis of entry port qualifications for specific labour market segments adds important information to the comparative analysis of the transition from higher education to work. Instead of focussing merely on institutions of the higher education system, such as institutional differentiation or occupational specificity, the examination of labour market segments shows how the graduate labour market is structured in different countries, and which role higher education plays in allowing entrance to the various labour market segments. The typology of professional/non-professional and public/private labour market segments developed in the theory chapter proved to be a valuable tool for identifying four different pathways from higher education to work. However, in contrast with research on vocational education to work transitions, where countries are classified exclusively either as OLMs or as ILMs (Gangl 2000b; 2002a; Marsden 1990; 1999), both OLM and ILM labour market characteristics can be found in the graduate labour markets of both countries. The main difference between Germany and Britain in this respect lies in the proportion of graduates entering each segment immediately after graduation and the specific higher education credential required for entry. The data therefore predicts a more complex relationship between higher education and labour market segments than the rigid bi-polar model suggested by previous research.

6.4.3 Mobility Within and Between Professional and Public Labour Market Segments

Turning to the occurrence of mobility between different labour market segments, Figure 21 reports the estimated Kaplan-Meyer failure functions for repeated job shifts between segments during the first five years after graduation for both countries. These curves strongly support the hypothesis that mobility between professional and public sectors is much lower in Germany than in Britain.

Figure 21: Changing the labour market segment during the first five years after graduation

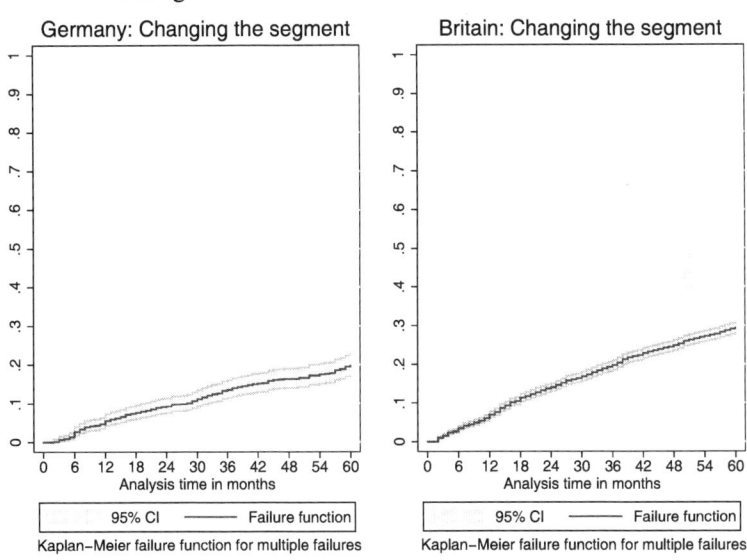

Data: SOEP, NCDS/BCS70

While less than 25 percent of German graduates find a new job in a different labour market segment, almost 50 percent of British job shifts occur between public and private and between professional and non-professional sectors. As expected, the four segments demonstrate a higher degree of social closure in Germany than in Britain. This fact has already been pointed out in the institutional analysis, according to which German professional and public sectors are more sheltered from market competition. In Britain, deregulation has reduced traditional career protection. Thus, even though public and professional segments are important destinations for British graduates, too, their permeability seems to have become much higher as a result of market liberalisation.

Another way of approaching the mobility between different labour market segments is to examine the distribution of labour market segments in relation to the segments of jobs previously held. Approached this way, labour market segments can again be considered less permeable in Germany than in Britain. In addition, the various segment types differ cross-nationally in their importance for between-segment mobility.

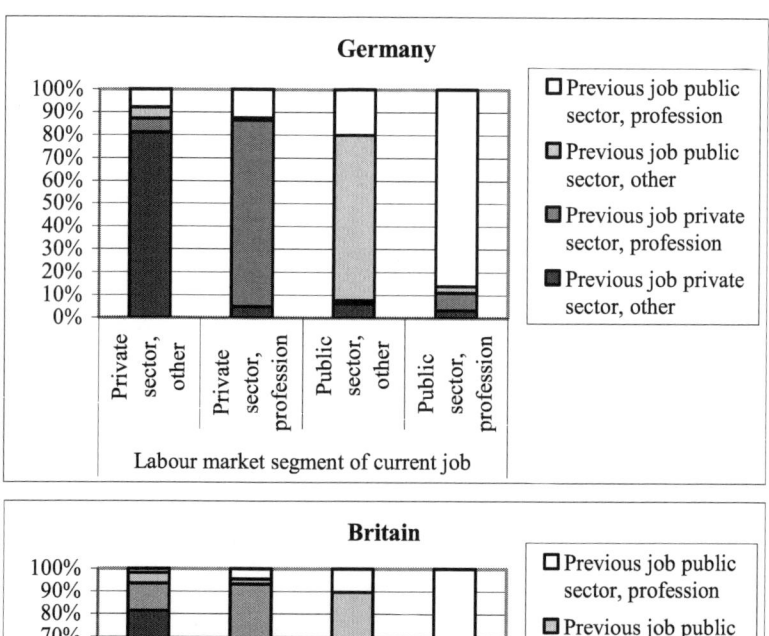

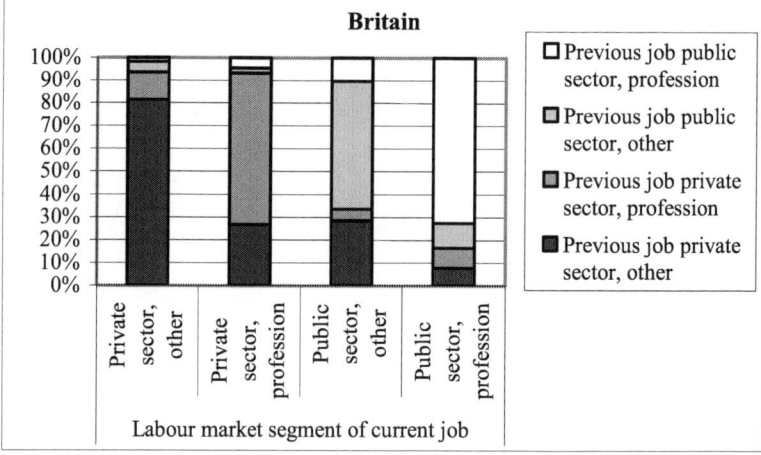

Data: SOEP, NCDS/BCS70

The upper panel of Figure 22 shows a high degree of career stability within the various labour market segments for Germany. On average, 80 percent of those changing the job remain within their same labour market segment during the first five years of their working lives. In Britain, the corresponding figure is lower, at around 70 percent. Interestingly, British graduates have a lower propensity to leave the private sector compared with the public, a finding that contradicts the assumption that internal labour markets have a higher degree of social closure. In Germany, hardly any differences in mobility patterns exist between graduates employed in the public or private sector or in professional and non-professional occupations, respectively. Thus none of the identified labour market segments seem to be substantially more permeable regarding entry and exit mobility, just as the theory of labour market segmentation predicts. Overall, however, in both countries, the majority of graduates remain within the same labour market segment after job changes.

Strong differences also exist in relation to the labour market segment of the previous job. Mobile German graduates are most likely to come from public sector professions, while mobile British graduates are most likely to come from the non-professional private sector. This might be merely related to the descriptive nature of the figures, since in both countries, the most mobile graduates come from segments where the majority of higher education graduates find a job after graduation. Yet, it might also be related to the specific nature of career mobility. For example, since higher education credentials in Britain rarely allow for entry into the professions straight away, graduates are more likely to obtain private sector jobs first. Entry into the OLM segment becomes possible only after having undergone specific professional training with the respective professional bodies, often on a part-time basis while already working.

These patterns are largely confirmed by the multivariate analysis of transition rates for changing the labour market segment reported in Table 13. To do so, repeated event logistic hazard ratios were estimated for both countries. The different types of previous labour market segments were included as independent variables into the models. Again, the two models generate some standard results on the determinants of sector mobility behaviour among those changing their jobs.

Consistent with the predictions of labour market segmentation theory, higher education credentials hardly influence transition rates, since further mobility within and between segments depends more on labour force experience within particular segments rather than qualifications. This is confirmed by the coefficients of sector-specific work experience, which demonstrates that job mobility rates decline with increasing labour market experience in both OLM and ILM sectors. In contrast, factors indicating a more discontinuous career development such as a high number of previous jobs or longer durations of unemployment increase the chances of changing the labour market segment. A high number of previously held jobs is a particularly strong signal of fragmented career development, which tends to foster further discontinuous employment patterns in both countries.

There are two important exceptions from the predicted pattern, however,. In Germany, the *Staatsexamen* almost doubles the chances of changing the segment. The reason for this might be that those studying for a *Staatsexamen* have to incorporate a phase of practical training within the public sector immediately after finishing the theoretical part of their degree course. Thereafter, they are free to decide whether to continue to work in this segment of the labour market or to change to another one. Examples of this kind of switch include medical doctors or lawyers who have to work in a public hospital or administration to acquire their degree but often obtain private sector employment thereafter, either by opening their own practice or working for a private law company. In Britain, in contrast, graduates from health and welfare programmes are less likely to change the segment, which indicates that jobs in these professions strongly follow the predicted pattern of OLMs.

The strongest difference between the two countries exists in relation to the labour market segment of the previous job. In Germany, previous labour market segments exhibit no influence whatsoever, indicating that all four segments are similar in their capacity to structure further career development. Thus, even the private non-professional sector remains rather closed in Germany, as Table 13 demonstrates.

Table 13: Changing the labour market segment

Changing the labour market segment	Germany	Britain
Importance of previous work experience for segment changes		
Work experience public sector (months)	0.969 (0.009)**	0.975 (0.003)**
Work experience profession (months)	0.976 (0.007)**	0.980 (0.002)**
Duration of unemployment (months)	1.016 (0.023)	0.990 (0.004)*
Further education (months)	0.978 (0.018)	1.007 (0.008)
Other activities (months)	0.991 (0.014)	0.995 (0.008)
No. of previous jobs	1.276 (0.116)**	1.571 (0.034)**
Segment of first job (Ref.: Private sector, other)		
Private sector, profession	0.969 (0.490)	0.937 (0.077)
Public sector, other	0.998 (0.632)	1.247 (0.126)*
Public sector, profession	1.297 (0.616)	1.048 (0.119)
Segment of previous job (Ref.: Private sector, other)		
Private sector, profession	1.565 (0.739)	3.455 (0.269)**
Public sector, other	2.470 (1.515)	3.162 (0.345)**
Public sector, profession	2.028 (0.913)	3.789 (0.449)**
Importance of higher education for segment changes		
Type of higher education institution (Ref.: *Fachhochschule*, polytechnic)		
University institution	*1.578 (0.353)*#	1.037 (0.058)
Type of degree (Ref.: Casmin 3a = *Fachhochschul*-degree (D), diploma/certificate (GB))		
Diplom, Magister (3b)	1.489 (0.350)	
Staatsexamen (3b)	1.899 (0.407)**	
Casmin3b low		0.964 (0.094)
Casmin3b high		1.029 (0.118)

Changing the labour market segment	Germany	Britain
Field of Study (Ref.: Humanities, Arts)		
Engineering, Technology	0.983 (0.319)	0.963 (0.101)
Science, Agriculture	0.559 (0.182)	0.942 (0.083)
Soc. Sc., Business, Law	1.179 (0.313)	0.991 (0.071)
Health, Welfare	0.989 (0.349)	0.771 (0.088)*
Education	0.783 (0.273)	1.056 (0.108)
Control variables		
Female	1.044 (0.198)	1.045 (0.058)
Female with child < 6 years old	0.899 (0.314)	0.731 (0.102)*
Non-German / Non-White	0.857 (0.239)	1.097 (0.135)
Father with higher degree / upper class	0.898 (0.175)	1.013 (0.053)
Vocational education	1.038 (0.238)	0.936 (0.069)
Yearly unemployment rate (%)	0.972 (0.094)	1.181 (0.028)**
Yearly change of GDP (%)	0.923 (0.041)	1.146 (0.023)**
Size of birth cohort (in 1.000)	1.009 (0.081)	1.041 (0.012)**
Age participation rate (%)	1.001 (0.001)	0.998 (0.004)
No. of observations (person months)	13489	202972
No. of failures	175	1910
Log-likelihood null model	-1107.4173	-10781.553
Log-likelihood end model	-900.11418	-9885.828
Likelihood Ratio Test Chi^2	414.61**	1791.45**

Models based on logistic regression, odds ratios reported, standard errors in parentheses
* significant at 5%; ** significant at 1%

Data: SOEP, NCDS/BCS70

In Britain, in contrast, transition rates out of the three supposedly more sheltered labour market segments are considerably higher than transition rates out of the private non-professional one, a finding which turns predictions about internal labour markets on their head. Apparently, the strong degree of deregulation and marketisation in these segments during past decades has had important consequences for career development. This assumption is supported by the macro control variables. First of all, they indicate that mobility between segments is strongly influenced by economic circumstances such as higher levels of unemployment and economic growth. However, the positive coefficient of the APR in particular signals that career mobility has become less stable in the course of higher education expansion. Instead of providing shelter from market mechanisms and a high level of closure for their work force, these segments have become more open in Britain, leading to a strong exchange of employees. Thus, mobility patterns in Britain do not at all follow the predicted pattern of internal labour markets anymore.

In conclusion, results from the previous sections show that only in Germany, the graduate labour market is strongly segmented along occupational and internal lines. This is supported by the analysis of entry port occupations, according to which specific credentials form the prerequisite for entering professional and public sectors. After entry into any of these segments, they only allow for minor change between them, while further career development mainly takes place within the segment of first placement. Just as it was the case for occupational specificity, labour market segmentation in Germany creates a strong lock-in effect. The segment of labour market entry strongly determines further career development and changes at a later point are hardly possible. This might be positive for the majority of graduates; however, those entering non-professional occupations of the private sector have little or no possibility of readjustment, even if their first placement was less optimal.

British graduate labour markets seem to be less divided into distinct public and professional spheres characterised by strong internal labour markets. Even though some higher education credentials are also important entry requirements for OLM and ILM segments and therefore follow the predicted pattern, subsequent mobility is less determined by the segment of the first job. Thus, both forms of internal labour markets have lost their capacity to shelter their members from the market, and mobility between different segments is much more common. With the exception of health care professionals, British graduates more strongly move between the various types of labour market segments during the first five years of their career and hence exhibit a more turbulent transition pattern. At the same time, the lower capacity of British ILM and OLM sectors to determine further career development also allows those who have started in less favourable positions to proceed to better jobs.

6.5 Labour Market Regulation and the Stability of Employment Positions

In addition to the institutional determinants of initial employment positions and the impact of different labour market segments on career mobility, the degree of labour market regulation and flexibility are important indicators to show the influence of institutional contexts in Germany and Britain. It has been demonstrated that the strictness of (un-)employment legislation varies strongly in both countries and should therefore have a significant impact on the duration of employment spells, the number of jobs, the incidence and consequences of unemployment as well as on upward and downward mobility patterns. The smoothness of labour market integration and the question whether unstable entry processes leave permanent marks on subsequent employment histories are likely to be strongly affected by national characteristics of labour market regulation.

In many respects, young people have been severely affected by the employment crisis of the 1980s and 1990s in both countries (Kohlrausch 2009). Especially in Britain, consistent levels of high youth unemployment have remained an important political issue, and latest active labour market programmes such as the "New Deal for Young People" have been specifically designed to tackle this problem. In Germany, even though the dual apprenticeship system still serves as an effective means of keeping youth unemployment at a lower level, certain groups of young people, e.g. those with migration background or those lacking the respective credentials are strongly at risk. However, the impact of different forms of labour market regulation on career mobility and the occurrence of unemployment are highly contended in empirical research. On the one hand, researchers emphasise the positive effects of a highly deregulated labour market as reflected by the rise in wages and occupational status with increasing labour market experience. It is argued that labour market entrants tend to profit from lower regulatory environments since young people are able to improve wages and occupational outcomes by changing employers more easily at the beginning of their careers and job hopping can be seen as a key mechanism of career development. On the other hand, other studies have pointed to more negative mobility effects, since job mobility in deregulated labour markets might also be associated with unemployment experiences and downward mobility. Job stability would certainly be the more preferable career outcome for young people involuntarily leaving their jobs or being caught in chains of contingent and secondary labour market segments (Gangl 2002b).

For the field of higher education, the impact of labour market regulation on graduate careers has not been tested systematically yet. So far, studies dealing with this issue commonly show that higher education graduates face lower risks of becoming unemployed when compared to the rest of the labour force, a phenomenon observable across countries (Brauns et al. 2000; Gangl 2002a; Hillmert 2001; Müller 1998; Teichler 1999). However, if unemployment rates are compared exclusively for graduates, cross-national differences become more pronounced. The comparison of graduate employment in ten European countries conducted with the CHEERS data showed that on average about 5% of the respondents were unemployed most of the time over the first four years after graduation. This percentage was marginal in six countries, such as Germany or Britain, but comprised around 9 percent in Italy and even 18 percent in Spain (Teichler 2007a). These results demonstrate that unemployment not only varies between different educational levels, but also between higher education graduates of different countries; however, is has not been analysed yet whether different forms of labour market regulation are decisive for the occurrence and consequences of graduate unemployment. Nor have the general patterns of career stability and status mobility been systematically linked to a country's institutional environment.

In order to assess the impact of different regulatory frameworks, the following analysis will have a closer look at the stability of career development, unemployment of higher education graduates and its consequences, and at experiences of upward and downward mobility in the course of career development. The institutional analysis has shown that unemployment and employment protection legislation are very strict in Germany. Since standard employment contracts cannot be easily dissolved, labour market positions of German graduates should be considerably stable and long-lasting, once employment is found. The strict dismissals protection is also likely to reduce involuntary job shifts. The generous unemployment benefit payments for up to one year are expected to influence re-employment patterns. It allows unemployed graduates to seek employment matching their qualifications and therefore should be similar to the one held before unemployment. At the same time, generous benefit levels are likely to reduce the overall risk of downward mobility. The negative side of a high degree of labour market regulation is its alleged tendency to hinder job creation. This lower flexibility in responding to economic changes is therefore also likely to restrict upward mobility. For Britain, it has been argued that its more flexible and deregulated labour market is likely to produce unstable entry positions with a series of stop-gap jobs during the first years after graduation. Only after finding employment matching their skills and/or experiences do British students experience a more stable career development. Lower levels of unemployment compensation paid for a shorter amount of time in combination with strict job acceptance rules will contribute to such a turbulent transition regime by increasing occupational mobility after spells of unemployment. British graduates simply cannot afford to wait until they find an adequate job, but have to accept any offer of re-employment. On the one hand, this might cause considerable downward status mobility in the long run. On the other hand, a more flexible institutional environment is more open to job creation in the upper status hierarchy, which could also lead to upward mobility rates.

6.5.1 Stability of Initial Employment Positions after Graduation

In order to assess the stability of labour market entry in both countries empirically, the duration of various spell types as well as the number of jobs held during the first five years after graduation will now be examined in more detail.

Figure 23 displays the mean duration in months that German and British graduates spend either in employment, unemployment, further education and training, or out of the labour force. It becomes apparent that for German graduates, full-time employment is the most prominent activity in their first five years. On average, they are employed full-time for four years, while spells of part-time employment, unemployment, further education, or spells out of the labour force are much shorter and do not last longer than 20 months. In Britain, in contrast, the average duration of full-time employment spells is 38 months, i.e. almost a year shorter than in Germany, while the time spent in other activities is longer. In the case of part-time employment, British graduates work on average for two years, while in Germany part-time jobs last little longer than one year on average. But despite the differences in mean spell length, part-time employment in both countries seems to be less prevalent than full-time employment, which indicates that obtaining a full-time job is more attractive, at least immediately after finishing higher education. A differentiation by gender demonstrates, however, that working on reduced hours is much more common for women in both countries (see Appendix E).

Unemployment experiences are comparatively short in both countries, even though British graduates on average tend to spend slightly longer periods in unemployment (8 months) than their German counterparts (5 months). This is in line with general findings on youth unemployment, which has been a substantial problem in Britain throughout the past decade, whilst young people in Germany have faced a lower risk of unemployment (Brauns et al. 2000). But despite these differences, graduates in both countries apparently do not face the risk of long-term unemployment (i.e. spells of unemployment lasting more than one year) immediately after graduation; short-term employment interruptions are more common. The occurrence and consequences of unemployment spells will be examined further in the next section.

Periods of further education are also similar in both countries, lasting on average about two years. Even though German graduates generally obtain a lower amount of additional training after graduation, the periods of further education are of comparable length. The strongest differences between the two countries can be observed in time spent outside the labour force, such as being on parental leave or home makers, having a gap year, or completing military service. German graduates opt out of the labour force for around 10 months on average, while their British counterparts for around two years on average. This might be due to the fact the British graduates are much younger when finishing their first degree and often take some time off before starting work life. But it might also be that leaving the labour force is a more permanent phenomenon in Britain, especially in cases when employment cannot easily be found.

Figure 23: Duration of spells and number of jobs after graduation

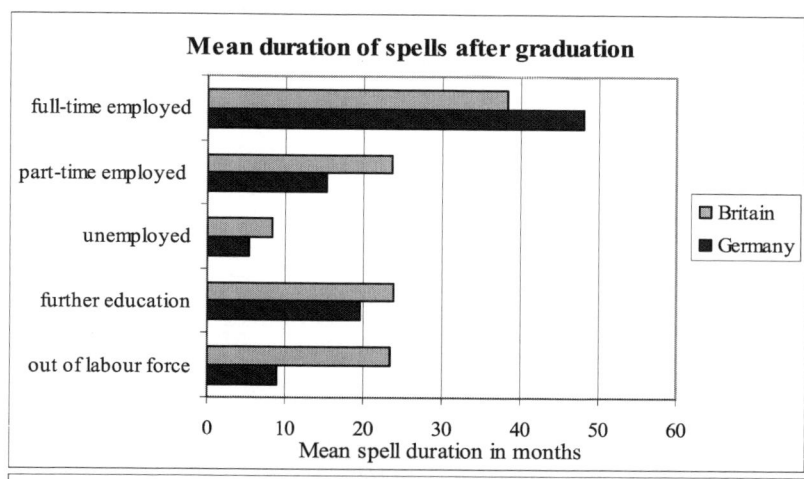

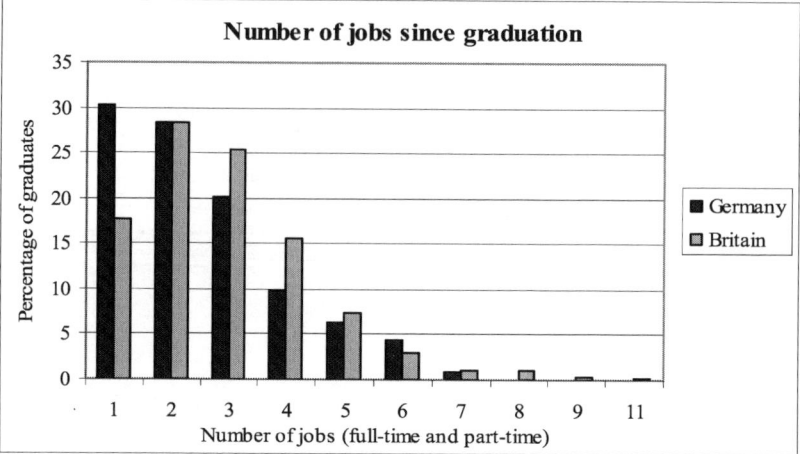

Data: SOEP, NCDS/BCS70, own calculations

Overall, these figures suggest that labour market entry in Germany can be considered relatively stable and continuous, since German graduates predominantly work full-time, while they spend much shorter periods in other activities. This can be taken as a first indicator of the fact that the high level of employment protection in Germany makes stable career development more feasible immediately after graduation. Once employment is obtained, the risk of losing the job again, is comparatively low. In Britain, in contrast, labour market entry can be characterised as a "patchwork" transition period that consists of many different activities of considerable length. Even though periods of full-time employment last the longest, spells of part-time employment, further education and spells out of the labour force make up for a considerable amount of time during the first five years following graduation. It seems that the low level of dismissals protection in the British labour market makes it more difficult for graduates to obtain stable employment positions.

In order to assess the stability of initial employment positions after graduation, it is important to look not only at the time spent in various activities inside and outside the labour market, but also at shifts within the labour market to account for the smoothness of the transition process. Figure 23 provides data on the number of full-time and part-time jobs held by graduates during the first five years after graduation in Germany and Britain. The reported number of individual jobs repeats the above results, showing a higher stability of job episodes in Germany, since 30 percent of all graduates keep their first job. In Britain, the first five years are much more turbulent for most graduates because less than 20 percent of the graduate population keep their first job and around a quarter have at least three different jobs.

This description again demonstrates that the high degree of labour market regulation in Germany guarantees a smoother labour market entry with higher job stability and fewer job shifts, while entry into the deregulated British labour market is marked by lower job stability and a sequence of stop-gap jobs. So far the results are in line with the theoretical arguments related to the strictness of labour market regulation set out in chapter 2. Apparently, the stricter employment protection legislation in Germany protects graduates from being made redundant soon after they found their first full-time employment. The shorter duration of part-time employment spells could in this regard be attributed to the lower degree of regulation of this type of employment in Germany. But it might also simply result from the fact that graduates prefer to work full-time and quit their part-time employment as soon as they find a full-time job. The generally low degree of employment protection in Britain is reflected in shorter spells of employment, and in the substantially higher number of job shifts British graduates experience immediately after graduation.

6.5.2 Occurrence and Effects of Unemployment

The results presented so far show that the occurrence of unemployment during the first years after graduation is relatively low in both countries. However, due to the descriptive nature of mean spell durations during the first five years, these results might also reflect completely different transition patterns and strongly react to outliers, which might cover cross-country variations. The estimation of transition rates to unemployment of more than three months after graduation in Figure 24 gives a more precise picture of the percentage of graduates at risk and the duration it takes to become unemployed.

Figure 24: Transition to unemployment after graduation

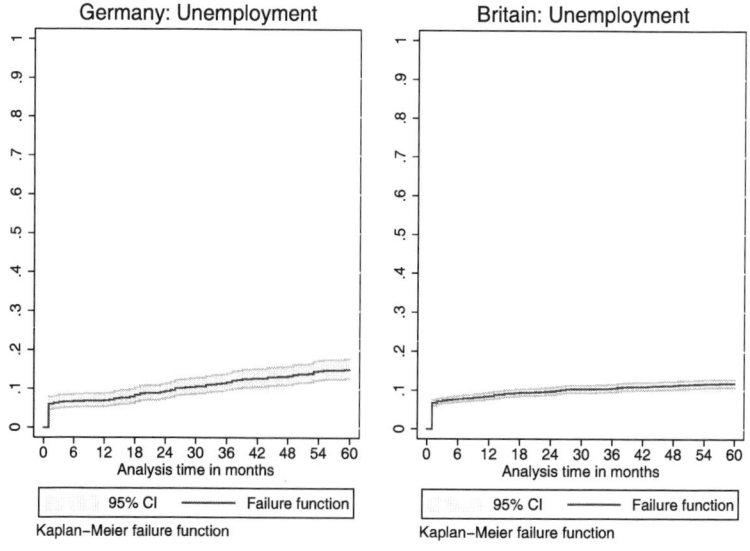

Data: SOEP, NCDS/BCS70

Approached from this perspective, however, the Kaplan-Meier failure functions also confirm that the occurrence of unemployment is rather low among German and British graduates. Figure 24 demonstrates that in both countries, only about 20 percent experience unemployment at all during the period of observation. At the same time, it shows that transition patterns are rather similar, since most students become unemployed in the first month after graduation, while transition rates thereafter decline. Even though this decline is seemingly larger in Britain, cross-country differences are insignificant according to the 95% confidence intervals. These findings are in line with other graduate surveys indicating the low incidence of unemployment among graduates in both countries (Teichler 2007a). This low occurrence also reflects the competitive advantage of people with a higher education degree as compared to those holding other qualifications (Brauns et al. 2000).

Even though the occurrence and duration of unemployment only marginally differs between the two countries, the seriousness of consequences might still vary. Clearly, concerns about exclusion from the labour market are justified, particularly at this early career stage, since they

230

are likely to have long-lasting consequences not only for the transition from higher education to work, but for the development of employment careers over the life course. In this regard, the description of activities before and after spells of unemployment exhibits strong differences between the two countries. In Figure 25, the occupational groups of jobs held before and after spells of unemployment were compared by using the same eight occupational categories as for the estimations on occupational mobility (see methods chapter), namely management occupations, professional occupations, technicians and associate professional occupations, clerks, service and market sales personnel, craft and related trades workers, plant and machine operators, and elementary occupations including skilled agricultural workers.

Figure 25: Occupational mobility after spells of unemployment

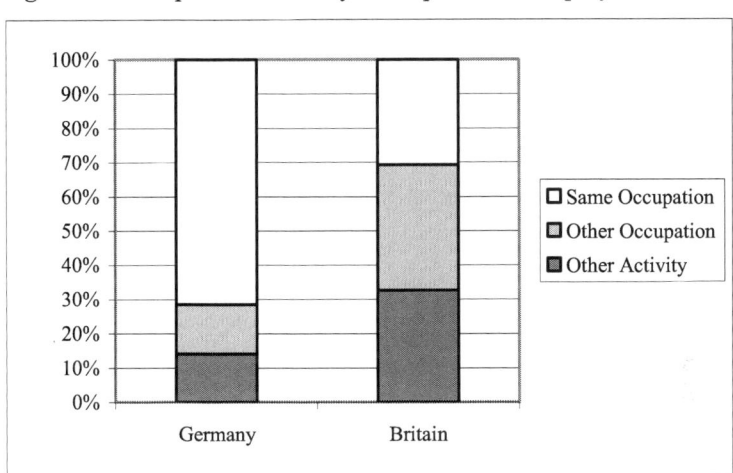

Activities after spells of unemployment, multiple spells per graduate possible

Data: SOEP, NCDS/BCS70[37]

In Germany, the vast majority of unemployed graduates are likely to continue to work in the same occupational group as before. Fewer than 30 percent change their occupation or even take up other activities, such as further education, or home making. In Britain, a larger proportion finds work in a different occupational group after experiencing unemployment. The proportion of unemployed that take up other activities is relatively high as well, however, making up for around one third of all unemployed British

---

37   Due to the low incidence of unemployment in both countries, the analysis had to stay at the descriptive level. Meaningful multivariate statistical modelling was not possible with the low number of cases, particularly in the German data set.

graduates. Obtaining further education might be a particular valid explanation for this pattern. Moving out of the labour force seems to be another likely exit option, however, as indicated by the long mean spell duration in Figure 23. The differentiation of this result by gender (see Appendix E) demonstrates that exit into economic inactivity is the most common option for British women, while British men more often tend to change their occupation. Patterns are much more equal between female and male graduates in Germany, even though German women are also slightly overrepresented among those taking up other activities after unemployment.

These findings might be taken to indicate that the generosity of unemployment benefits and the duration of benefit entitlement indeed have an impact on occupational mobility after phases of unemployment. As expected, the high unemployment benefits in the German system, which are paid for more or less one year and in addition depend on one's former wage level, allows higher education graduates to search for jobs that match their qualifications. And at least until 1998, unemployed individuals also had the option of turning down job offers that were below their skill level and/or in non-matching occupations. British graduates, in contrast, are driven back into any kind of employment soon after becoming unemployed due to low unemployment benefits and the short durations of benefit claims. Contrary to their German counterparts, they do not have the option of turning down offers in different occupational fields, with lower wages, or those not matching their qualifications. At the same time, opting out of the labour force seems to be a common solution for British graduates, most probably since new employment is not found easily after becoming unemployed.

Overall, these results stay in line with the predictions of labour market regulation in chapter 5. In Germany, high levels of employment protection and generous unemployment benefits are important factors for stabilising career development after graduation. Longer phases of full-time employment, fewer job shifts and less occupational mobility after unemployment also result from a high level of labour market regulation. In Britain, even though the occurrence and the level of unemployment are similar to Germany, the low level of regulation of labour market institutions leads to a more turbulent labour market entry. It consists of shorter spells of full-time employment, a large number of job shifts, a high degree of occupational mobility, and even exit to economic inactivity as a response to unemployment.

Thus, higher or lower degrees of labour market regulation help to explain variations both in the transition from higher education to work in the transition from vocational education and training to work. The major difference between the two educational levels lies in the incidence of unemployment. While highly unregulated labour markets such as the British one have to struggle with high levels of youth unemployment, particularly among the least qualified, more regulated environments such as the German

232

one prohibit such high levels, mainly through the provision of occupation-specific skills (Brauns et al. 2000, Gangl 2002a). For those with higher education qualifications, the risk of unemployment is low in both countries, indicating that higher education in general provides a competitive advantage and better shelter from the risk of unemployment. Here, the regulation of the labour market more generally influences career stability and turbulence, be it in form of job shifts or occupational mobility.

Bringing the different levels of occupational specificity back in, these results also confirm the findings in previous sections, namely that the German labour market is much more strongly segmented along occupational lines. Even after spells of unemployment, German graduates keep working in the same occupational group as before. The generosity of unemployment benefits and the long duration of entitlements support such an occupation-specific mobility pattern by making sure that interruptions do not strongly increase occupational mobility. Estévez-Abe and her colleagues (2001) explain this aspect of the German political economy by identifying strong institutional complementarities between a specific skill system and a high degree of skill protection provided through the labour market. Even at the level of higher education, these complementarities seem to be in place. The British example of graduate career mobility follows the overall pattern inherent to liberal market economies. Even though one cannot speak of lower levels of skills, the less specific orientation of higher education in Britain makes British graduates move in and out of various occupational groups, be it with or without the experience of unemployment. The highly deregulated labour market complements this more turbulent transition phase by not protecting specific skill investment, but rather making flexible responses to changing economic circumstances more common.

6.5.3 Upward and Downward Labour Market Mobility

Shifting its attention from the relationship between unemployment and occupational mobility to status mobility in general, the analysis now addresses patterns of upward and downward mobility occurring after first placement in relation to various forms of labour market regulation. In doing so, this section again relies on the application of the EGP class scheme, differentiating between the high service class (EGP class I), the low service class (EGP class II) and lower classes (all other EGP classes) in order to measure more or less advantageous status positions and the mobility between them. Apart from the determinants of employment stability and the incidence of unemployment, it is the direction of status mobility that is important for assessing the influence of varying degrees of labour market regulation in Germany and Britain. The specific institutional environments of both countries should have a strong impact on upward and downward mobility patterns. It has been argued that the more flexible and market-driven labour market in Britain is likely to produce lower status mobility. On the one hand, it does not shelter graduates from downward mobility since they are forced to accept a much larger variety of jobs, particularly after phases of unemployment. On the other hand, upward mobility should be more prevalent, since job creation is much easier in flexible environments as a response to changing economic circumstances. In Germany, the highly regulated labour market should generally provide protection from downward mobility in that it encourages stable employment positions and lower occupational mobility. However, since the highly regulated framework affects turnover levels in the total work force, strict labour market regulation should also have the indirect effect of lowering overall vacancy levels in the labour market, thus shortening mobility chains on the market and restricting upward mobility.

The distinction between these different forms of status mobility gives insight into the sources of career stability and instability in both countries. Status mobility is measured through a comparison of EGP classes held before and after job shifts or career interruptions due to unemployment. Upward mobility occurs if the EGP class of the next job is higher, and downward mobility takes place if it is lower than the previous job. No mobility is measured if a graduate finds a new job in the same EGP class as before. Figure 26 reveals the country differences of job mobility patterns during the first five years after graduation. Again, Germany is marked by a higher degree of stability than Britain. Almost half of all job shifts take place within the same EGP class, which does not necessarily mean that the kind of occupation stays the same, but rather that the class of occupation does not differ. The proportion of graduates changing the occupational class upward or downward is quite low. In Britain, in contrast, almost 50 percent of graduates experience job shifts with downward mobility. The degree of upward mobility, however, is also higher than in Germany. Only about a quarter of graduates remain in the same status class after finding a new job.

Looking at the EGP class of "previous job held" reveals that observed country mobility patterns are fairly equally distributed across classes. But again, it is noteworthy that British career mobility is much more turbulent and flexible. Obtaining an EGP class I job in Britain is by no means a guarantee for obtaining subsequent jobs in the same class. On the contrary, only 15 percent of graduates maintain their occupational status, while the rest faces downward mobility. Even though this guarantee is not given in Germany either, downward mobility occurs at a much lower scale. The same holds true for upward mobility, where a much higher proportion of British graduates in lower class positions move up the occupational ladder than their German counterparts. Obviously, the institutional framework influences career mobility as expected.

Figure 26: Upward and downward mobility after job shifts in Germany and Britain

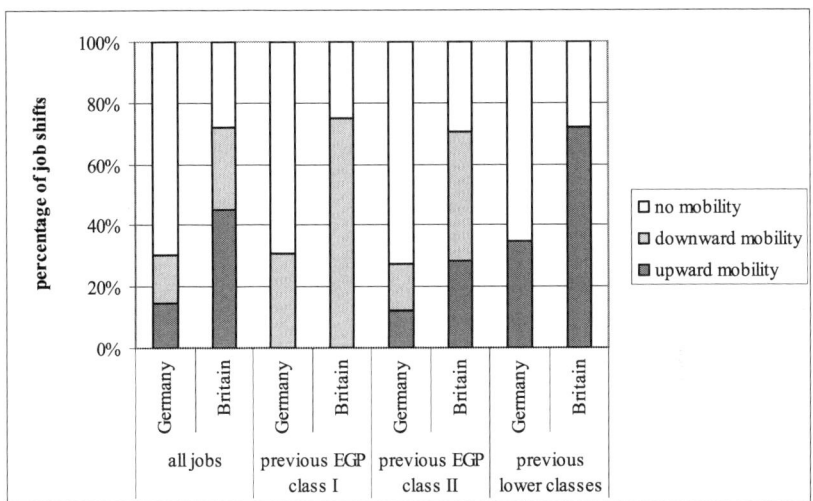

Data: SOEP, NCDS/BCS70

The highly regulated labour market in Germany is effective in restraining employer-initiated turnover and subduing involuntary job mobility, which reduces the associated risk of downward mobility. However, the indirect effect of an inflexible framework also restricts upward mobility by shortening mobility chains. In Britain, the highly deregulated labour market does not provide shelter from downward mobility processes by stabilising current employment relationships. At the same time, it does not restrict overall turnover levels in the labour market and thereby increases opportunities for upward mobility.

Taken together, the previous sections have shown that the regulation of labour markets influences graduate career development in the predicted pattern. The strictness of employment protection legislation and the high levels and durations of unemployment benefits ensure that German higher education graduates face a more stable career development marked by fewer job shifts, few occupational shifts and less downward mobility. At the same time, these inflexible structures also serve to constrain upward mobility, since they tend to entrap graduates in their current status positions. Thus, previous employment positions strongly influence career dynamics and subsequent positions held. Based on this mechanism, strict labour market regulation serves to lock-in status and occupational positions of German graduates, ensuring career stability but at the same time preventing correction of more unfavourable starting positions. In Britain, a more turbulent transition regime results from the flexible labour market environment. Graduates change their occupations more frequently after phases of unemployment, and upward and downward mobility is common. At the same time, this means that previous employment positions are less important for subsequent occupational and status outcomes, allowing for later correction of initial skill mismatches.

7.   Smooth Path or Long and Winding Road?

The previous chapters have demonstrated that national institutions indeed matter; they have a strong influence on the development of graduate careers. In Germany, the transition from higher education to work follows a smooth path, while in Britain it is more comparable to a long and winding road. This final chapter will summarise key findings of the empirical analysis in order to construct a common point of reference, to compare the incomparable national specificities by seeking again a more theoretical explanation for the overall transition patterns in both countries. Just as Hall and Soskice (2001) have identified specific institutional complementarities between vocational training and work, it is the goal of these final considerations to link the empirical findings back to Germany and Britain's different political economies in order to construct specific institutional complementarities between higher education and the labour market.

7.1   The Importance of National Institutions for the Transition Process

The opening point made in this study was that the connection between higher education and work exhibits similarities and differences across Europe. At the societal macro level, all countries have recently experienced a large increase in number of students and strong transformations in their labour markets, but these changes differed in scope and scale. At the individual level, it is generally easy for higher education graduates to find employment, but the quality of initial employment outcomes differs considerably across countries. Following these observations, the main statement of the introduction was that the national institutional set-up of both higher education systems and the graduate labour market should be important points of reference for explaining country-specific transition patterns. So far, cross-national studies on graduate employment have not systematically considered the institutional environment in any systematic fashion.

Responding to this research gap, this book developed a novel theoretical model which applied concepts from research on VET to work transitions and the Varieties of Capitalism approach to the transition from higher education to work. In a first step, four institutional spheres were identified: stratification, occupational specificity, labour market segmentation, and labour market regulation. The possible impact of those institutional dimensions on graduate career mobility was then theorised. In order to examine the theoretical model empirically, two countries representing the key varieties of capitalism, Germany as CME and Britain as LME, were analysed. The preliminary hypotheses held that the higher education system and the labour market in CMEs should be tightly coupled and, accordingly, lead to a relatively smooth transition from higher education to work. A rather loose coupling between higher education and the labour market in LMEs, in contrast, should result in a more turbulent labour market entry.

The analysis of higher education and labour market institutions in Germany and Britain in Chapter 4 confirmed these initial assumptions. The comparison was based on a secondary analysis of previous research on the four institutional spheres and on a secondary analysis of official documents and national statistics. Since a broad array of institutional features was included, such an approach runs the risk of producing very general findings, while more specific national characteristics are ignored. Nevertheless, the analysis showed that Germany and Britain vary considerably regarding the four institutional dimensions. In Germany, a weakly differentiated higher education system builds upon a highly stratified secondary education system, the primary source for sorting students into a stratified occupational structure. This institutional set-up should, in combination with moderate levels of higher education expansion, guarantee generally more favourable entry positions, which are weakly stratified along higher education structures and hardly change over time. In addition, the high importance of occupation-specific training provided by German higher education institutions should be a prerequisite for a close match between a higher education credential, the occupation obtained, and a low level of occupational mobility thereafter. The close coupling between higher education and the professional and public sector was expected to make entry into these segments uncomplicated after graduation. Careers within these segments should follow the logic of internal labour markets. Finally, a high degree of labour market regulation should at the same time lead to a stable career development with low occupational mobility after spells of unemployment and low status mobility in general.

In Britain, the weakly stratified secondary school system complements a highly stratified higher education system, which should have a strong capacity to structure labour market outcomes. In combination with high levels of higher education expansion, this set-up should lead to generally less favourable employment positions for British graduates, which are assumed to worsen over time. Selection takes place through the highly differentiated higher education system, which guarantees favourable labour market outcomes only for a small proportion of graduates. At the same time, the lower importance of occupation-specific training makes initial matches between higher education credentials and occupations more problematic, leading to a higher degree of mismatches and occupational mobility. This should particularly be the case for careers in the professional and public sector, since training has to a large extent been organised outside universities. The lower importance of occupation-specific training should also make it more difficult to enter these occupations straight after graduation. In addition, the strong level of deregulation in these segments over the past decades should increase between-sector mobility. What is more, the low regulation in the British labour market in general should make unstable career development, i.e. numerous job shifts, occupational mobility after unemployment, and strong status mobility, more likely.

The analysis of individual transitions from higher education to work in Germany and Britain demonstrated that the four institutional concepts – stratification, occupational specificity, labour market segmentation, and labour market regulation – are highly valuable for explaining cross-national similarities and differences in career mobility. On the whole, findings confirmed the expected relations, but also revealed that the story is sometimes not as simple as assumed initially. The longitudinal analysis of first five years after graduation was conducted by means of event history modelling. Compared to cross-sectional strategies, this method has an advantage in so far as it captures the duration dependence of careers in addition to the correlation between respective covariates. Thus, the general nature of the transition process could be examined instead of merely contrasting labour market outcomes at a particular point in time. Results indicated that German higher education graduates in general face better career outcomes immediately after graduation when compared to their British counterparts. As expected, status outcomes by different types of higher education institutions and degrees are weakly stratified in Germany and highly in Britain.

However, the role of higher education expansion was smaller than assumed in both countries, which leads to the conclusion that the stratification of secondary education in Germany and higher education in Britain is more important for explaining EGP class differences. The increase in the student population in Britain only influences the fact whether or not employment is found in general, but not the EGP class of the first job. In Germany, higher education expansion has not lead to less favourable employment conditions of higher education graduates either, which overall suggests that the rising numbers of higher education graduates does not necessarily tighten the labour market, but is accompanied by an upgrading of the occupational structure. Elias and Purcell (2003) offer a likely explanation for this finding, at least for Britain. They identify two new and separate groups of occupations where the proportion of graduates has risen rapidly over the past twenty-five years, namely modern graduate occupations and new graduate occupations (Elias and Purcell 2003). Even though, compared with the former and traditional graduate jobs, the latter category has slightly lower earnings, both are areas considered adequate for graduate employment.

An unexpected finding was the fact that fields of study strongly stratify labour market outcomes in Germany, even though at first sight, they only constitute a horizontal differentiation. This result could only be explained by the importance of occupation-specific training in Germany, which significantly puts graduates with more general subjects at a significant disadvantage. This pattern is observable in Britain, too, but not to the same extent, following from the lower degree of occupational specificity. On the whole, though, the different values attached to occupation-specific training and the applicability of knowledge lead, as expected, to a tight match between higher education credentials and occupational outcomes with low occupational mobility in Germany. In contrast, British graduates experience lower initial matches and therefore hop between different types of occupations in the beginning of their careers. These findings contradict the assumption of some scholars that higher education in general confers general rather than specific skills. Different institutional environments produce higher education systems with varying degrees of occupational specificity, just as it is the case for vocational training. This holds true even though estimations were based on rather broad subject clusters with very diverse occupational outcomes due to data restrictions. It is therefore suggested that models are replicated with other data sets to allow for more refined field of study categories and an objective assessment of the congruence between subjects and occupations.

The country-specific importance of occupation-specific training also helped to explain the impact of internal and occupational labour market segments on graduate career mobility. In this regard, the four-cluster typology of private, public, professional and non-professional spheres has proved to be highly valuable for characterising a segmented graduate labour market. Since in Germany, a higher education degree has traditionally been a prerequisite for entering professional occupations and jobs in the public sector, the majority of graduates succeed at the entry ports of these segments and thereafter pursue careers within the segment of the first job. The coupling between British higher education and the professional or public sector is much looser, since entry certificates are mainly obtained after finishing higher education. Therefore, the majority of graduates starts in the private sector and only later moves on into the more internal labour market segments. At the same time, the deregulation of these labour market sectors in Britain during the past two decades has strongly reduced their social closure. Therefore, they have lost their capacity to provide internal and occupational lines of career progress, and determine further career development to a lesser extent than in Germany.

The different degrees of labour market regulation in both countries also strongly influenced the transition process of higher education graduates. Strict employment and unemployment legislation in Germany leads to stable career trajectories, with long phases of full-time employment, few job shifts, little occupational mobility after periods of unemployment, and shelter from downward mobility. At the same time, upward mobility is restricted as well, since job creation is far less dynamic than in the flexible British system. There, the low degree of labour market regulation leads to a stop-gap-job pattern immediately after graduation with shorter spells of employment, a lot of job shifts, and strong patterns of mobility, be they upward or downward or between different occupations. The only similarities in this regard are related to the incidence and duration of unemployment after graduation, which is low and short in both countries. It would be worthwhile for further research to include additional indicators of labour market flexibility into the estimations, such as type of employment contract or self-employment, both of which have been shown to vary considerably in both countries among higher education graduates (Kim and Kurz 2001).

Overall, these results demonstrate that both higher education and labour market institutions matter for the transition from higher education to work. However, there are some aspects of graduate employment which need more in-depth investigation and are therefore recommended for further research. First of all, the importance of standardisation for graduate career mobility could not be explored in the present study due to data limitations. It would be of great value for understanding country-specific transition patterns if this theoretical concept was explored further. By means of standardisation, it would be possible to incorporate different forms of higher education governance resulting from more centralised or decentralised political structures into the explanatory model. Beyond the standardisation of occupation-specific contents, the application of this concept would provide a basis for analysing the extent to which standardised examination or marking procedures shape the transition process.

The interaction between different institutional spheres and the socio-structural background of students has so far not been explored sufficiently due to data and space restrictions. Initial results have shown that the transition process is clearly gendered in both countries. Quite surprisingly, though, gender differences are strong within countries, while the pattern of gender inequalities is rather similar in Germany and Britain. In both countries, women have a higher risk of working part-time and of obtaining lower status positions after graduation. Generally, they tend to study subjects with lower labour market returns and work more often in the public service than their male counterparts. Thus, even though strong cross-national differences in overall transition patterns exist, patterns of gender inequality seem to be more universal across countries. A more thorough investigation of sex segregation in graduate labour markets and the ways in which it is influenced by different institutional environments would first of all mean applying more gender-sensitive concepts to the transition process than the ones used so far. Introducing theoretical approaches that also account for cross-national similarities will give further important insights in the understanding of how gender inequalities come about, particularly among highly skilled women and men.

What also remains largely untouched in this study is the relationship between parental socio-economic background and graduate career prospects. The analysis of the stratification of education systems has already shown that the channelling of students into different education tracks leading to differences in their subsequent labour market chances occurs at different stages. Since these selection processes are strongly influenced by parental choice, cross-national variations of the reproduction of social inequalities should vary according to the institutional framework of different political economies. Initial evidence for this assumption was given by the British results on stratified labour market returns, which showed that parental socio-economic status is indeed important for obtaining high service class positions, even if the institutional dimensions of higher education are controlled for. Finally, data restrictions did not allow for an exploration of the effects of ethnicity and nationality in full detail, aspects that are therefore recommended for further research.

7.2 Building Institutional Complementarities between Higher Education and Work

By and large, a general result of this study is that the application of the four institutional concepts to the transition from higher education to work provides a theoretical framework for conducting more expedient cross-national comparisons of graduate employment than before. However, it was argued that the application of these concepts alone cannot account for overall transition regimes prevailing in different political economies. Analysing the degree of coupling between the different institutional spheres and building institutional complementarities makes it possible to grasp the overall logic of the transition from higher education to work. Combining all results, the following picture emerges: In Germany, the close coupling between higher education institutions and the graduate labour market is based on a highly stratified school system and a weakly stratified higher education, which, in combination, serve to make graduate employment more elitist. At the same time, the prevalence of strong internal labour markets, such as those found in the professions and the public service, when combined with a relatively well regulated labour market, guarantee career stability for labour market entrants. This tight coupling ensures that German graduates in general have more favourable and more matching entry processes than their British counterparts. It is more common for German graduates to find employment in high status positions, matching occupations and internal labour market segments. In addition, German graduates experience smoother and more stable career development with little occupational and status mobility, even after spells of unemployment.

In Britain, higher education is more disconnected from the labour market, due to the historical emphasis on general education, but also due to linkages with particular occupations and professions that have only recently been established and a low level of overall labour market regulation. Only the upper tiers of the vertically stratified higher education institutions ensure matching processes similar to those in Germany. The majority of British graduates start their careers in lower status positions, which match their higher education credentials to a lesser degree, while entry into professional and public sectors is more restricted. Higher education credentials are generally less important for job placements, while additional signals such as demographic variables are used for matching students to jobs. In the course of their early careers, British graduates perform extensive job hopping between different occupations and status positions, either to obtain better matching jobs, or because they are forced to do so by the highly flexible labour market environment.

In order to capture the nature of a looser or tighter coupling between higher education and labour markets in both countries more precisely and to make sense of these divergent transition patterns at a more abstract level, it is useful to return to the institutional complementarities between vocational training and the labour market in Germany and Britain. According to the Varieties of Capitalism approach, CMEs are rich in institutions that lock economic actors into long-term relationships, while LMEs lack such institutions and more strongly depend on market relations. In CMEs, the strong degree of cooperation between the state, trade unions, and employer associations guarantees the provision of specific skills through a standardised vocational education and training system, which complements a highly segmented labour market along occupations and industries. Strict labour market regulation helps to protect the investment in specific skills. Hence, those institutions that lock economic actors into long-term relationships make it possible for workers and employers to commit to a high-skill equilibrium, which in the long run ensures a high level of specific skill protection. The absence of such cooperative structures in LMEs makes general skills more important. They are complementary to a labour market weakly segmented along occupations and industries, but more strongly segmented in relation to internal firm hierarchies. A high degree of regulation is not necessary, since no specific skills have to be protected. Accordingly, the strong reliance on markets and hierarchies results in a low-skill equilibrium with a low degree of specific skill protection.

It becomes immediately apparent that the connection between higher education and labour markets follows a similar logic. Germany, as an example of CMEs, more strongly corresponds to a specific skill system. It is mainly the government that guarantees, in cooperation with professional associations and bodies, the provision of specific skills through the higher education system. This is complemented by a highly segmented graduate labour market, also strongly corresponding to occupations, but in addition characterised by distinct internal labour markets in the professional and public sector. Both segments ensure a high degree of market protection in graduate labour markets. And as for the field of vocational training, a highly regulated labour market helps to protect individual skill investments by reducing occupational mobility. In Britain, which serves as an example of LMEs, the connection between higher education and the labour market more strongly represents a general skill system. The more general training of higher education graduates corresponds to a graduate labour market that is less segmented along occupations. This makes matching processes a more individual endeavour, less reliant on specific credentials and more dependent on discretionary employer recruitment. In addition, the low degree of labour market regulation does not protect specific skill investments for the majority of graduates. An important confinement of this general pattern lies in the fact that some forms of cooperation between public higher education institutions and professional bodies have developed in LMEs as well. But even the traditionally more sheltered public and professional segments have become deregulated and open to market competition.

By and large, the observed institutional complementarities between higher education and graduate labour markets correspond to the overall logic of different political economies. However, there are also important differences between vocational training and higher education. One is related to the degree of specific skills. Even though higher education in CMEs provides on the whole more specific skills than in LMEs, skills provided through higher education are in general less specific than it is the case for skills obtained through vocational training. The other difference refers to the varying degrees of protection inherent in both types of political economies. Even though labour market regulation is decisive for skill protection at the level of higher education, the particular structure of graduate labour market makes it also possible to provide varying degrees of *status protection.*

The empirical results have shown that the connection between higher education and the graduate labour market in CMEs tends to be more "decommodified" and protected from market competition as compared to both vocational training in CMEs and higher education in LMEs. This higher degree of status protection in CMEs relies on a mixture of institutional structures. First of all, the combination of a highly stratified secondary education system and a weakly stratified higher education system ensures that higher education remains more elitist in character, even in the course of higher education expansion. In addition, the high level of protection of internal labour market segments from market processes in sectors important for graduate employment, coupled with a highly regulated labour market in general ensures a high protection of initial status positions in the further course of graduate careers. Taken together, such a high level of status protection guarantees a smooth transition process, consisting of higher status entry positions, stable career development, and little status mobility.

Graduate labour markets in LMEs are less sheltered from market competition, and therefore institutional complementarities between higher education and labour markets offer only a low degree of status protection. This is prepared by a weakly stratified education system and complemented by higher degrees of higher education expansion, which increases competition among graduates and reduces status returns. In addition, the absence of strong internal labour market segments, i.e. public and professional sectors with a lower degree of social closure, do not guarantee status protection of employment positions, even if a job is obtained in these segments. The lower-level protection of status positions is reinforced by a high degree of deregulation in the labour market in general, which makes skills investments more risky and outcomes less stable. On the whole, this low degree of status protection is associated with a more turbulent labour market entry of higher education graduates, consisting of generally lower status outcomes, more stop-gap jobs, and more status mobility.

The various degrees of status protection that were found in CMEs and LMEs fit neatly with the Varieties of Capitalism thesis. Britain and Germany thus exhibit distinct equillibria between higher education systems and graduate labour markets. This is also supported by the particular patterns of labour market exclusion found in both countries. In the coordinated market economy of Germany, the downside of a high degree of status protection is a tendency to create social exclusion by three different lock-in effects. First, the high degree of stratification locks graduates into specific status positions. Second, the high degree of occupational specificity locks graduates into specific occupations. Third, the high degree of labour market segmentation locks graduates into specific labour market segments. All of these lock-in effects are reinforced by a high degree of labour market regulation, which does not allow for later corrections of the initial placement, since it reduces occupational and status mobility. As a consequence, the high status protection of institutional arrangements in CMEs generally leads to more favourable starting positions and stable career development. Yet, the lock-in of initial position makes latter mobility difficult. It excludes those with less favourable starting positions and restricts later correction of initial mismatches. This process of exclusion was shown to be more pronounced for graduates with more general fields of study and for female graduates.

The importance of lock-in effects and subsequent exclusion of particular social groups is also observable in the field of vocational training in CMEs. There, the high level of skill protection guarantees generally more favourable starting positions, but only for those with vocational certificates. Those finishing education without the respective credentials are systematically excluded from labour market participation. But despite these apparent similarities between the various educational levels, differences in the mechanisms of exclusion prevail between higher education and training: while exclusion patterns during the transition from higher education to work strongly depend on the initial position obtained in the labour market, exclusion patterns during the transition from VET to work strongly depend on the qualification obtained in the education system. In LMEs, neither status nor skill protection produce such strong lock-in effects for career prospects. Only one aspect of higher education systems in CMEs, its high degree of stratification, seems to create a distinct pattern of exclusion, since higher class positions are mainly obtained by students with higher socio-economic backgrounds. But this again corresponds to the general exclusion patterns in LMEs, which, according to Estévez-Abe et al. (2001), reproduce class inequalities to a higher degree. Table 14 summarises the institutional determinants of graduate employment in different political economies.

Table 14: The institutional determinants of transition patterns in CMEs and LMEs

	CMEs	LMEs
Stratification of secondary schooling	High	Low
	+	+
Stratification of higher education	Low	High
	+	+
Occupational specificity	High	Low
	+	+
Degree of labour market segmentation	High	Low
	+	+
Degree of labour market regulation	High	Low
	↓	↓
Institutional complementarities	Specific skill equilibrium, high status protection	General skill equilibrium, low status protection
	↓	↓
Transition regime	High status positions, good initial matches, stable career development, low occupational and status mobility, high lock-in	Low status positions, bad initial matches, unstable career development, high occupational and status mobility, low lock-in

7.3 National Paths in Transition?

Overall, the Varieties of Capitalism thesis requires looking at the specific historical circumstances and institutional contexts that form complementarities between higher education and graduate labour markets. It is only by conducting such an analysis that one can begin to understand the social dynamics which will enable a more comprehensive Varieties of Capitalism thesis – in particular the implications of the institutional complementarities – as it applies to the relationship between labour markets and higher education. The previous analysis has shown that the type of skill equilibrium and the degree of status protection create distinct institutional complementarities between higher education and work and therefore are crucial for determining the career prospects of higher education graduates.

Applying this framework to countries other than Germany and Britain should lead to similar results, depending on whether countries are classified as CMEs or LMEs. Some critics of the Varieties of Capitalism approach, however, have argued that it is more capable of explaining a dualism rather than a range of varieties (Boyer 2005), so applying it for countries that cannot be clearly classified as CMEs and LMEs is more complex. As a consequence, more comprehensive cross-country comparisons might show that CMEs and LMEs only represent two types of a larger variety of political economies. Table 15 demonstrates that the combination of different types of skill regimes and different levels of status protection theoretically allows for identifying four distinct types of institutional complementarities between higher education and work.

Table 15: Institutional complementarities between higher education and work

		Type of skill equilibrium	
		Specific skill equilibrium	General skill equilibrium
Level of status protection	High status protection	Germany	
	Low status protection		Britain

Further research in this regard will have to establish whether more distinct models of transition regimes exist, just as it is the case for welfare state typologies, which also identify a Social-Democratic and a Southern European model. It might be that the influence of the four institutional spheres on graduate career trajectories does no follow the same neat pattern in the Scandinavian or Southern European countries as it is the case for Germany and Britain, but rather exhibit more mixed directions of institutional outcomes. Analysis of the CHEERS data, which provides a most comprehensive attempt to follow graduates during the first four years after graduation in a broader range of countries, would most probably yield interesting results.

Apart from its theoretical applicability for cross-national research on graduate employment, this study also poses some practical questions for further developments in Germany and Britain. Just as for the field of vocational education and training, German institutional arrangements seem to be more positive for labour market outcomes and career mobility. In Britain, the low degree of status protection and the general skill equilibrium makes the individual transition from higher education to work a more vulnerable process. Even though higher education in Britain by and large still guarantees better labour market chances as compared to lower educational qualifications, the comparative results of this study clearly show that the strong labour market reforms over the last decades have considerably worsened the career prospects of graduates. Effects of the high degree of deregulation and liberalisation of the graduate labour market and of higher education are only beginning to be perceived and might become more severe in the future, creating unstable career prospects for those working in occupations of particular importance to the public interest, such as professionals or civil servants.

However, the ongoing expansion of higher education participation, which aims at achieving an enrolment rate of 50 percent of those aged 18–30 by 2010 (DfES 2003), might also have considerable consequences for graduate career prospects in the future. Even though results have so far only pointed towards a slight decrease in overall employment chances in the course of higher education expansion, a further deterioration of career outcomes might occur in the future. The high level of stratification of the British higher education system might then strongly contribute to the sorting of students into jobs, creating a more diversified class structure between a small higher education elite, graduating from high-profile university institutions with postgraduate degrees, and the majority of graduates. British undergraduate students from less reputable institutions may then be likely to obtain jobs far below their educational level.

In Germany, the high degree of status protection seems to have maintained the relative advantage of higher education graduates as compared to holders of other certificates. However, in this case, changes have to be closely monitored as well, particularly against the background of the Bologna Process. The introduction of a vertically differentiated degree structure in the German higher education system, similar to the one existing in Britain, is likely to produce a higher stratification of labour market outcomes between undergraduate and postgraduate credentials in the future. It remains to be seen whether German undergraduate students will experience a similar level of status protection as graduates holding an "old" German degree have in the past. If not, graduates with a Bachelor degree may have to compete with graduates from the dual apprenticeship system.

The channelling of students into particular occupational strata then becomes even more pronounced. If a highly stratified school system is accompanied by a highly stratified higher education system, sorting occurs twice in course of an individual education process. Since German education inequalities are the highest among all OECD member status (OECD 2003) and since it is well-established that the tripartite structure of German secondary schooling is the decisive factor in reproducing these social inequalities (Allmendinger and Aisenbrey 2002; Blossfeld and Shavit 1993), this propensity is likely to increase through the introduction of a stratified higher education system. It might be that this additional sorting process will encourage only students from upper socio-economic backgrounds to stay on at higher education institutions and study for a postgraduate degree, which, as the British case has shown, is likely to yield better labour market returns. The aim of German education policy to increase age participation rates also has to be viewed against the background of a double-stratified education system. As this study has shown, the stratified secondary school system sets an institutional barrier to higher education expansion. Since the German apprenticeship system offers a worthwhile alternative for pupils holding the *Abitur*, the increase of numbers of students in Germany is unlikely to match the corresponding increase in Britain.

Finally, cross-national differences in the relationship between higher education and labour markets will have to be closely monitored against the background of the Bologna Process, which aims at harmonising the structures of higher education systems across Europe. Many scholars expect a convergence of the career prospects of higher education graduates, since from now on higher education credentials are supposed to be more easily transferable across countries. What this perspective fails to take into account, however, is the institutional set-up of graduate labour markets as well as the existence of path dependencies in the higher education system. This study has demonstrated that in the two decades prior to Bologna, similar experiences of higher education expansion across the nation were crucially mediated by institutional dynamics. This indicates that the national higher education reform projects initiated by the Bologna Process are likely to follow a tortuous route to convergence. This study sought to enable a better understanding of some of the obstacles that stand in the way.

References

(1944). *Education Act*, Act of Parliament No. 7 & 8 Geo. 6.

(1969). *Gesetz über die Gemeinschaftsaufgabe Ausbau und Neubau von Hochschulen (Hochschulbauförderungsgesetz)*, Bundesministerium für Bildung und Forschung (BGBl. I, p. 1556).

(1988). *Education Reform Act 1988*, Act of Parliament No. 1988 c. 40.

(1992). *Further and Higher Education Act 1992*, Act of Parliament No. 1992 c. 13.

(1998). *Competition Act*, Act of Parliament No. 1998, c. 41.

(2002). *Hochschulrahmengesetz*, Fassung der Bekanntmachung vom 19. Januar 1999 (BGBl. I S. 18), zuletzt geändert durch Artikel 1 des Gesetzes vom 8. August 2002 (BGBl. I, p. 3138).

Abbott, A. D. (1988). *The System of Professions*. Chicago, London: The University of Chicago Press.

Allison, P. D. (1984). *Event History Analysis: Regression for Longitudinal Data*. Beverly Hills, London: Sage Publications.

Allmendinger, J. (1989a). Career Mobility Dynamics: A Comparative Study of the United States, Norway and Germany, *Max Planck Institute for Human Development Discussion Papers*. Berlin: MPIfG.

Allmendinger, J. (1989b). Educational Systems and Labour Market Outcomes. *European Sociological Review*, 5, pp. 231-250.

Allmendinger, J.; Aisenbrey, S. (2002). Soziologische Bildungsforschung. In R. Tippelt (Ed.), *Handbuch für Bildungsforschung*. Opladen: Leske & Budrich, pp. 41-60.

Allmendinger, J.; Hinz, T. (1998). Occupational Careers under Different Welfare Regimes: West Germany, Great Britain and Sweden. In L. Leisering & R. Walker (Eds.), *The Dynamics of Modern Society*. Bristol: The Policy Press, pp. 63-84.

Altbach, P. G.; McGill Peterson, P. (1999). *Higher Education in the 21st Century: Global Challenge and National Response*. New York: IIE Books.

Althauser, R. P. (1989). Internal Labor Markets. *Annual Review of Sociology*, 15, pp. 143-161.

Althauser, R. P.; Kalleberg, A. L. (1981). Firms, Occupations and the Structure of Labor Markets: A Conceptual Analysis. In R. P. Althauser & A. L. Kalleberg (Eds.), *Sociological Perspectives on Labor Markets*. Orlando: Academic Press, pp. 1483-1536.

Alwin, D. F.; McCammon, R. J. (2003). Generations, Cohorts, and Social Change. In J. T. Mortimer & M. J. Shanahan (Eds.), *Handbook of the Life Course*. New York: Kluwer Academic Publishers, pp. 23-49.

Amable, B. (2000). Institutional Complementarity and Diversity of Social Systems of Innovation and Production. *Review of International Political Economy*, 7, pp. 645-687.

Archer, M. (1972). *University and Society*. London: Heinemann Educational Books.

Ardy, B.; Umbach, G. (2004). *Employment Policies in Germany and the UK: The Impact of Europeanisation*. London: Anglo-German Foundation for the Study of Industrial Society.

Babb, P.; Butcher, H.; Church, J.; Zealey, L. (2006). Social Trends 36, *Office for National Statistics*. Houndmills, Basingstoke, New York: Palgrave Macmillan.

Barlow, L. (1946). Scientific Manpower: Report of a Special Committee appointed by the Lord President of the Council. London: HMSO.

Becker, G. S. (1962). Investment in Human Capital: A Theoretical Analysis. *The Journal of Political Economy*, 70, pp. 9-49.

Becker, G. S. (1964). *Human Capital. A Theoretical and Empirical Analysis, with Special Reference to Education*. New York: Columbia University Press for NBER.

Becker, R. (1993). *Staatsexpansion und Karrierechancen. Berufsverläufe im öffentlichen Dienst und in der Privatwirtschaft*. Frankfurt/M., New York: Campus Verlag.

Ben-David, J. (1977). *Centers of Learning: Britain, France, Germany, United States*. New York: McGraw-Hill.

Bernardi, F.; Gangl, M.; van de Werfhorst, H. G. (2004). The From-School-To-Work Dynamics. Timing of Work and Quality of Work in Italy, the Netherlands and the United States, 1980-1998, *CEACS Working Paper*. Madrid: Fundación Juan March.

Bleiklie, I.; Byrkjeflot, H. (2002). Changing Knowledge Regimes: Universities in a New Research Environment. *Higher Education*, 44, pp. 519-532.

Blossfeld, H.-P.; Becker, R. (1988). Arbeitsmarktprozesse zwischen öffentlichem und privatwirtschaftlichem Sektor. *Mitteilungen aus der Arbeitsmarkt- und Berufsforschung*, 22, pp. 233-246.

Blossfeld, H.-P.; Mayer, K. U. (1988). Arbeitsmarktsegmentation in der Bundesrepublik Deutschland. Eine empirische Überprüfung von Segmentationstheorien aus der Persepktive des Lebenslaufs. *Kölner Zeitschrift für Sozialpsychologie*, 40, pp. 262-283.

Blossfeld, H.-P.; Rohwer, G. (1995). *Techniques of Event-History Modeling. New Approaches to Causal Analysis*. Mahwah, NJ: Erlbaum.

Blossfeld, H.-P.; Shavit, Y. (1993). *Persisting Barriers: Changes in Educational Opportunities in Thirteen Countries*. Boulder, CO: Westview Press.

BMBF (2004). *Basic and Structural Data 2003/2004*, Berlin, Bonn: BMBF Publications and Website Division.

BMBF (2007). Higher Education Pact, *Online documents*. Berlin: Bundesministerium für Bildung und Forschung.

Booth, C. (1999). The Rise of the "New" Universities in Britain. In D. Smith & A. K. Langslow (Eds.), *The Idea of a University*. London, Bristol, Philadelphia: Jessica Kingsley Publishers.

Boudon, R. (2003). Beyond Rational Choice Theory. *Annual Review of Sociology*, 29, pp. 1-21.

Boyer, R. (2005). How and Why Capitalisms Differ, *Max Planck Institute for the Study of Societies Discussion Papers*. München: MPIfG.

Brater, M.; Beck, U. (1981). Berufe als Organisationsform menschlichen Arbeitsvermögens. In W. Littek, W. Rammert & G. Wachtler (Eds.), *Einführung in die Arbeits- und Industriesoziologie*. Frankfurt/M., New York: Campus Verlag, pp. 208-224.

Brauns, H.; Gangl, M.; Scherer, S. (2000). The Educational Stratification of Unemployment Risks at the Beginning of Working Life: Results from France, the United Kingdom and West Germany, *Beitrag zur 2. Nutzerkonferenz "Forschung mit dem Mikrozensus: Analysen zur Sozialstruktur und zum Arbeitsmarkt"*. Mannheim.

Brauns, H.; Haun, D.; Steinmann, S. (1997a). Die Konstruktion eines international vergleichbaren Klassenschemas (EGP). Erwerbsstatistische Besonderheiten am Beispiel von Labour Force Surveys der Bundesrepublik Deutschland, Frankreichs, Großbritanniens und Ungarns, *Working Papers Mannheimer Zentrum für Sozialforschung*. Mannheim: MZES.

Brauns, H.; Müller, W.; Steinmann, S. (1997b). Educational Expansion and Returns to Education. A Comparative Study on Germany, France, the UK, and Hungary, *Working Papers Mannheimer Zentrum für Sozialforschung*. Mannheim: MZES.

Brauns, H.; Steinmann, S. (1997). Educational Reform in France, West-Germany, the United Kingdom and Hungary: Updating the CASMIN Educational Classification, *Working Papers Mannheimer Zentrum für Sozialforschung*. Mannheim: MZES.

Breen, R.; Hannan, D. F.; O'Leary, R. (1995). Returns to Education: Taking Account of Employers' Perceptions and Use of Educational Credentials. *European Sociological Review*, 11, pp. 59-73.

Brennan, J.; Kogan, M.; Teichler, U. (1996a). *Higher Education and Work*. London, Bristol, Pennsylvania: Jessica Kingsley Publishers.

Brennan, J.; Lyon, S.; Schomburg, H.; Teichler, U. (1996b). Employment and Work of British and Germany Graduates. In J. Brennan, M. Kogan & U. Teichler (Eds.), *Higher Education and Work*. London, Bristol, Pennsylvania: Jessica Kingsley Publishers, pp. 47-98.

Briedis, K.; Minks, K.-H. (2004). Zwischen Hochschule und Arbeitsmarkt. Eine Befragung der Hochschulabsolventinnen und Hochschulabsolventen des Prüfungsjahres 2001. Hannover: HIS Hochschul-Informations-System.

Büchel, F.; De Grip, A.; Mertens, A. (2003). *Overeducation in Europe: Current Issues in Theory and Policy*. Cheltenham, UK: Edward Elgar.

Butz, M. (2000). Lohnt Bildung noch? Die Einkommensungleichheiten der unterschiedlichen Bildungsklassen in der Bundesrepublik Deutschland im Zeitvergleich 1982-1995. In P. A. Berger & D. Konietzka (Eds.), *Neue Ungleichheiten der Erwerbsgesellschaft*. Opladen: Leske & Budrich, pp. 95-117.

Bynner, J.; Butler, N.; Ferri, E.; Shepherd, P.; Smith, K. (2001). The Design and Conduct of the 1999-2000 Surveys of the National Child Development Study and the 1970 British Cohort Study, *CLS Cohort Studies Working Papers*. London: Centre for Longitudinal Studies.

Chevalier, A.; Conlon, G. (2003). Does it Pay to Attend a Prestigious University? Centre for the Economics of Education, London School of Economics and Political Science, London.

Clark, B. R. (1995). *Places of Inquiry. Research and Advanced Education in Modern Universities*. Berkeley, CA: University of California Press.

Clasen, J. (2005). *Reforming European Welfare States. Germany and the United Kingdom Compared*. Oxford, New York: Oxford University Press.

Coleman, J. S. (1994). *Foundations of Social Theory*. Cambridge MA., London: The Belknap Press of Harvard University Press.

Collins, R. (1979). *The Credential Society*. New York: Academic Press.

CRE (2000). The Bologna Declaration on the European Space for Higher Education: An Explanation. Paris: Confederation of EU Rectors' Conferences and the Association of European Universities.

Davies, S.; Guppy, N. (1997). Field of Study, College Selectivity, and Student Inequalities in Higher Education. *Social Forces*, 75, pp. 1417-1438.

Deakin, S.; Reed, H. (2003). River Crossing or Cold Bath? Deregulation and Employment in Britain in the 1980s and 1990s. In G. Esping-Andersen & M. Regini (Eds.), *Why Deregulate Labour Markets?* Oxfort, New York: Oxford University Press.

Dearing Report (1997). Higher Education in the Learning Society, *Report submitted to the Secretaries of State for Education and Employment, Wales, Scotland*

and Northern Ireland in July 1997. http://www.leeds.ac.uk/educol/ncihe/: The National Committee of Inquiry into Higher Education.

Dekker, R.; de Grip, A.; Heijke, H. (2002). The Effects of Training and Overeducation on Career Mobility in a Segmented Labour Market. *International Journal of Manpower*, 23, pp. 106-125.

Derlien, H.-U. (2003). German Public Administration: Weberian despite "Modernization". In K. K. Tummala (Ed.), *Comparative Bureaucratic Systems*. Lanham, Boulder, New York, Oxford: Lexington Books, pp. 97-122.

DES (1966). *A Plan for Polytechnics and Other Colleges. Higher Education in the Further Education System (Cm. 3006)*, Great Britain. Parliament. House of Commons. London: HMSO.

DES (1991). *Higher Education: A New Framework. Cm. Paper/Bill Number: 1541*, Great Britain. Parliament. House of Commons. London: HMSO.

DfE (1985). *The Development of Higher Education into the 1990s (Cm. 9524)*, Great Britain. Parliament. House of Commons. London: HMSO.

DfE (1994). *Student Numbers in Higher Education - Great Britain 1982/83 to 1992/93*, Great Britain. Parliament. House of Commons. London: HMSO.

DfEE (1998). *Green Paper: The Learning Age: A Renaissance for a New Britain*, Great Britain. Parliament. House of Commons. London: HMSO.

DfES (2003). *The Future of Higher Education. Government White Paper presented to Parliament by the Secretary of State for Education and Skills by Command of Her Majesty*, Great Britain. Parliament. House of Commons. London: HMSO.

Doeringer, P. B. (1967). Determinants of the Structure of Industrial Type Internal Labour Markets. *Industrial Relations Review*, 20, pp. 206-220.

Doeringer, P. B.; Piore, M. (1971). *Internal Labor Markets and Manpower Analysis*. Lexington (MA): Heath.

Dolton, P.; McIntosh, S. (2003). Public and Private Sector Labour Markets. In R. Dickens, P. Gregg & J. Wadsworth (Eds.), *The Labour Market under New Labour: The State of Working Britain*. Houndmills, Basingstoke, New York: Palgrave Macmillan, pp. 214-232.

Dowding, K. (1995). *The Civil Service*. London, New York: Routledge.

Ebbinghaus, B. (2005). Can Path Dependence Explain Institutional Change?, *Max Planck Institute for Study of Societies Discussion Papers*. Berlin: MPIfG.

Ebbinghaus, B.; Manow, P. (2001). Introduction. Studying Varieties of Welfare Capitalism. In B. Ebbinghaus & P. Manow (Eds.), *Comparing Welfare Capitalism. Social Policy and Political Economy in Europe, Japan and the USA*. London: Routledge, pp. 1-24.

Elder, G. H. (1985). Perspectives on the Life Course. In G. H. Elder (Ed.), *Life Course Dynamics. Trajectories and Transitions, 1968-1980*. Ithaca: Cornell University Press, pp. 23-49.

Elder, G. H. (1992). The Life Course. In E. Borgatta & M. Borgatta (Eds.), *The Encyclopedia of Sociology, Volume 3*. Houndmills, Basingstoke, New York: Palgrave Macmillan, pp. 1120-1130.

Elder, G. H. (1994). Time, Human Agency, and the Social Change: Perspectives on the Life Course. *Social Psychology Quarterly*, 57, pp. 4-15.

Elder, G. H.; Johnson Kirkpatrick, M.; Crosnoe, R. (2003). The Emergence and Development of Life Course Theory. In J. T. Mortimer & M. J. Shanahan (Eds.), *Handbook of the Life Course*. New York: Kluwer Academic Publisher, pp. 3-19.

Elias , P. (1997). Occupational Classification (ISCO-88): Concepts, Methods, Reliability, Validity and Cross-national Comparability. *OECD Labour Market and Social Policy Occasional Papers*, 20, pp. 1-23.

Elias, P.; Purcell, K. (2003). Measuring Change in the Graduate Labour Market. *Project Paper 'Researching Graduate Careers Seven Years On'*, 1.

Ellwein, T. (1985). *Die deutsche Universität. Vom Mittelalter bis zur Gegenwart*. Königstein: Athenäum Verlag.

Enders, J. (2004). Higher Education, Internationalisation, and the Nation-State: Recent Developments and Challenges to Governance Theory. *Higher Education*, 47, pp. 361-382.

Erikson, R.; Goldthorpe, J. H. (1992). *The Constant Flux. A Study of Class Mobility in Industrial Societies*. Oxford: Clarendon Press.

Erikson, R.; H., G. J.; Portocarero, L. (1979). Intergenerational Class Mobility in Three Western European Societies. *British Journal of Sociology*, 30, pp. 415-441.

Estévez-Abe, M.; Iversen, T.; Soskice, D. (2001). Social Protection and the Formation of Skills: A Reinterpretation of the Welfare State. In P. A. Hall & D. Soskice (Eds.), *Varieties of Capitalism. The Institutional Foundations of Comparative Advantage*. Oxford, New York: Oxford University Press, pp. 145-183.

European Commission (2004). Employment in Europe 2004. Recent Trends and Prospects. Luxembourg: Office for Official Publications of the European Communities.

Eurydice (2000). *Two Decades of Reform in Higher Education in Europe: 1980 Onwards*. Brussels: Eurydice, the Information Network on Education in Europe.

Eurydice (2006). *Structures of Education, Vocational Training and Adult Education Systems in Europe - 2006 Edition.* Brussels: Eurydice, the Information Network on Education in Europe.

Falk, S.; Sackmann, R.; Struck, O.; Weymann, A.; Windzio, M.; Wingens, M. (2000). Gemeinsame Startbedingungen in Ost und West? Risiken beim Berufseinstieg und deren Folgen im weiteren Erwerbsverlauf *Working Paper Series*. Bremen: Collaborative Research Center "Status Passages and Risks in the Life Course" (Sfb 186).

Fuchs, S.; Schettkat, R. (2003). Germany: A Regulated Flexibility. In G. Esping-Andersen & M. Regini (Eds.), *Why Deregulated Labour Markets?* Oxford, New York: Oxford University Press.

Gangl, M. (2000a). Education and Labour Market Entry across Europe: The Impact of Institutional Arrangements in Training Systems and Labour Markets, *Working Papers Mannheimer Zentrum für Sozialforschung*. Mannheim: MZES.

Gangl, M. (2000b). European Perspectives on Labour Market Entry: A Matter of Institutional Linkages and Labour Markets?, *Working Papers Mannheimer Zentrum für Sozialforschung*. Mannheim: MZES.

Gangl, M. (2001). European Perspectives on Labour Market Entry: A Dichotomy of Occupationalized versus Non-Occupationalized Systems? *European Societies*, 3, pp. 471-494.

Gangl, M. (2002a). Changing Labour Markets and Early Career Outcomes: Labour Market Entry in Europe over the Past Decade. *Work, Employment and Society*, 16, pp. 67-90.

Gangl, M. (2002b). The Only Way is Up? Employment Protection and Job Mobility among Recent Entrants to European Labour Markets, *Working Papers Mannheimer Zentrum für Sozialforschung*. Mannheim: MZES.

Gangl, M. (2004). Institutions and the Structure of Labour Market Matching in the United States and West Germany. *European Sociological Review*, 20, pp. 171-187.

Grimshaw, D.; Ward, K. G.; Rubery, J.; Beynon, H. (2001). Organisations and the Transformation of the Internal Labour Market. *Work, Employment and Society*, 15, pp. 25-54.

Hage, J. (2000). Path Dependencies of Education Systems and the Division of Labour within Organisations. In M. Maurice & A. Sorge (Eds.), *Embedding Organisations. Societal Analysis of Actors, Organisations and Socio-Economic Context*. Amsterdam, Philadelphia: John Benjamins Publishing Company.

Haisken-DeNew, J. P.; Frick, J. R. (2005). *DTC Desktop Companion to the German Socio-Economic Panel Study (SOEP)*. Berlin: DIW.

257

Hall, P. A.; Soskice, D. (2001). An Introduction to Varieties of Capitalism. In P. A. Hall & D. Soskice (Eds.), *Varieties of Capitalism. The Institutional Foundations of Comparative Advantage.* Oxford: University Press, pp. 1-68.

Hammouya, M. (1999). Statistics on Public Sector Employment: Methodology, Structures and Trends, *ILO Bureau of Statistics Working Paper.* Geneva: International Labour Office.

Hannan, D. F.; Raffe, D.; Rutjes, H.; Willems, E.; Mansuy, M.; Müller, W.; Amor, T. (1999). A Comparative Analysis of Transitions from Education to Work in Europe (CATEWE) - A Conceptual Framework, *ESRI Working Paper* Dublin: European Studies Research Insitute.

Hartmann, J. (1997). Komplexes Stichprobendesign und Ereignisanalyse. Zur Notwendigkeit einer Gewichtung bei disproprtional geschichteter Stichprobenziehung, *Working Papers Mannheimer Zentrum für Sozialforschung.* Mannheim: MZES.

Heckman, J. J. (2002). Flexibility and Job Creation: Lessons for Germany, *National Bureau of Economic Research Working Paper Series.* Cambridge (MA): NBER.

Heidenreich, M. (1999). Berufskonstruktion und Professionalisierung. Erträge der soziologischen Forschung. In H.-J. Apel, K.-P. Horn, P. Lundgreen & U. Sandfuchs (Eds.), *Professionalisierung pädagogischer Berufe im historischen Prozess.* Bad Heilbrunn: Julius Klinkhardt, pp. 35-58.

Heinz, W. R. (1996). Status Passages as Micro-Macro Linkages in Life Course Research. In A. Weymann & W. R. Heinz (Eds.), *Society and Biography.* Weinheim: DSV, pp. 51-66.

Heinz, W. R. (1999). *From Education to Work: Cross-National Perspectives.* Cambridge: Cambridge University Press.

Hesse, J. J. (2003). Stability Turned Regidity. Paradoxes in German Public Sector Reform. In J. J. Hesse, C. Hood & B. G. Peters (Eds.), *Paradoxes in Public Sector Reform. An International Comparison.* Berlin: Duncker & Humblot, pp. 197-214.

Hill, D. H. (1997). Adjusting for Attrition in Event-History Analysis. *Sociological Methodology,* 27, pp. 393-416.

Hillmert, S. (2001). *Ausbildungssysteme und Arbeitsmarkt : Lebensverläufe in Großbritannien und Deutschland im Kohortenvergleich.* Wiesbaden: Westdeutscher Verlag.

Hillyard, P.; Sim, J.; Tombs, S.; Whyte, D. (2003). Leaving a "Stain Upon the Silence": Critical Ciminology and the Politics of Dissent, *"Tough on Crime" ... Though on Freedoms? From Community to Global Interventions.* Centre for Studies in Crime and Social Justice (Edge Hill), Chester, England.

Hood, C. (1995). The "New Public Management" in the 1980s: Variations on a Theme. *Accounting, Organizations and Society*, 20, pp. 93-109.

Hood, C. (2003). From Public Bureaucracy State to Re-regulated Public Service: The Paradox of British Public Sector Reform. In J. J. Hesse, C. Hood & B. G. Peters (Eds.), *Paradoxes in Public Sector Reform. An International Comparison*. Berlin: Duncker & Humblot, pp. 127-148.

Horton, S. (2000). Human Resources Flexibilities in UK Public Services. In D. Farnham & S. Horton (Eds.), *Human Resources Flexibilities in the Public Services*. Houndmills, Basingstoke, New York: Palgrave Macmillan.

Huisman, J.; Maassen, P.; Neave, G. (2001). *Higher Education and the Nation State. The International Dimension on Higher Education*. Oxford: Pergamon.

Humboldt, W. v. (1956). Über die innere und äußere Organisation der höheren wissenschaftlichen Anstalten in Berlin (1810). In n.a. (Ed.), *Die Idee der deutschen Universität: Die fünf Grundschriften aus der Zeit ihrer Neubegründung durch klassischen Idealismus und romantischen Idealismus*. Darmstadt: Wissenschaftliche Buchgesellschaft.

Hussmanns, R.; Mehran, F.; Verma, V. (1990). *Surveys of Economically Active Population, Employment, Unemployment and Underemployment: An ILO Manual on Concepts and Methods*. Geneva: International Labour Organization.

Jahr, V.; Schomburg, H.; Teichler, U. (2003). *Internationale Mobilität von Absolventinnen und Absolventen europäischer Hochschulen*. Kassel: Wissenschaftliches Zentrum für Berufs- und Hochschulforschung.

Jenkins, S. P. (2004). Survival Analysis, *Manuscript of the Essex Summer School in SSCA*. University of Essex, Colchester.

Jongbloed, B. (2004). Funding Higher Education: Options, Trade-Offs and Dilemmas. *Fulbright Brainstorms - New Trends in Higher Education*. CHEPS, University of Twente, the Netherlands.

Jovanovic, B. (1979). Job Matching and the Theory of Turnover. *The Journal of Political Economy*, 5, pp. 972-990.

Kalleberg, A. L.; Sorensen, A. B. (1979). The Sociology of Labor Markets. *Annual Review of Sociology*, 5, pp. 351-379.

Keller, A. (2003). Von Bologna nach Berlin. Perspektiven eines Europäischen Hochschulraums im Rahmen des Bologna-Prozesses am Vorabend des europäischen Hochschulgipfels 2003 in Berlin. Berlin.

Kerckhoff, A. C. (1996). Building Conceptual and Empirical Bridges between Studies of Educational and Labour Force Careers. In A. C. Kerckhoff (Ed.), *Generating Social Stratification: Toward a New Research Agenda*. Boulder: Westview Press, pp. 37-56.

Kerckhoff, A. C. (2001). Education and Social Stratification. Processes in Comparative Perspective. *Sociology of Education*, Extra Issue 2001, pp. 3-18.

Kerr, C. (1954). The Balkanization of Labor Markets. In E. W. Bakke, P. M. Hauser, G. L. Palmer, C. A. Myers, D. Yoder & C. Kerr (Eds.), *Labor Mobility and Economic Opportunity* Cambridge (MA): Technology-Press of MIT, pp. 92-110.

Kerst, C.; Minks, K.-H. (2003). Fünf Jahre nach dem Studienabschluss - Berufsverlauf und aktuelle Situation von Hochschulabsolventinnen und Hochschulabsolventen des Prüfungsjahrgangs 1997. In H. Hochschul-Informations-System (Ed.), *HIS Projektbericht*. Hannover: HIS.

Kim, A.; Kim, K.-W. (2003). Returns to Tertiary Education in Germany and the UK: Effects of Fields of Study and Gender, *Working Papers Mannheimer Zentrum für Sozialforschung*. Mannheim: MZES.

Kim, A.; Kurz, K. (2001). Precarious Employment, Education and Gender: A Comparison of Germany and the United Kingdom, *Working Papers Mannheimer Zentrum für Sozialforschung*. Mannheim: MZES.

Kivinen, O.; Nurmi, J. (2003). Unifying Higher Education for Different Kinds of Europeans. Higher Education and Work: A Comparison of Ten Countries. *Comparative Education*, 39, pp. 83-103.

Klemm, K. (2000). Bildung. In J. Allmendinger & W. Ludwig-Mayerhofer (Eds.), *Soziologie des Sozialstaates*. Weinheim: Juventa, pp. 145-166.

Kogan, I.; Müller, W. (2003). School-to-Work Transitions in Europe: Analyses of the EU LFS 2000 Hoc Module. Introduction. In I. Kogan & W. Müller (Eds.), *School-to-Work Transitions in Europe: Analyses of the EU LFS 2000 Hoc Module*. Mannheim: MZES.

Kohli, M. (1985). Die Institutionalisierung des Lebenslaufs: Historische Befunde und theoretische Argumente. *Kölner Zeitschrift für Soziologie und Sozialpsychologie*, 37, pp. 1-29.

Kohlrausch, B. (2007). *A Ticket to Work? Active Labour Market Policy for the Young Unemployed in Britain and Germany*. Dissertation, University of Bremen.

Kohlrausch, B. (2009). *A Ticket to Work? Policies for the Young Unemployed in Britain and Germany*. Frankfurt/M., New York Campus Verlag.

Korsnes, O. (2000). Towards a Relational Approach to the Study of the Variety in Situated Creativity of Economic Actors. In M. Maurice & A. Sorge (Eds.), *Embedding Organizations. Societal Analysis of Actors, Organisations and Socio-economic Context*. Amsterdam, Philadelphia: John Benjamins Publishing Company, pp. 71-88.

Krais, B. (1996). Bildungsexpansion und soziale Ungleichheit in der Bundesrepublik Deutschland. In A. Bolder, W. R. Heinz & K. Rodex (Eds.), *Die*

Wiederentdeckung der Ungleichheit. Jahrbuch '96 Bildung und Arbeit.
Opladen: Leske & Budrich, pp. 118-146.

Kuhlmann, S.; Röber, M. (2004). Civil Service in Germany: Characteristics of Public Employment and Modernization of Public Personnel Management, *Modernization of State and Administration in Europe: A France-Germany Comparison.* Bordeaux, France: Goethe-Institut.

Lane, C. (1989). *Management and Labour in Europe: The Industrial Enterprise in Germany, Britain and France.* Aldershot: Edward Elgar Publishing Limited.

Lane, C.; Potton, M.; Littek, W. (2000). The Professions between State and Market. A Cross-national Study of Convergence and Divergence. *ESRC Working Paper.*

Lane, C.; Wilkinson, F.; Littek, W.; Heisig, U.; Brown, J.; Burchell, B.; Mankelow, R.; Potton, M.; Tutschner, R. (2004). The Future of Professionalised Work in Britain and Germany. Solicitors and Advocates. In Anglo-German Foundation for the Study of Industrial Society (Ed.), *Anglo-German Foundation Reports.* London.

Leff, G. (1993). Die Artes Liberales. In W. Rüegg (Ed.), *Geschichte der Universität in Europa. Band 1.* München: Beck.

Leisering, L.; Leibfried, S. (1999). *Time and Poverty in Western Welfare States.* Cambridge: Cambridge University Press.

Leuze, K. (2007). Sex or Subject? What Makes the Difference for Sex Segregation in Graduate Labour Markets?, *3rd International SOEP Young Scholars Symposium.* Hanse Institute for Advanced Studies, Delmenhorst, Germany.

Li, Y. (2002). Falling off the Ladder? Professional and Managerial Career Trajectories and Unemployment Experiences. *European Sociological Review*, 18, pp. 253-270.

Lindberg, M. E. (2007). Connections between the Differentiation of Higher Education Participation and the Distribution of Occupational Status. A Comparative Study of Seven European Countries. *European Societies*, 9, pp. 551-572.

Lutz, B.; Sengenberger, W. (1974). *Arbeitsmarktsegmentation und öffentliche Beschäftigungspolitik.* Göttingen: Otto Schwarz.

Lutz, B.; Sengenberger, W. (1980). Segmentationsanalyse und Beschäftigungspolitik. *WSI-Mitteilungen*, 5, pp. 291-299.

MacDonald, K. (1995). *The Sociology of the Professions.* Beverly Hills, London: Sage Publications.

March, J. G.; Olson, J. P. (1989). *Rediscovering Institutions.* New York: The Free Press.

Marsden, D. (1990). Institutions and Labour Mobility: Occupational and Internal Labour Markets in Britain, France, Italy and West Germany. In R. Brunetta

& C. Dell'Aringa (Eds.), *Labour Relations and Economic Performance.* Houndmills, Basingstoke, New York: Palgrave Macmillan, pp. 414-438.

Marsden, D. (1999). *A Theory of Employment Systems: Micro-Foundations of Societal Diversity.* Oxford: Oxford University Press.

Martens, K.; Rusconi, A.; Leuze, K. (2007). *New Arenas of Education Governance. The Impact of International Organizations and Markets on Educational Policymaking.* Houndmills, Basingstoke, New York: Palgrave Macmillan.

Mason, G. (2000). Production Supervisors in Britain, Germany and the United States: Back from the Dead Again? *Work, Employment and Society,* 14, pp. 625-645.

Maurice, M. (2000). The Paradox of Societal Analysis. A Review of the Past and Prospects for the Future. In M. Maurice & A. Sorge (Eds.), *Embedding Organisations. Societal Analysis of Actors, Organisations and Socio-economic Context.* Amsterdam, Philadelphia: John Benjamins Publishing Company, pp. 13-37.

Maurice, M.; Sellier, F.; Silvestre, J.-J. (1986). *The Social Foundations of Industrial Power: A Comparison of France and Germany.* Cambridge, MA: MIT Press.

Mayer, K. U. (2001). The Paradox of Global Social Change and Institutional Path Dependencies. In A. Woodward & M. Kohli (Eds.), *Inclusions and Exclusions in European Societies.* London, New York: Routlegde, pp. 89-110.

Mayer, K. U.; Müller, W. (1989). Lebensverläufe im Wohlfahrtsstaat. In A. Weymann (Ed.), *Handlungsspielräume. Untersuchungen zur Individualisierung und Institutionalisierung von Lebensläufen in der Moderne.* Stuttgart: Enke, pp. 41-61.

Meyer, J. W. (1977). The Effects of Education as an Institution. *American Journal of Sociology,* 83, pp. 55-77.

Meyer, J. W.; Ramirez, F. O.; Soysal, Y. N. (1992). World Expansion of Mass Education, 1870-1980. *Sociology of Education,* 65, pp. 128-149.

Meyer, J. W.; Rowan, B. (1977). Institutionalized Organizations: Formal Structures as Myth and Ceremony. *American Journal of Sociology,* 83, pp. 340-363.

Mincer, J. (1970). The Distribution of Labor Incomes: A Survey With Special Reference to the Human Capital Approach. *Journal of Economic Literature,* 8, pp. 1-26.

Moraw, P. (1993). Der Lebensweg der Studenten. In W. Rüegg (Ed.), *Geschichte der Universität in Europa. Band 1.* München: Beck.

Moraw, P. (2005). Die Universitäten in Europa und Deutschland. Anfänge und Schritte auf einem langen Weg. In U. Sieg & D. Korsch (Eds.), *Die Idee der Universität heute.* München: K.G. Saur, pp. 25-41.

Müller, W. (1998). Erwartete und unerwartete Folgen der Bildungsexpansion. In J. Friedrichs, M. R. Lepsius & K. U. Mayer (Eds.), *Die Diagnosefähigkeit der Soziologie, Sonderheft 38 der Kölner Zeitschrift für Soziologie*. Opladen: Leske & Budrich, pp. 81-112.

Müller, W. (2000). Education and Labour Market Outcomes: Commonality or Divergence? In M. Haller (Ed.), *The Making of the European Union. Contributions of the Social Sciences*. Berlin, Heidelberg, New York: Springer-Verlag, pp. 287-308.

Müller, W.; Bruns, H.; Steinemann, S. (2002). Expansion und Erträge tertiärer Bildung in Deutschland, Frankreich und im Vereinigten Königreich. *Berliner Journal für Soziologie*, 12, pp. 37-62.

Müller, W.; Gangl, M. (2003). *Transitions from Education to Work in Europe. The Integration of Youth into EU Labour Markets*. Oxford, New York: Oxford University Press.

Müller, W.; Shavit, Y. (1998). The Institutional Embeddedness of the Stratification Process. A Comparative Study of Qualifications and Occupations in Thirteen Countries. In Y. Shavit & W. Müller (Eds.), *From School to Work*. Oxford: Clarenden Press, pp. 1-48.

Neal, M.; Morgan, J. (2000). The Professionalization of Everyone? A Comparative Study of the Development of the Professions in the United Kingdom and Germany. *European Sociological Review*, 16, pp. 9-26.

Neave, G. (2001). The European Dimension of Higher Education. In J. Huisman, P. Maassen & G. Neave (Eds.), *Higher Education and the Nation State. The International Dimension on Higher Education*. Oxford: Pergamon.

North, D. C. (1990). *Institutions, Institutional Change and Economic Performance*. Cambridge: Cambridge University Press.

OECD (2002). *Highlights of Public Sector Pay and Employment Trends: 2002 Update*. Paris: OECD Publishing.

OECD (2003). *Learning for Tomorrow's World - First Results from PISA 2003*. Paris: OECD Publishing.

OECD (2004a). *Education at a Glance. OECD Indicators 2004*. Paris: OECD Publishing.

OECD (2004b). *OECD Handbook for Internationally Comparative Education Statistics: Concepts, Standards, Definitions and Classifications*. Paris: OECD Publishing.

OECD (2004c). Public Sector Modernisation: Modernising Public Employment. In OECD (Ed.), *Policy Brief July 2004*. Paris: OECD Publishing.

Pierson, P. (2001). Post-Industrial Pressures on the Mature Welfare States. In P. Pierson (Ed.), *The New Politics of the Welfare State*. Oxford, New York: Oxford University Press, pp. 80-104.

Pierson, P. (2004). *Politics in Time. History, Institutions, and Social Analysis.* Princeton: Princeton University Press.

Pissarides, C. A. (2003). Unemployment in Britain: A European Success Story, *Unemployment in Europe: Reasons and Remedies.* Munich: Yrjo Jahnsson Foundation and CESifo.

Plewis, I.; Calderwood, L.; Hawkes, D.; Nathan, G. (2004). National Child Development Study and 1970 British Cohort Study Technical Report: Changes in the NCDS and BCS70 Populations and Samples over Time. 1st Edition London: Centre for Longitudinal Studies Bedford Group for Lifecourse and Statistical Studies, Institute of Education, University of London.

Prime Minister, G. B. (1995). The Civil Service: Taking Forward Continuity and Change (Cm2748), *Great Britain. Parliament. House of Commons.* London: HMSO, pp. 35-45.

Ragin, C. (1987). *The Comparative Method. Moving beyond Qualitative and Quantitative Strategies.* Berkeley: Berkeley University Press.

Ragin, C. (1994). *Constructing Social Research.* Thousand Oaks: Pine Forge Press.

Ramirez, F. O.; Meyer, J. W. (1980). Comparative Education: The Social Construction of the Modern World System. *Annual Review of Sociology,* 6, pp. 369-399.

Robbins, L. (1963). Higher Education Report of the Committee appointed by the Prime Minister under the Chairmanship of Lord Robbins 1961-1963. London: HMSO.

Röber, M.; Löffler, E. (2000). Germany: The Limitations of Flexibility Reforms. In D. Farnham & S. Horton (Eds.), *Human Resources Flexibilities in the Public Services. International Perspectives.* Houndmills, Basingstoke, New York: Palgrave Macmillan, pp. 115-134.

Rosenbaum, J. E.; Kariya, T. (1991). Do School Achievements Affect the Early Jobs of High School Graduates? Results from the High School and Beyond Survey in the US and Japan. *Sociology of Education,* 64, pp. 78-95.

Rosenfeld, R. (1992). Job Mobility and Career Processes. *Annual Review of Sociology,* 18, pp. 39-61.

Rothenbacher, F. (1999). Der öffentliche Dienst in Europa - ein schrumpfender Sektor? Sozialstruktur, Einkommen und soziale Sicherheit. *Informationsdienst Soziale Indikatoren,* 21, pp. 1-4.

Rothenbacher, F. (2001/2002). The Public Service and Social Protection in Europe: A Comparative Research Project. *Eurodata Newsletter,* 14/15.

Rubery, J.; Grimshaw, D. (2003). *The Organization of Employment. An International Perspective.* Houndmills, Basingstoke, New York: Palgrave Macmillan.

Ryder, N. B. (1965). The Cohort as Concept in the Study of Social Change. *American Sociological Review*, 30, pp. 843-861.

Sackmann, R.; Wingens, M. (2003). From Transitions to Trajectories. In W. R. Heinz & V. W. Marshall (Eds.), *Social Dynamics of the Life Course: Transitions, Institutions, and Interrelations.* New York: Walter de Gruyter, pp. 93-116.

Sattinger, M. (1993). Assignment Models of the Distribution of Earnings. *Journal of Economic Literature*, 31, pp. 831-880.

Scherer, S. (2001). Early Career Patterns: A Comparison of Great Britain and West Germany. *European Sociological Review*, 17, pp. 119-144.

Scherer, S. (2005). Patterns of Labour Market Entry - Long Wait or Career Instability? An Empirical Comparison of Italy, Great Britain and West Germany. *European Sociological Review*, 21, pp. 427-440.

Schomburg, H. (2007). The Professional Success of Higher Education Graduates. *European Journal of Education*, 42, pp. 35-57.

Schomburg, H.; Teichler, U. (2006). *Higher Education and Graduate Employment in Europe. Results of Graduate Surveys from 12 Countries.* Berlin, Heidelberg, New York: Springer-Verlag.

Schultz, T. W. (1961). Investment in Human Capital. *American Economic Review*, 51, pp. 1-17.

Scott, D. K. (2002). General Education for an Integrative Age. *Higher Education Policy*, 15, pp. 7-18.

Scott, J.; Alwin, D. F. (1998). Retrospective Versus Prospective Measurements of Life Histories in Longitudinal Research. In G. H. Elder & J. Geile, Z. (Eds.), *Crafting Life Studies: Intersection of Personal and Social History.* Beverly Hills, London: Sage Publications, pp. 98-127.

Scott, P. (1995). *The Meanings of Mass Higher Education.* Buckingham, Bristol: Open University Press.

Scott, R. W. (2001). *Institutions and Organizations. Second Edition.* Beverly Hills, London: Sage Publications.

Shavit, Y.; Müller, W. (1998). *From School to Work: A Comparative Study of Educational Qualifications and Occupational Destinations.* Oxford: Clarenden Press.

Siedentopf, H. (1990). The Public Service. In K. König, H. J. von Oertzen & F. Wagener (Eds.), *Public Administration in the Federal Republic of Germany.* Baden-Baden: Nomos, pp. 235-246.

Smith, D.; Langslow, A. K. (1999). *The Idea of a University.* London, Bristol, Philadelphia: Jessica Kingsley Publishers.

Solga, H. (2001). Longitudinal Surveys and the Study of Occupational Mobility: Panel and Retrospective Design in Comparison. *Quality & Quantity*, 35, pp. 291-309.

Sorensen, A. B. (1977). The Structure of Inequality and the Process of Attainment. *American Sociological Review*, 42, pp. 965-978.

Sorensen, A. B.; Tuma, N. B. (1981). Labor Market Structures and Job Mobility. *Research in Social Stratification and Mobility*, 1, pp. 67-94.

Spence, M. (1973). Job Market Signalling. *The Quarterly Journal of Economics*, 87, pp. 355-374.

Sporn, B. (1999). Current Issues and Future Priorities for European Higher Education Systems. In P. G. M. P. Altbach, Patti (Ed.), *Higher Education in the 21st Century: Global Challenge and National Response*. New York: IIE Books.

Streeck, W.; Thelen, K. (2005). Institutional Change in Advanced Political Economies. In W. Streeck & K. Thelen (Eds.), *Beyond Continuity: Institutional Change in Advanced Political Economies*. Oxford, New York: Oxford University Press, pp. 1-39.

Teichler, U. (1988). *Changing Patterns of the Higher Education System. The Experience of Three Decades*. London: JKP.

Teichler, U. (1996). *Higher Education and Graduate Employment in Europe. Select Findings from Previous Decades*. Kassel: Wissenschaftliches Zentrum für Berufs- und Hochschulforschung der Universität Gesamthochschule Kassel.

Teichler, U. (1999). Research on the Relationships between Higher Education and the World of Work: Past Achievements, Problems and New Challenges. *Higher Education*, 38, pp. 169–190.

Teichler, U. (2000). Graduate Employment and Work in Selected European Countries. *European Journal of Education*, 35, pp. 141-155.

Teichler, U. (2002a). Diversification of Higher Education Institutions and the Profile of the Individual Institution. *Higher Education Management and Policy*, 14, pp. 177-188.

Teichler, U. (2002b). Graduate Employment and Work in Europe: Diverse Situations and Common Perceptions. *Tertiary Education and Management*, 8, pp. 199-216.

Teichler, U. (2007a). Does Higher Education Matter? Lessons from a Comparative Graduate Survey. *European Journal of Education*, 42, pp. 11-34.

Teichler, U. (2007b). *Higher Education Systems. Conceptual Frameworks, Comparative Perspectives*. Rotterdam: Sense-Publishers

Thurow, L. C. (1975). *Generating Inequality: Mechanisms of Distribution in the U.S. Economy*. New York: Basic Books.

Tuma, N. B. (1985). Effects of Labor Market Structure on Job Shift Patterns. In J. J. Heckman & B. Singer (Eds.), *Longitudinal Analysis of Labor Market Data*. Cambridge: Cambridge University Press, pp. 327-363.

UNESCO (1997). *International Standard Classification of Education ISCED 1997*. Paris: UNESCO Publishing.

van de Werfhorst, H. G.; Kraaykamp, G. (2001). Four Field-Related Educational Resources and Their Impact on Labor, Consumption, and Sociopolitical Orientation. *Sociology of Education*, 74, pp. 296-317.

Verger, J. (1993). Grundlagen. Die Entstehung der Universitäten. In W. Rüegg (Ed.), *Geschichte der Universität in Europa. Band 1*. München: Beck.

Weymann, A. (1989). *Handlungsspielräume. Untersuchungen zur Individualisierung und Institutionalisierung von Lebensläufen in der Moderne*. Stuttgart: Enke.

Weymann, A. (2003a). Future of the Life Course. In J. T. Mortimer & M. J. Shanahan (Eds.), *Handbook of the Life Course*. New York: Kluwer Academic Publisher, pp. 703-714.

Weymann, A. (2003b). The Life Course, Institution, and Life-Course Policy. In W. Heinz & V. W. Marshall (Eds.), *Social Dynamics of the Life Course: Transitions, Institutions, and Interrelations*. New York: Walter de Gruyter, pp. 703-714.

Wolbers, M. H. (2003). Job Mismatches and their Labour-Market Effects among School-Leavers in Europe. *European Sociological Review*, 19, pp. 249-266.

Wood, S. (2001). Labour Market Regimes under Threat? Sources of Continuity in Germany, Britain, and Sweden. In P. Pierson (Ed.), *The New Politics of the Welfare State*. Oxford, New York: Oxford University Press, pp. 368-409.

Zucker, L. G. (1977). The Role of Institutionalization in Cultural Persistence. *American Sociological Review*, 42, pp. 726-743.

Appendix

Appendix A: Description of German and British Data Sets

	SOEP	NCDS/BSC70
Number of graduates	878	3805
Years of graduation	1984 – 2001	1979 – 1997
Years of labour market careers	1984 – 2005	1979 – 2000
Sample NCDS	n.a.	43.44 %
Old graduation cohort (before 1990)	24.00 %	38.00 %
Females	40.66 %	50.09 %
Females with children under six years	2.05 %	3.89 %
Non-German (Ger) / Non-White (GB)	8.20 %	4.26 %
Father with higher education (Ger) / employment in EGP class I or II (GB)	26.65 %	46.02 %
Vocational Training	19.93 %	26.41 %
Mean age of graduation (Std. Dev.)	28 (4.102)	24 (3.160)
Graduation in East Germany	17.00 %	n.a.
University graduates	65.49 %	55.77 %
Casmin 3b (high)	65.49 %	17.08 %
Diplom, Magister	46.36 %	n.a.
Staatsexamen	19.13 %	n.a.
Casmin 3b (low)	n.a.	71.67 %
Casmin 3a (gen)	34.51 %	11.25 %
Engineering	26.88 %	11.14 %
Science	14.46 %	16.95 %
Soc. Sc., Business, Law	34.05 %	32.27 %
Health, Welfare	7.86 %	9.67 %
Humanities, Arts	9.57 %	20.05 %
Education	7.18 %	9.91 %

Appendix B: The Erikson-Goldthorpe Class Scheme

Classes	Occupations included
I	Higher-grade professionals, administrators, and officials; managers in large industrial establishments; large proprietors
II	Lower grade professionals, administrators, and officials; higher-grade technicians; managers in small industrial establishments; supervisors of non-manual employees
IIIa	Routine non-manual employees, higher grade (in administration and commerce)
IIIb	Routine non-manual employees, lower grade (sales and services)
IVab	Small proprietors and artisans with or without employees
IVc	Farmers and smallholders; other self-employed in primary production
V	Lower-grade technicians; supervisors of manual workers
VI	Skilled manual workers
VIIa	Semi- and unskilled manual workers (not in agriculture)
VIIb	Agricultural and other workers in primary production

(Source: Erikson, Robert and Goldthorpe 1992: 38f)

Appendix C: The New Casmin Educational Classification

Qualification		Description
1a		Inadequately completed general education
1b		General elementary education
1c		Basic vocational qualification or general elementary education and vocational qualification
2a		Intermediate vocational qualification or intermediate general qualification and vocational qualification
2b		Intermediate general qualification
	2c_gen	General maturity certificate
	2c_voc	Vocational maturity certificate/General maturity certificate and vocational qualification
3a		Lower tertiary education
	3a_gen	Lower tertiary education – general diplomas
	3b_voc	Lower tertiary education – diplomas with vocational emphasis
3b		Higher tertiary education
	3b_low	Higher tertiary education – lower level
	3b_high	Higher tertiary education – higher level

Appendix D: Vocational Training in Germany and Britain

In Germany, the main characteristic of the so-called "dual system" of apprenticeship is the combination of school-based theoretical education with practical learning in the work place, normally lasting for three and a half years. Its organisation is based on the cooperation between state, trade unions and employers, who jointly set the curricular standards, practical requirements and further particulars. Due to the orientation of the dual system towards occupation-specific skills that can directly be utilised in particular occupations available in the German labour market, transition to work has traditionally been rather easy (Allmendinger and Aisenbrey 2002; Blossfeld and Mayer 1988; Müller 1998; Müller and Gangl 2003). The smoothness of the transition process has worsened recently, however, due to tightened labour market conditions, rapid changes in skill demand, and the increasing unwillingness of employers to train young people themselves (Kohlrausch 2007). In addition, the *Hauptschule* has undergone an enormous decline in social acceptance for the labour market during the last two decades (Müller 1998). While during the 1970s it was normal for *Hauptschul*-graduates to obtain an apprenticeship, nowadays they frequently face problems in meeting the requirements for vocational training. Nevertheless, the German dual system is still considered a worthy alternative to higher education even for leavers from the *Gymnasium*. In 2002, around 50 per cent of a given age cohort were enrolled in the dual system (OECD 2004a: Table C2.5) and about 25 percent graduated from tertiary education. Over the last 15 years, these trends in educational attainment of the 25- to 64-year-old population have been surprisingly stable (OECD 2004a: Table A3.4a).

With respect to British vocational education and training, substantial changes have taken place during the last three decades (Brauns and Steinmann 1997). In the mid 1970s, the VET system was highly criticised for not producing an adequate number of highly skilled individuals compared to international competitors and compared to requirements of the labour market. Also during this decade, Britain experienced increasing and politically unacceptable levels of youth unemployment, particularly among unskilled school leavers. Both issues were related to the fact that the training offered was lacking any organised structure and regulation, taking place predominantly in form of training-on-the-job. After the Conservatives won power in 1979, the Thatcher Government reformed the VET system radically by introducing several vocational education programmes. However, these new measures were far from being standardised or of high quality. By the late 1980s, about 6000 different pre-vocational and vocational qualifications existed in Britain, awarded by different qualifying bodies competing in overlapping occupational areas, while the standards achieved by young people often were to be questioned.

In order to rationalise British vocational training, the National Council of Vocational Qualifications (NCVQ) was established in 1986. Its main tasks were to develop a unified framework of national qualifications based on national standards, the development of quality assurance mechanisms, and the development of National Vocational Qualifications (NVQ) in co-operation with the most important awarding bodies such as The Business and Technician Education Council (BTEC) and The City and Guilds of London Institute (CGLI). The established framework of National Vocational Qualifications includes five levels of qualifications reflecting the level of competence and achieved skills. The NVQ are usually directed at specific occupations, and assessment of actual performance takes place in a realistic work environment, normally the workplace itself. By 1991 the Government introduced the General National Vocational Qualifications (GNVQ) as a kind of 'bridge' between the traditional 'academic' qualifications like GCSE and A level on the one hand and the NVQ framework on the other establishing a triple track of educational provision. In contrast to the NVQ, the GNVQs are more broadly based education awards than specific in competence of a particular occupation. Furthermore, GNVQ assess educational achievement whereas the assessment of NVQ of actual performance takes places in the workplace. Even though there are serious concerns about the reliability and validity of criteria-referenced assessment used in NVQ and GNVQ, they represent the first attempt to establish a VET system based on national standards and geared towards teaching occupation-specific knowledge. Despite these reforms, British VET has never reached the same levels of standardisation and occupation-specific training as in Germany.

Appendix E: Gender-specific Transition Patterns

Figure 27: Transition to part-time employment after graduation by gender

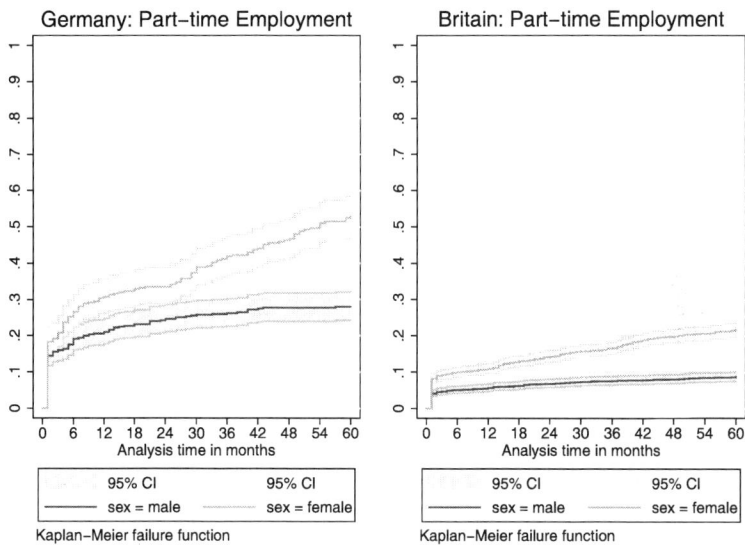

Data: SOEP, NCDS/BCS70

Table 16: Number of spells in Germany by spelltyp and gender

Spelltyp	Male	Female	Total
Full-time Employment	647	442	1089
Part-time Employment	178	253	431
Unemployment	184	141	325
Education, training	162	127	289
Paternal leave, homemaker	33	148	181
Other	157	85	242
Total	1361	1196	2557

Table 17: Activities after unemployment in Britain by gender (in %)

Spells after unemployment	Male	Female
Same occupation	49.70	31.11
Different occupation	32.34	29.38
Other activity	17.96	39.51

List of Tables

Table 1: Objective and subjective measures of graduate employment in Western Europe 27

Table 2: The institutional determinants of VET transition patterns in political economies 66

Table 3: Matching fields of study and occupations 93

Table 4: Institutional differentiation and the stratification of labour market returns 124

Table 5: Occupational specificity and the matching of students to jobs..140

Table 6: Importance of internal labour market segments for graduate careers 155

Table 7: Impact of labour market regulation on career mobility 166

Table 8: Transition to first employment and first employment in EGP class I (both full-time and part-time) 182

Table 9: Obtaining an occupation matching the field of study after graduation 196

Table 10: Making a job shift within or between occupations 203

Table 11: Transition to ILM and OLM labour market segments after graduation 215

Table 12: Credentials important for entering different labour market segments 217

Table 13: Changing the labour market segment 222

Table 14: The institutional determinants of transition patterns in CMEs and LMEs 246

Table 15: Institutional complementarities between higher education and work 247

Table 16: Number of spells in Germany by spelltyp and gender 273

Table 17: Activities after unemployment in Britain by gender (in %) 273

List of Figures

Figure 1: Theoretical model for studying the transition from higher education to work 42

Figure 2: Segmentation of graduate labour markets 60

Figure 3: Number of German and British students enrolled in higher education 104

Figure 4: German and British age participation rates in higher education 106

Figure 5: Share of public employment over total employment in Germany and Britain 153

Figure 6: Employment ratio of the population aged 16 – 64 years in Germany and Britain 159

Figure 7: Annual unemployment rates 1971-2004 in Germany and Britain 163

Figure 8: Unemployment among higher education degree holders in Germany and Britain 165

Figure 9: Activities during the first five years after graduation in Germany and Britain 169

Figure 10: Transition to first employment in Germany and Britain 176

Figure 11: Transition to first employment in the service class in Germany and Britain 178

Figure 12: EGP class distribution in Germany and Britain 180

Figure 13: Predicted probabilities of entering EGP class I by field of study and type of degree 189

Figure 14: Transition to a first job matching the field of study 193

Figure 15: Field of study distribution at graduation and after finding a matching job 194

Figure 16: Predicted failure functions by field of study in Germany and Britain 198

Figure 17: Survivor functions for making a job shift within or between occupations 201

Figure 18: Labour market segment of first job in Germany and Britain 209

Figure 19: Transition to public and professional labour market segments in Germany and Britain 210

Figure 20: Labour market segments and class of first job in Germany and Britain 213

Figure 21: Changing the labour market segment during the first five years after graduation 219

Figure 22: Mobility within and between labour market segments in Germany and Britain 220

Figure 23: Duration of spells and number of jobs after graduation 228

Figure 24: Transition to unemployment after graduation 230

Figure 25: Occupational mobility after spells of unemployment 231

Figure 26: Upward and downward mobility after job shifts in Germany and Britain 235

Figure 27: Transition to part-time employment after graduation by gender 273

List of Abbreviations

BA	Bachelor of Arts
BA	Bundesagentur für Arbeit (German Labour Agency)
BMBF	Bundesministerium für Bildung und Forschung
BSc	Bachelor of Science
BTEC	Business and Technology Education Council
CGLI	City and Guilds of London Institute
CME	Coordinated Market Economy
CSYS	Certificate of Sixth Year Studies (Scotland)
DfES	Department for Education and Skills
DPhil / PhD	Doctorate of Philosophy
EdD	Doctorate of Education
EU	European Union
GCE A Level	General Certificate of Education Advanced Level
GCE AS Level	General Certificate of Education Advanced Supplementary Level
GCSE	General Certificate of Secondary Education
GNVQ	General National Vocational Qualification
HRK	Hochschulrektorenkonferenz
ILM	Internal Labour Market
KMK	Kultusministerkonferenz der Länder
LEA	Local Education Authority
LME	Liberal Market Economy
MA	Master of Arts
MBA	Master of Business Administration
MEd	Master of Education
MMedSci	Master of Medical Sciences
MMusA	Master of Musical Arts
MSc	Master of Science
MSW	Master of Social Work
NCVQ	National Council of Vocational Qualifications
NPM	New Public Management
NVQ	National Vocational Qualifications
OECD	Organisation for Economic Cooperation and Development
OLM	Occupational Labour Market
PCFC	Polytechnics and Colleges Funding Council
PGCE	Postgraduate Certificate
UNESCO	United Nations Education, Scientific and Cultural Organisation
VCE	Vocational Certificate of Education
VET	Vocational Education and Training

Notes

Notes

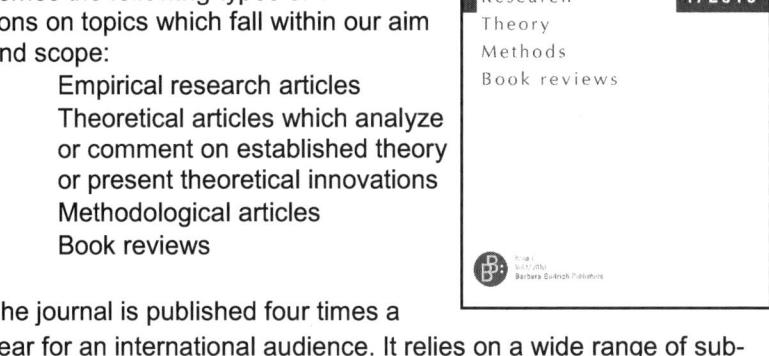

Early Childhood & Family

PAMELA OBERHUEMER & INGE SCHREYER & MICHELLE J. NEUMAN
Professionals in early childhood education and care systems
European profiles and perspectives
2010. 522 S. Kt. 49,90 €, US$ 58.00, GBP 36.95
ISBN 978-3-86649-249-3
In a European context of rapidly expanding early education/care provision for young children, the staffing of these services is a critical quality issue. What are the requirements for professional education and training? How alike or how varied are the qualification profiles and fields of work? Through detailed country reports and comparative analyses across 27 countries, this book provides answers to these questions.

OLAF KAPELLA & CHRISTIANE RILLE- PFEIFFER & MARINA RUPP & NORBERT F. SCHNEIDER (EDS.)
Family Diversity: Collection of the 3rd European Congress of Family Science
2010. 392 pp. Hc. 49,90 €, US$75,95, GBP 46,95
ISBN 978-3-86649-299-8
International experts provide an overview of the current state-of-the-art of European family research and outline the multiple formations, structures and configurations of family in Europe. Four aspects are discussed in depth: family images, sex/gender roles, globalisation and family development processes.

Verlag Barbara Budrich • Barbara Budrich Publishers
Stauffenbergstr. 7. D-51379 Leverkusen Opladen
Tel +49 (0)2171.344.594 • Fax +49 (0)2171.344.693 • info@budrich-verlag.de
US-office: Uschi Golden • 28347 Ridgebrook • Farmington Hills, MI 48334 • USA •
ph +1.248.488.9153 • info@barbara-budrich.net • www.barbara-budrich.net

www.barbara-budrich.net